Latte with Luke

SANDRA GLAHN

Coffee Cup Bible Studies
Latte with Luke

Published by AMG Publishers.

Published in association with the literary
agency of MacGregor and Luedeke, P.O. Box 1316, Manzanita, OR 97130

ISBN: 978-1-61715-565-9

Editing and typesetting by Rick Steele Editorial Services, Ringgold, GA
(https://steeleeditorialservies.myportfolio.com)

Coffee Cup Bible Studies® series interior design: PerfecType, Nashville, TN

Cover Design: Jonathan Lewis, Jonlin Creative, Pekin, IL

Printed in the United States of America

Acknowledgments

Special thanks to:

Gary, my love—for partnering with me in every way.

Members of Biblical Studies Foundation (bible.org) and translators of the NET Bible—for your help, apart from which the Coffee Cup Bible Study series would have been impossible. Thank you for laboring without earthly compensation so others might grow in the Word. May God reward you in this life and in the next.

Ver-lee Cheneweth—for being a great teaching assistant, faithful friend, consistent prayer supporter, and fine researcher.

Victoria Aguas—for great editing support, lending solid Bible knowledge, and concrete encouragement.

Misty Hedrick—for editing the manuscript, providing feedback, and creating original poetry for this study.

Christine Prater—for generously allowing the inclusion of your poem, which appeared first in *Fathom* Mag.

The editorial and production team at AMG Publishers—for expertise in both the biblical text and in editing content.

And thanks to all who pray that God will use the Word through this series to change lives. You know who you are, and your contribution is not forgotten. May the Lord reward in public what you have done in secret.

Contents

Week 1 of 7

Introduction and Overview: Luke 1–24

Sunday: Meet Luke

Scripture: "Only Luke is with me." (2 Tim. 4:11)

Since Luke will guide our study through the life of Christ, let's get to know the good doctor. Who was Luke? Although not included among the twelve apostles, tradition that dates to about the third century says this man was a disciple who penned more of the New Testament than any other human—writing more than a quarter of it. "The Gospel of Luke" or "the Gospel according to St. Luke" or simply "Luke" is attributed to the man by the same name mentioned numerous times by Paul. Luke's name also appears in the heading on the oldest known manuscript of the Gospel attributed to him. And all the early church fathers who mention authorship of the book attribute it to Luke.

Luke based his work on eyewitness accounts and research (Luke 1:1–4). Although he probably was not an eyewitness of the events of Jesus's life, he had access to many eyewitnesses. He recorded their stories in his Gospel and continued the story in the Book of Acts.

We meet Luke himself in the writings of the apostle Paul. In this apostle's letter to the believers in Colossae, Paul sent the church this salutation:

"Aristarchus, my fellow prisoner, sends you greetings, as does Mark, the cousin of Barnabas (about whom you received instructions; if he comes to you, welcome him). And Jesus who is called Justus also sends greetings. In terms of Jewish converts, these are the only fellow workers for the kingdom of God, and they have been a comfort to me." (Col. 4:10–11)

Notice that in this list of fellow Jewish converts to Christianity, Paul does not include Luke. But when Paul goes on to mention his other coworkers, whom we assume were Gentile, we do find Luke's name:

"Epaphras, who is one of you and a slave of Christ, greets you. He is always struggling in prayer on your behalf, so that you may stand mature and fully assured in all the will of God. For I can testify that he has worked hard for you and for those in Laodicea and Hierapolis. Our dear friend Luke the physician and Demas greet you." (vv. 12–14)

Putting these statements together, we see Paul directly and indirectly identifying Luke as **1)** a dear friend; **2)** a physician; and **3)** a Gentile Christian.

Probably in the same mail pouch with the letter Paul wrote to the Colossians, he sent a personal epistle to a man named Philemon, whose runaway slave was returning with Paul's commendation. In that letter Paul wrote this to Philemon: "Mark, Aristarchus, Demas and Luke, my colaborers, greet you too" (v. 24).

So, we add a fourth descriptor of Luke: someone whom the apostle Paul considered a "colaborer."

All additional information we discover about Luke comes from writings historically attributed to him: The Gospel of Luke and The Book of Acts. After telling the story of Jesus's life, death, burial, and resurrection, the writer of Acts picks up the story where the Gospel ends it, starting with Jesus's ascension and the Day of Pentecost. Writing in third person, Luke takes the reader through the events of Paul's conversion and missionary journeys, all the way to Troas in Asia Minor (today: Turkey). There a shift happens. Watch for the change from "them" and "they" to "us" and "we" in Luke's narrative:

"They went through the region of Phrygia and Galatia, having been prevented by the Holy Spirit from speaking the message in the province of Asia. When they came to Mysia, they attempted to go into Bithynia, but the Spirit of Jesus did not allow them to do this, so they passed through Mysia and went down to Troas. A vision appeared to Paul during the night: A Macedonian man was standing there urging him, 'Come over to Macedonia and help us!' After Paul saw the vision, we attempted immediately to go over to Macedonia, concluding that God had called us to proclaim the good news to them. We put out to sea from Troas . . . ." (Acts 16:6–12)

The group goes from Troas to Philippi, where Lydia becomes Europe's first documented convert to Christianity. Then Paul leaves Luke with the new believers in Philippi (17:1)—some think for about five years—and Paul continues to finish out his second missionary journey. The language describing the rest of that journey switches back to third person, describing "them," as Luke is no longer an eyewitness. But later, when Paul is in the middle of his third missionary journey, another shift occurs in the language: "We sailed from Philippi" (20:6). We. Luke has rejoined the travelers.

After an arduous journey complete with a shipwreck, eventually the mission team makes it to Rome, where Paul ministers under house arrest. Eventually, according to tradition, he is released, but later re-arrested during the reign of Nero. And near the end of Paul's life, which was perhaps about ten years after Luke rejoined Paul in Philippi, the apostle pens these words from prison to Timothy, his protégé in Ephesus:

"Make every effort to come to me soon. For Demas deserted me, since he loved the present age, and he went to Thessalonica. Crescens went to Galatia and Titus to Dalmatia. Only Luke is with me. Get Mark and bring him with you, because he is a great help to me in ministry" (2 Tim. 4:9–11).

How lonely Paul must have felt when he wrote from prison that "only Luke is with me." How much worse if Luke had departed with Demas and left Paul completely alone! Instead, though, Luke remained a faithful coworker and beloved friend to the end.

Every year on October 18, the Catholic and Orthodox Churches set aside a day to honor Luke and his legacy. Some believe Luke was martyred at the age of 84 in Greece, while others think he was executed shortly after the death of Paul. Some say he was beheaded; many say he was hung from an olive tree. But whatever the details, Luke was faithful to the end, this Godfearing Gentile transformed by the mercy of God, standing in the cloud of witnesses cheering us on.

For memorization: "From generation to generation he is merciful to those who fear him" (Luke 1:50).

Prayer: *Heavenly Father, thank you for our brother, Luke, through whom we learn of Elizabeth and Zechariah, Mary and Joseph, Anna and Simeon, the prodigal Son, and most of all Jesus, the Son of Man. Thank you for sending Jesus, fully human and fully divine, and for Luke's faithful detailing of the events. Thank you for Jesus's love for us, for his genuine compassion for all. And may your Spirit use Luke's Gospel to help us see, trust, and obey the Lord Jesus Christ. Through the power of Your Spirit. Amen.*

Monday: First Things

1. Pray for insight and read the content below, which will give you an introduction to the Coffee Cup series and specifically to Luke's Gospel.

> **The precepts of the Lord are right, rejoicing the heart;**
> **The commandment of the Lord is pure, enlightening the eyes. (Psalm 19:8)**

Congratulations! You have chosen wisely. By selecting a book in the Coffee Cup Bible Study series, you are choosing to spend time learning that which will rejoice the heart and enlighten the eyes. Let's consider some ways to help you maximize your study time.

About Coffee. You don't actually have to drink coffee to benefit from using one of the Coffee Cup Bible Study series books. You don't even have to like coffee. Tea works, too. So does milk. Or water. Or nothing. Coffee is just a metaphor: Take a "coffee break"—a bit of "down" time, away from the routine, designed to refresh you. And you can imbibe alone, but you might benefit from interaction with a group.

Life Rhythms. Most participants in Bible studies say they find it easier to keep up on weekdays than on the weekends, when the routine often changes. That's why each study in the Coffee Cup series contains weekday Bible study questions that require active involvement, while the weekend segments consist of short, passive readings that draw application from the texts you've been studying. Still, the specified days as laid out here serve as mere suggestions. Some people prefer to attend a Bible study one day and follow a four-day-a-week study schedule along with weekend readings. Others prefer to take twice as long to get through Luke's Gospel, cutting each day's selection roughly in half, spreading a seven-week study over fourteen weeks. Adapt the structure of days to fit your own needs.

Community. While you can complete this study individually, consider going through it with others. If you don't already belong to a Bible study group, find some friends and start one—whether meeting in person or virtually or a hybrid of of options.

Aesthetics. At the author's web site (www.aspire2.com) in a section designed for the Coffee Cup series, you can find links to art and resources that relate to each study. The more senses you engage in your interaction with Scripture, the more you will remember truth, apply it, and enjoy it. Because Jesus told so many stories that Luke recorded, we have "an embarrassment of riches" when it comes to art that illustrates Jesus's parables and narratives.

Convenience. Rather than flipping through a printed Bible to look up verses or scrolling through an app, you'll find the entire biblical text for each day included in this Coffee Cup Bible Study book. While it's important to know our way around the Word, we designed the series this way so you can stash it in a purse, diaper bag, briefcase, or backpack. You can also use it on the subway, at a coffee shop, or in a doctor's waiting room. And hopefully you won't get distracted during group time by having seven different translations to work through on a given text. In this study I use the NET (New English Translation).

Why does the Coffee Cup Series use the NET? Accessible online from anywhere in the world with internet access, the NET Bible is a modern translation from the ancient Greek, Hebrew, and Aramaic texts. A team of biblical-language scholars volunteered their time to prepare the NET because they shared a vision to make the Bible available worldwide without the high cost of permissions usually required for using copyrighted materials. Any other translation, with the exception of the King James Version (KJV), would have made the cost of including the Bible's actual words (translated) prohibitive. Only through the generosity of the Biblical Studies Foundation and the NET Bible translators is this convenience possible. For more information on this ministry, go to www.bible.org.

Selections for Memorization. In the second decade of this century, an Ebola crisis raged in Africa. And Nancy Writebol, a clinical nurse associate, became one of the first Americans to fall ill with the wasting disease. After her evacuation from Liberia, doctors admitted her to an isolation unit at Emory University Hospital in Atlanta. And months later after her recovery, she challenged her American audiences to memorize Scripture. "We never know when we will be unable to access it," she said. Ebola affected her vision, making reading nearly impossible for her. And her husband could not join her in isolation to read her the Bible. So, she lay alone at night, crying out to God and wondering if she would survive. But the verses she'd memorized came to mind and ministered to her.

No matter where we live, we need God's Word in our hearts to help us stand strong in every situation. Each week in the Coffee Cup series you'll find a verse or two to memorize.

Sensitivity to time-and-culture considerations. Many Bible studies, though well intentioned, often skip an important step in the process of study and application—the "timelessness" step. Such studies might start by instructing readers to observe and interpret the words written to the original audience. And that's great. But sometimes readers are told that the next step is to apply the words directly to their own settings ("what this means to me"). The result is sometimes misunderstanding and misapplication. For example, one might observe that Paul told slaves to obey their masters, and the resulting application might be "it's okay to own people," or "we need to obey our employers." Yet enslaving people is not treating them as we would want to be treated. Today's bosses don't own employees as slaveholders owned their slaves, nor do today's employers and employees typically share the same household, as was true in ancient master/slave relationships. Thus, it's more accurate to use the voluntary "submit" rather than the obligatory "obey" when applying Scripture to an employment context—after we've also established that the master/slave is not God's ideal authority structure. In the Coffee Cup series, our aim is to look at the original setting and audience, find the timeless truth, and then apply it to our lives.

Sensitivity to literary genre. Rather than crafting a series in which each study is laid out exactly like all the others, each Coffee Cup study explores the genre in which the Bible book being considered was written—whether epistle, poetry, history, narrative, prophecy, apocalypse, or Gospel. That means the way we study Luke, one of the four Gospels, differs from how we would study the compact poetry in Song of Songs or an historical narrative like the Book of Judges or a letter like Colossians. For this reason, while the studies in the

Coffee Cup series may have similar elements, no two take the same approach. In fact, while many people explore the Gospels by creating a timeline of events using stories found in other Gospel accounts, in this study we will resist doing so—except in our introduction to John the Baptist—to limit our focus to the unique picture of Jesus that Luke wants his readers to see. Luke emphasizes the humanity of the God-man Jesus. That might explain why Luke's is the only Gospel to trace Jesus's genealogy all the way back to the first man, Adam. Luke is also the only Gospel writer to include the nativity of Jesus, essential to the doctrine of the incarnation—God becoming human. Of all the titles Jesus used to refer to himself, Luke repeatedly records that Jesus called himself "the Son of Man" (Luke 5:24; 6:5; 7:34; 9:22, 26, 44, 58; 11:30; 12:8, 10, 40; 17:22, 24, 26, 30; 18:8, 31; 19:10; 21:27, 36; 22:22, 69; 24:7), instead of the Son of God—which we find in John's Gospel (e.g., 1:49).

What was Luke's purpose? He begins his Gospel with a description of what he set out to do and why:

> Now many have undertaken to compile an account of the things that have been fulfilled among us, like the accounts passed on to us by those who were eyewitnesses and servants of the word from the beginning. So it seemed good to me as well, because I have followed all things carefully from the beginning, to write an orderly account for you, most excellent Theophilus, so that you may know for certain the things you were taught (Luke 1:1–4).

Who is Theophilus? Some think that Theophilus, meaning "friend of God" in Greek, was an honorary title used to address anyone who fit the category of friend. Others think someone named Theophilus commissioned Luke to research and write Jesus's story. Or perhaps Luke took it upon himself to gather the stories on behalf of a friend. What we do know from the author's own testimony is that he has purposely collected the details to compile "an orderly account." Historians think Luke wrote his narrative about three decades after Jesus's resurrection.

Of the four Gospel writers—Matthew, Mark, Luke, and John—Luke appears to be the only non-Jewish author among them. Luke's Gentile status might explain his focus on Jesus's ministry to "outsiders," helping readers see how God has kept his promise to one day bless all nations through Abraham's descendants. Luke shows how Jesus lived righteously in a hostile world and how God calls Jesus's followers to do the same.

The Backstory

The Scriptures tell one grand narrative of God's glory and his redemption of humanity. Where does the Gospel of Luke fit into that big story?

Thousands of years before the events in Luke's Gospel occurred, God created our first parents and charged them with the blessing of filling and ruling the earth. The earth was to be filled with the glory of God. But a tempter in the Garden coaxed the humans to rebel, which they did. So God warned that tempter about someone to come who would descend from the mother of all living: "I will put hostility between you and the woman and between your offspring and her offspring; he will strike your head, and you will strike his heel" (Gen. 3:15). This descendant would one day bring reconciliation and restoration between God and humans.

God chose a family from whom this promised restorer would come—Abram and Sarai—later renamed Abraham and Sarah. Although childless, this couple received God's "impossible" promise that they would become a great nation through whom the entire world would be blessed (see Gen. 12). God kept his promise starting with their miracle-son, Isaac, and then through Isaac's son Jacob, who had twelve sons and a daughter. The fourth son of Jacob received a prophecy from his father that he, Judah, would be the one through whom the promised blessing would come:

> The scepter will not depart from Judah,
> nor the ruler's staff from between his feet,
> until he comes to whom it belongs;
> the nations will obey him. (Gen. 49:10)

Jacob pronounced this blessing while his entire extended family resided in Egypt, where God had preserved him and his descendants through a time of famine. Over a period of more than four hundred years, this family became enslaved to Egyptians, and the people came to number more than a million. God heard their cries for help and raised up Moses to lead them through the Red Sea back to their original country—the Promised Land (see Exodus). But when their time came to enter the Promised Land, the people refused to obey God, so they ended up spending forty years in the wilderness before that desert-wandering generation died out and their progeny finally entered the land. Before Moses died, he appointed Joshua as his successor.

Under Joshua's leadership (see the Book of Joshua), Israel

marched in and claimed their territory. Eventually, Joshua retired after a decorated military career, and the Lord led the nation through localized leaders called judges (this style of leadership with God as king was the Lord's preference; see the Book of Judges) rather than human monarchs. Eventually the people rebelled and insisted on having a king, so God let them have it their way (read 1 and 2 Kings and 1 and 2 Chronicles).

King Saul, then King David, and then King Solomon reigned over one united kingdom. But under Solomon's son, Rehoboam, the nation split into a northern kingdom (Israel) and a southern kingdom (Judah), each having its own king. For the next five hundred years, good and bad kings—mostly bad—ruled over these two kingdoms.

As the people increasingly embraced idolatry, God disciplined them by sending other nations to drive his people into exile. But in 538 BC, Cyrus—king of Persia—decreed that the exiles from Judah could return to their homeland. After three groups went back to this southern kingdom, God sent Malachi to prophesy to them. The prophet proclaimed judgment due to the people's corruption, but he promised that God would send another messenger—one who would prepare the way for the Promised One (see Mal. 2:17–3:1).

On this side of history, we know something they didn't—that four hundred years after Malachi's prediction, God would fulfill this promise through His messenger, the son of an elderly infertile couple named Elizabeth and Zechariah. The Gospel of Luke opens with their story, followed by the foretelling and birth of the Son of God and Son of Man, Jesus the Christ. The descendant foretold in the beginning, the one bringing reconciliation and restoration, is the promised Messiah born to Mary and Joseph. Luke's narrative then follows the life and ministry of Jesus, who is born fully human, dies a physical death, is raised from the dead, and physically ascends into heaven.

The Book of Acts opens with the Ascension, followed by the sending of the Holy Spirit on the Day of Pentecost. Today the Holy Spirit indwells all who believe in Jesus, making each Christ-follower a temple intended to glorify God in all the earth. In this era, we gather as the church. But at the end of the age, Christ will return as Judge and King of the earth, and he will restore all things. The whole earth will finally be full of worshipers proclaiming the glory of Father, Son, and Holy Spirit.

With that as our big picture, let's begin to focus on the life of Christ on earth, which is the focus of Luke's Gospel.

1. This week we will read a lot more than in the weeks that follow. Unlike epistles such as Philippians or Ephesians that have six or fewer chapters, Luke has twenty-four chapters. And it's important to read the whole Gospel instead of just "hunting and pecking" for details or learning about Luke without reading Luke itself. So, sit back and read the text for each day as you would any other story. It will take you about as long to read each passage in Luke as it does to read a lengthy magazine article. To start, read Luke chapter 1 (below). As you read, circle references to prayer and to names of women. Put a star by sections where someone speaks a prophecy.

> 1:1 Now many have undertaken to compile an account of the things that have been fulfilled among us, 2 like the accounts passed on to us by those who were eyewitnesses and servants of the word from the beginning. 3 So it seemed good to me as well, because I have followed all things carefully from the beginning, to write an orderly account for you, most excellent Theophilus, 4 so that you may know for certain the things you were taught.
>
> 5 During the reign of Herod king of Judea, there lived a priest named Zechariah who belonged to the priestly division of Abijah, and he had a wife named Elizabeth, who was a descendant of Aaron. 6 They were both righteous in the sight of God, following all the commandments and ordinances of the Lord blamelessly. 7 But they did not have a child because Elizabeth was barren, and they were both very old.
>
> 8 Now while Zechariah was serving as priest before God when his division was on duty, 9 he was chosen by lot, according to the custom of the priesthood, to enter the Holy Place of the Lord and burn incense. 10 Now the whole crowd of people were praying outside at the hour of the incense offering. 11 An angel of the Lord, standing on the right side of the altar of incense, appeared to him. 12 And Zechariah, visibly shaken when he saw the angel, was seized with fear. 13 But the angel said to him, "Do not be afraid, Zechariah, for your prayer has been heard, and your wife Elizabeth will bear you a son; you will name him John. 14 Joy and gladness will come to you, and many will rejoice at his birth, 15 for he will be great in the sight of the Lord. He must never drink wine or strong drink, and he will be filled with the Holy Spirit, even before his birth. 16 He will turn many of the people of Israel to the Lord their God. 17 And he will go as forerunner before the Lord in the spirit and power of Elijah, to turn the hearts of the fathers back to their children and the disobedient to the wisdom of the just, to make ready for the Lord a people prepared for him."

18 Zechariah said to the angel, "How can I be sure of this? For I am an old man, and my wife is old as well." 19 The angel answered him, "I am Gabriel, who stands in the presence of God, and I was sent to speak to you and to bring you this good news. 20 And now because you did not believe my words, which will be fulfilled in their time, you will be silent, unable to speak, until the day these things take place."

21 Now the people were waiting for Zechariah, and they began to wonder why he was delayed in the Holy Place. 22 When he came out, he was not able to speak to them. They realized that he had seen a vision in the Holy Place because he was making signs to them and remained unable to speak. 23 When his time of service was over, he went to his home.

24 After some time his wife Elizabeth became pregnant, and for five months she kept herself in seclusion. She said, 25 "This is what the Lord has done for me at the time when he has been gracious to me, to take away my disgrace among people."

26 In the sixth month of Elizabeth's pregnancy, the angel Gabriel was sent by God to a town of Galilee called Nazareth, 27 to a virgin engaged to a man whose name was Joseph, a descendant of David, and the virgin's name was Mary. 28 The angel came to her and said, "Greetings, favored one, the Lord is with you!" 29 But she was greatly troubled by his words and began to wonder about the meaning of this greeting. 30 So the angel said to her, "Do not be afraid, Mary, for you have found favor with God! 31 Listen: You will become pregnant and give birth to a son, and you will name him Jesus. 32 He will be great and will be called the Son of the Most High, and the Lord God will give him the throne of his father David. 33 He will reign over the house of Jacob forever, and his kingdom will never end." 34 Mary said to the angel, "How will this be, since I have not been intimate with a man?" 35 The angel replied, "The Holy Spirit will come upon you, and the power of the Most High will overshadow you. Therefore the child to be born will be holy; he will be called the Son of God.

36 "And look, your relative Elizabeth has also become pregnant with a son in her old age—although she was called barren, she is now in her sixth month! 37 For nothing will be impossible with God." 38 So Mary said, "Yes, I am a servant of the Lord; let this happen to me according to your word." Then the angel departed from her.

39 In those days Mary got up and went hurriedly into the hill country, to a town of Judah, 40 and entered Zechariah's house and greeted Elizabeth. 41 When Elizabeth heard Mary's greeting, the baby leaped in her womb, and Elizabeth was filled with the Holy

Spirit. 42 She exclaimed with a loud voice, "Blessed are you among women, and blessed is the child in your womb! 43 And who am I that the mother of my Lord should come and visit me? 44 For the instant the sound of your greeting reached my ears, the baby in my womb leaped for joy. 45 And blessed is she who believed that what was spoken to her by the Lord would be fulfilled."

46 And Mary said,

"My soul exalts the Lord,

47 and my spirit has begun to rejoice in God my Savior,

48 because he has looked upon the humble state of his servant.

For from now on all generations will call me blessed,

49 because he who is mighty has done great things for me, and holy is his name;

50 from generation to generation he is merciful to those who fear him.

51 He has demonstrated power with his arm; he has scattered those whose pride wells up from the sheer arrogance of their hearts.

52 He has brought down the mighty from their thrones, and has lifted up those of lowly position;

53 he has filled the hungry with good things, and has sent the rich away empty.

54 He has helped his servant Israel, remembering his mercy,

55 as he promised to our ancestors, to Abraham and to his descendants forever."

56 So Mary stayed with Elizabeth about three months and then returned to her home.

57 Now the time came for Elizabeth to have her baby, and she gave birth to a son. 58 Her neighbors and relatives heard that the Lord had shown great mercy to her, and they rejoiced with her. 59 On the eighth day they came to circumcise the child, and they wanted to name him Zechariah after his father. 60 But his mother replied, "No! He must be named John." 61 They said to her, "But none of your relatives bears this name." 62 So they made signs to the baby's father, inquiring what he wanted to name his son. 63 He asked for a writing tablet and wrote, "His name is John." And they were all amazed. 64 Immediately Zechariah's mouth was opened and his tongue released, and he spoke, blessing God. 65 All their neighbors were filled with fear, and throughout the entire hill country of Judea all these things were talked about. 66 All who heard these things kept them in their hearts, saying, "What then will this child be?" For the Lord's hand was indeed with him.

67 Then his father Zechariah was filled with the Holy Spirit and prophesied,

68 "Blessed be the Lord God of Israel,
because he has come to help and has redeemed his people.

69 For he has raised up a horn of salvation for us in the house of his servant David,

70 as he spoke through the mouth of his holy prophets from long ago,

71 that we should be saved from our enemies
and from the hand of all who hate us.

72 He has done this to show mercy to our ancestors,
and to remember his holy covenant—

73 the oath that he swore to our ancestor Abraham.
This oath grants 74 that we, being rescued from the hand of our enemies,
may serve him without fear,

75 in holiness and righteousness before him for as long as we live.

76 And you, child, will be called the prophet of the Most High.
For you will go before the Lord to prepare his ways,

77 to give his people knowledge of salvation through the forgiveness of their sins.

78 Because of our God's tender mercy,
the dawn will break upon us from on high

79 to give light to those who sit in darkness and in the shadow of death,
to guide our feet into the way of peace."

80 And the child kept growing and becoming strong in spirit, and he was in the wilderness until the day he was revealed to Israel.

2. Now read Luke 2. Circle names of women. Put a star by prophecies.

2:1 Now in those days a decree went out from Caesar Augustus to register all the empire for taxes. 2 This was the first registration, taken when Quirinius was governor of Syria. 3 Everyone went to his own town to be registered. 4 So Joseph also went up from the town of Nazareth in Galilee to Judea, to the city of David called Bethlehem, because he was of the house and family line of David. 5 He went to be registered with Mary, who was promised in marriage to him, and who was expecting a child. 6 While they were there, the time came for her to deliver her child. 7 And she gave birth to her firstborn son and wrapped him in strips of cloth and laid him in a manger, because there was no place for them in the inn.

8 Now there were shepherds nearby living out in the field, keeping guard over their flock at night. 9 An angel of the Lord

appeared to them, and the glory of the Lord shone around them, and they were absolutely terrified. 10 But the angel said to them, "Do not be afraid! Listen carefully, for I proclaim to you good news that brings great joy to all the people: 11 Today your Savior is born in the city of David. He is Christ the Lord. 12 This will be a sign for you: You will find a baby wrapped in strips of cloth and lying in a manger." 13 Suddenly a vast, heavenly army appeared with the angel, praising God and saying,

14 "Glory to God in the highest,
and on earth peace among people with whom he is pleased!"

15 When the angels left them and went back to heaven, the shepherds said to one another, "Let us go over to Bethlehem and see this thing that has taken place, that the Lord has made known to us." 16 So they hurried off and located Mary and Joseph, and found the baby lying in a manger. 17 When they saw him, they related what they had been told about this child, 18 and all who heard it were astonished at what the shepherds said. 19 But Mary treasured up all these words, pondering in her heart what they might mean. 20 So the shepherds returned, glorifying and praising God for all they had heard and seen; everything was just as they had been told.

21 At the end of eight days, when he was circumcised, he was named Jesus, the name given by the angel before he was conceived in the womb.

22 Now when the time came for their purification according to the law of Moses, Joseph and Mary brought Jesus up to Jerusalem to present him to the Lord 23 (just as it is written in the law of the Lord, "Every firstborn male will be set apart to the Lord"), 24 and to offer a sacrifice according to what is specified in the law of the Lord, a pair of doves or two young pigeons.

25 Now there was a man in Jerusalem named Simeon who was righteous and devout, looking for the restoration of Israel, and the Holy Spirit was upon him. 26 It had been revealed to him by the Holy Spirit that he would not die before he had seen the Lord's Christ. 27 So Simeon, directed by the Spirit, came into the temple courts, and when the parents brought in the child Jesus to do for him what was customary according to the law, 28 Simeon took him in his arms and blessed God, saying,

29 "Now, according to your word, Sovereign Lord,
permit your servant to depart in peace.
30 For my eyes have seen your salvation
31 that you have prepared in the presence of all peoples:
32 a light,
for revelation to the Gentiles
and for glory to your people Israel."

33 So the child's father and mother were amazed at what was said about him. 34 Then Simeon blessed them and said to his mother Mary, "Listen carefully: This child is destined to be the cause of the falling and rising of many in Israel and to be a sign that will be rejected. 35 Indeed, as a result of him the thoughts of many hearts will be revealed—and a sword will pierce your own soul as well!"

36 There was also a prophetess, Anna the daughter of Phanuel, of the tribe of Asher. She was very old, having been married to her husband for seven years until his death. 37 She had lived as a widow since then for eighty-four years. She never left the temple, worshiping with fasting and prayer night and day. 38 At that moment, she came up to them and began to give thanks to God and to speak about the child to all who were waiting for the redemption of Jerusalem.

39 So when Joseph and Mary had performed everything according to the law of the Lord, they returned to Galilee, to their own town of Nazareth. 40 And the child grew and became strong, filled with wisdom, and the favor of God was upon him.

41 Now Jesus' parents went to Jerusalem every year for the Feast of the Passover. 42 When he was twelve years old, they went up according to custom. 43 But when the feast was over, as they were returning home, the boy Jesus stayed behind in Jerusalem. His parents did not know it, 44 but (because they assumed that he was in their group of travelers) they went a day's journey. Then they began to look for him among their relatives and acquaintances. 45 When they did not find him, they returned to Jerusalem to look for him. 46 After three days they found him in the temple courts, sitting among the teachers, listening to them and asking them questions. 47 And all who heard Jesus were astonished at his understanding and his answers. 48 When his parents saw him, they were overwhelmed. His mother said to him, "Child, why have you treated us like this? Look, your father and I have been looking for you anxiously." 49 But he replied, "Why were you looking for me? Didn't you know that I must be in my Father's house?" 50 Yet his parents did not understand the remark he made to them. 51 Then he went down with them and came to Nazareth, and was obedient to them. But his mother kept all these things in her heart.

52 And Jesus increased in wisdom and in stature and in favor with God and with people.

3. Look at your own notations. How did God use women to fulfill His promise?

___

___

4. What role did prayer and prophecy play in the story of Jesus's birth and early life?

___

___

5. Pray for your own spiritual life and growth in trusting God.

Tuesday: Jesus the Powerful

1. Pray for insight and read Luke, chapters 3–9.

> 3:1 In the fifteenth year of the reign of Tiberius Caesar, when Pontius Pilate was governor of Judea, and Herod was tetrarch of Galilee, and his brother Philip was tetrarch of the region of Iturea and Trachonitis, and Lysanias was tetrarch of Abilene, 2 during the high priesthood of Annas and Caiaphas, the word of God came to John the son of Zechariah in the wilderness. 3 He went into all the region around the Jordan River, preaching a baptism of repentance for the forgiveness of sins.

[In this section, circle all references to Christ as God's son. Put a star next to prophecies.]

> 4 As it is written in the book of the words of the prophet Isaiah,
> *"The voice of one shouting in the wilderness:*
> *'Prepare the way for the Lord,*
> *make his paths straight.*
> *5 Every valley will be filled,*
> *and every mountain and hill will be brought low,*
> *and the crooked will be made straight,*
> *and the rough ways will be made smooth,*
> *6 and all humanity will see the salvation of God.'"*

7 So John said to the crowds that came out to be baptized by him, "You offspring of vipers! Who warned you to flee from the coming wrath? 8 Therefore produce fruit that proves your repentance, and don't begin to say to yourselves, 'We have Abraham as our father.' For I tell you that God can raise up children for Abraham from these stones! 9 Even now the ax is laid at the root of the trees, and every tree that does not produce good fruit will be cut down and thrown into the fire."

10 So the crowds were asking him, "What then should we do?" 11 John answered them, "The person who has two tunics must share with the person who has none, and the person who has food must do likewise." 12 Tax collectors also came to be baptized, and they said to him, "Teacher, what should we do?" 13 He told them, "Collect no more than you are required to." 14 Then some soldiers also asked him, "And as for us—what should we do?" He told them, "Take money from no one by violence or by false accusation, and be content with your pay."

15 While the people were filled with anticipation and they all wondered whether perhaps John could be the Christ, 16 John answered them all, "I baptize you with water, but one more powerful than I am is coming—I am not worthy to untie the strap of his sandals. He will baptize you with the Holy Spirit and fire. 17 His winnowing fork is in his hand to clean out his threshing floor and to gather the wheat into his storehouse, but the chaff he will burn up with inextinguishable fire."

18 And in this way, with many other exhortations, John proclaimed good news to the people. 19 But when John rebuked Herod the tetrarch because of Herodias, his brother's wife, and because of all the evil deeds that he had done, 20 Herod added this to them all: He locked up John in prison.

21 Now when all the people were baptized, Jesus also was baptized. And while he was praying, the heavens opened, 22 and the Holy Spirit descended on him in bodily form like a dove. And a voice came from heaven, "You are my one dear Son; in you I take great delight."

23 So Jesus, when he began his ministry, was about thirty years old. He was the son (as was supposed) of Joseph, the son of Heli, 24 the son of Matthat, the son of Levi, the son of Melchi, the son of Jannai, the son of Joseph, 25 the son of Mattathias, the son of Amos, the son of Nahum, the son of Esli, the son of Naggai, 26 the son of Maath, the son of Mattathias, the son of Semein, the son of Josech, the son of Joda, 27 the son of Joanan, the son of Rhesa, the son of Zerubbabel, the son of Shealtiel, the son of Neri, 28 the son of Melchi, the son of Addi, the son of Cosam,

the son of Elmadam, the son of Er, 29 the son of Joshua, the son of Eliezer, the son of Jorim, the son of Matthat, the son of Levi, 30 the son of Simeon, the son of Judah, the son of Joseph, the son of Jonam, the son of Eliakim, 31 the son of Melea, the son of Menna, the son of Mattatha, the son of Nathan, the son of David, 32 the son of Jesse, the son of Obed, the son of Boaz, the son of Sala, the son of Nahshon, 33 the son of Amminadab, the son of Admin, the son of Arni, the son of Hezron, the son of Perez, the son of Judah, 34 the son of Jacob, the son of Isaac, the son of Abraham, the son of Terah, the son of Nahor, 35 the son of Serug, the son of Reu, the son of Peleg, the son of Eber, the son of Shelah, 36 the son of Cainan, the son of Arphaxad, the son of Shem, the son of Noah, the son of Lamech, 37 the son of Methuselah, the son of Enoch, the son of Jared, the son of Mahalalel, the son of Kenan, 38 the son of Enosh, the son of Seth, the son of Adam, the son of God.

[Underline all references to the supernatural in this section—the Spirit, the devil.]

4:1 Then Jesus, full of the Holy Spirit, returned from the Jordan River and was led by the Spirit in the wilderness, 2 where for forty days he endured temptations from the devil. He ate nothing during those days, and when they were completed, he was famished. 3 The devil said to him, "If you are the Son of God, command this stone to become bread." 4 Jesus answered him, "It is written, 'Man does not live by bread alone.'"

5 Then the devil led him up to a high place and showed him in a flash all the kingdoms of the world. 6 And he said to him, "To you I will grant this whole realm–and the glory that goes along with it, for it has been relinquished to me, and I can give it to anyone I wish. 7 So then, if you will worship me, all this will be yours." 8 Jesus answered him, "It is written, 'You are to worship the Lord your God and serve only him.'"

9 Then the devil brought him to Jerusalem, had him stand on the highest point of the temple, and said to him, "If you are the Son of God, throw yourself down from here, 10 for it is written, 'He will command his angels concerning you, to protect you,' 11 and 'with their hands they will lift you up, so that you will not strike your foot against a stone.'" 12 Jesus answered him, "It is said, 'You are not to put the Lord your God to the test.'" 13 So when the devil had completed every temptation, he departed from him until a more opportune time.

14 Then Jesus, in the power of the Spirit, returned to Galilee, and news about him spread throughout the surrounding countryside. 15 He began to teach in their synagogues and was praised by all.

[Put a star next to words of prophesy and fulfillment in this section.]

16 Now Jesus came to Nazareth, where he had been brought up, and went into the synagogue on the Sabbath day, as was his custom. He stood up to read, 17 and the scroll of the prophet Isaiah was given to him. He unrolled the scroll and found the place where it was written,

18 *"The Spirit of the Lord is upon me,*
because he has anointed me to proclaim good news to the poor.
He has sent me to proclaim release to the captives
and the regaining of sight to the blind,
to set free those who are oppressed,
19 to proclaim the year of the Lord's favor."

20 Then he rolled up the scroll, gave it back to the attendant, and sat down. The eyes of everyone in the synagogue were fixed on him. 21 Then he began to tell them, "Today this scripture has been fulfilled even as you heard it being read." 22 All were speaking well of him, and were amazed at the gracious words coming out of his mouth. They said, "Isn't this Joseph's son?" 23 Jesus said to them, "No doubt you will quote to me the proverb, 'Physician, heal yourself!' and say, 'What we have heard that you did in Capernaum, do here in your hometown too.'" 24 And he added, "I tell you the truth, no prophet is acceptable in his hometown. 25 But in truth I tell you, there were many widows in Israel in Elijah's days, when the sky was shut up three and a half years and there was a great famine over all the land. 26 Yet Elijah was sent to none of them, but only to a woman who was a widow at Zarephath in Sidon. 27 And there were many lepers in Israel in the time of the prophet Elisha, yet none of them was cleansed except Naaman the Syrian." 28 When they heard this, all the people in the synagogue were filled with rage. 29 They got up, forced him out of the town, and brought him to the brow of the hill on which their town was built, so that they could throw him down the cliff. 30 But he passed through the crowd and went on his way.

31 So he went down to Capernaum, a town in Galilee, and on the Sabbath he began to teach the people. 32 They were amazed at his teaching because he spoke with authority.

33 Now in the synagogue there was a man who had the spirit of an unclean demon, and he cried out with a loud voice, 34 "Ha!

Leave us alone, Jesus the Nazarene! Have you come to destroy us? I know who you are—the Holy One of God." 35 But Jesus rebuked him: "Silence! Come out of him!" Then, after the demon threw the man down in their midst, he came out of him without hurting him. 36 They were all amazed and began to say to one another, "What's happening here? For with authority and power he commands the unclean spirits, and they come out!" 37 So the news about him spread into all areas of the region.

38 After Jesus left the synagogue, he entered Simon's house. Now Simon's mother-in-law was suffering from a high fever, and they asked Jesus to help her. 39 So he stood over her, commanded the fever, and it left her. Immediately she got up and began to serve them.

40 As the sun was setting, all those who had any relatives sick with various diseases brought them to Jesus. He placed his hands on every one of them and healed them. 41 Demons also came out of many, crying out, "You are the Son of God!" But he rebuked them and would not allow them to speak because they knew that he was the Christ.

42 The next morning Jesus departed and went to a deserted place. Yet the crowds were seeking him, and they came to him and tried to keep him from leaving them. 43 But Jesus said to them, "I must proclaim the good news of the kingdom of God to the other towns too, for that is what I was sent to do." 44 So he continued to preach in the synagogues of Judea.

[Put a star next to miracles that happen in this section.]

5:1 Now Jesus was standing by the Lake of Gennesaret, and the crowd was pressing around him to hear the word of God. 2 He saw two boats by the lake, but the fishermen had gotten out of them and were washing their nets. 3 He got into one of the boats, which was Simon's, and asked him to put out a little way from the shore. Then Jesus sat down and taught the crowds from the boat. 4 When he had finished speaking, he said to Simon, "Put out into the deep water and lower your nets for a catch." 5 Simon answered, "Master, we worked hard all night and caught nothing! But at your word I will lower the nets." 6 When they had done this, they caught so many fish that their nets started to tear. 7 So they motioned to their partners in the other boat to come and help them. And they came and filled both boats, so that they were about to sink. 8 But when Simon Peter saw it, he fell down at Jesus' knees, saying, "Go away from me, Lord, for I am a sinful man!" 9 For Peter and all who were with him were astonished at the catch of fish that they had taken, 10 and so were James and John, Zebedee's sons, who were Simon's business partners. Then Jesus said to Simon, "Do not be afraid; from now on you will be catching people!" 11 So when they had brought their boats to shore, they left everything and followed him.

12 While Jesus was in one of the towns, a man came to him who was covered with leprosy. When he saw Jesus, he bowed down with his face to the ground and begged him, "Lord, if you are willing, you can make me clean." 13 So he stretched out his hand and touched him, saying, "I am willing. Be clean!" And immediately the leprosy left him. 14 Then he ordered the man to tell no one, but commanded him, "Go and show yourself to a priest, and bring the offering for your cleansing, as Moses commanded, as a testimony to them." 15 But the news about him spread even more, and large crowds were gathering together to hear him and to be healed of their illnesses. 16 Yet Jesus himself frequently withdrew to the wilderness and prayed.

17 Now on one of those days, while he was teaching, there were Pharisees and teachers of the law sitting nearby (who had come from every village of Galilee and Judea and from Jerusalem), and the power of the Lord was with him to heal. 18 Just then some men showed up, carrying a paralyzed man on a stretcher. They were trying to bring him in and place him before Jesus. 19 But since they found no way to carry him in because of the crowd, they went up on the roof and let him down on the stretcher through the roof tiles right in front of Jesus. 20 When Jesus saw their faith, he said, "Friend, your sins are forgiven." 21 Then the experts in the law and the Pharisees began to think to themselves, "Who is this man who is uttering blasphemies? Who can forgive sins but God alone?" 22 When Jesus perceived their hostile thoughts, he said to them, "Why are you raising objections within yourselves? 23 Which is easier, to say, 'Your sins are forgiven,' or to say, 'Stand up and walk'? 24 But so that you may know that the Son of Man has authority on earth to forgive sins"—he said to the paralyzed man—"I tell you, stand up, take your stretcher and go home." 25 Immediately he stood up before them, picked up the stretcher he had been lying on, and went home, glorifying God. 26 Then astonishment seized them all, and they glorified God. They were filled with awe, saying, "We have seen incredible things today."

27 After this, Jesus went out and saw a tax collector named Levi sitting at the tax booth. "Follow me," he said to him. 28 And he got up and followed him, leaving everything behind.

[Underline references to sin, repentance, and miracles in this section. Circle the phrase "Son of Man."]

29 Then Levi gave a great banquet in his house for Jesus, and there was a large crowd of tax collectors and others sitting at the table with them. 30 But the Pharisees and their experts in the law complained to his disciples, saying, "Why do you eat and drink with tax collectors and sinners?" 31 Jesus answered them, "Those who are well don't need a physician, but those who are sick do. 32 I have not come to call the righteous, but sinners to repentance."

33 Then they said to him, "John's disciples frequently fast and pray, and so do the disciples of the Pharisees, but yours continue to eat and drink." 34 So Jesus said to them, "You cannot make the wedding guests fast while the bridegroom is with them, can you? 35 But those days are coming, and when the bridegroom is taken from them, at that time they will fast." 36 He also told them a parable: "No one tears a patch from a new garment and sews it on an old garment. If he does, he will have torn the new, and the piece from the new will not match the old. 37 And no one pours new wine into old wineskins. If he does, the new wine will burst the skins and will be spilled, and the skins will be destroyed. 38 Instead new wine must be poured into new wineskins. 39 No one after drinking old wine wants the new, for he says, 'The old is good enough.'"

6:1 Jesus was going through the grain fields on a Sabbath, and his disciples picked some heads of wheat, rubbed them in their hands, and ate them. 2 But some of the Pharisees said, "Why are you doing what is against the law on the Sabbath?" 3 Jesus answered them, "Haven't you read what David did when he and his companions were hungry— 4 how he entered the house of God, took and ate the sacred bread, which is not lawful for any to eat but the priests alone, and gave it to his companions?" 5 Then he said to them, "The Son of Man is lord of the Sabbath."

6 On another Sabbath, Jesus entered the synagogue and was teaching. Now a man was there whose right hand was withered. 7 The experts in the law and the Pharisees watched Jesus closely to see if he would heal on the Sabbath, so that they could find a reason to accuse him. 8 But he knew their thoughts, and said to the man who had the withered hand, "Get up and stand here." So he rose and stood there. 9 Then Jesus said to them, "I ask you, is it lawful to do good on the Sabbath or to do evil, to save a life or to destroy it?" 10 After looking around at them all, he said to the man, "Stretch out your hand." The man did so, and his hand was restored.

11 But they were filled with mindless rage and began debating with one another what they would do to Jesus.

[Circle the word "pray" in this section along with references to miracles.]

12 Now it was during this time that Jesus went out to the mountain to pray, and he spent all night in prayer to God. 13 When morning came, he called his disciples and chose twelve of them, whom he also named apostles: 14 Simon (whom he named Peter), and his brother Andrew; and James, John, Philip, Bartholomew, 15 Matthew, Thomas, James the son of Alphaeus, Simon who was called the Zealot, 16 Judas the son of James, and Judas Iscariot, who became a traitor.

17 Then he came down with them and stood on a level place. And a large number of his disciples had gathered along with a vast multitude from all over Judea, from Jerusalem, and from the seacoast of Tyre and Sidon. They came to hear him and to be healed of their diseases, 18 and those who suffered from unclean spirits were cured. 19 The whole crowd was trying to touch him because power was coming out from him and healing them all.

[Circle the words *blessed and woe in this section.]*

20 Then he looked up at his disciples and said:

"Blessed are you who are poor, for the kingdom of God belongs to you.

21 Blessed are you who hunger now, for you will be satisfied.

Blessed are you who weep now, for you will laugh.

22 Blessed are you when people hate you, and when they exclude you and insult you and reject you as evil on account of the Son of Man! 23 Rejoice in that day, and jump for joy because your reward is great in heaven. For their ancestors did the same things to the prophets.

24 But woe to you who are rich, for you have received your comfort already.

25 Woe to you who are well satisfied with food now, for you will be hungry.

Woe to you who laugh now, for you will mourn and weep.

26 Woe to you when all people speak well of you, for their ancestors did the same things to the false prophets.

[Circle all references to love in this section.]

27 "But I say to you who are listening: Love your enemies, do good to those who hate you, 28 bless those who curse you, pray for those who mistreat you. 29 To the person who strikes you on the cheek, offer the other as well, and from the person who takes away your coat, do not withhold your tunic either. 30 Give to everyone who asks you, and do not ask for your possessions back from the person who takes them away. 31 Treat others in the same way that you would want them to treat you.

32 "If you love those who love you, what credit is that to you? For even sinners love those who love them. 33 And if you do good to those who do good to you, what credit is that to you? Even sinners do the same. 34 And if you lend to those from whom you hope to be repaid, what credit is that to you? Even sinners lend to sinners, so that they may be repaid in full. 35 But love your enemies, and do good, and lend, expecting nothing back. Then your reward will be great, and you will be sons of the Most High, because he is kind to ungrateful and evil people. 36 Be merciful, just as your Father is merciful.

[Underline all commands in this section.]

37 "Do not judge, and you will not be judged; do not condemn, and you will not be condemned; forgive, and you will be forgiven. 38 Give, and it will be given to you: A good measure, pressed down, shaken together, running over, will be poured into your lap. For the measure you use will be the measure you receive."

39 He also told them a parable: "Someone who is blind cannot lead another who is blind, can he? Won't they both fall into a pit? 40 A disciple is not greater than his teacher, but everyone when fully trained will be like his teacher. 41 Why do you see the speck in your brother's eye, but fail to see the beam of wood in your own? 42 How can you say to your brother, 'Brother, let me remove the speck from your eye,' while you yourself don't see the beam in your own? You hypocrite! First remove the beam from your own eye, and then you can see clearly to remove the speck from your brother's eye.

43 "For no good tree bears bad fruit, nor again does a bad tree bear good fruit, 44 for each tree is known by its own fruit. For figs are not gathered from thorns, nor are grapes picked from brambles. 45 The good person out of the good treasury of his heart produces good, and the evil person out of his evil treasury produces evil, for his mouth speaks from what fills his heart.

46 "Why do you call me 'Lord, Lord,' and don't do what I tell you?

47 "Everyone who comes to me and listens to my words and puts them into practice—I will show you what he is like: 48 He is like a man building a house, who dug down deep and laid the foundation on bedrock. When a flood came, the river burst against that house but could not shake it because it had been well built. 49 But the person who hears and does not put my words into practice is like a man who built a house on the ground without a foundation. When the river burst against that house, it collapsed immediately and was utterly destroyed!"

[Put a star by miracles in this section.]

7:1 After Jesus had finished teaching all this to the people, he entered Capernaum. 2 A centurion there had a slave who was highly regarded, but who was sick and at the point of death. 3 When the centurion heard about Jesus, he sent some Jewish elders to him, asking him to come and heal his slave. 4 When they came to Jesus, they urged him earnestly, "He is worthy to have you do this for him 5 because he loves our nation and even built our synagogue." 6 So Jesus went with them. When he was not far from the house, the centurion sent friends to say to him, "Lord, do not trouble yourself, for I am not worthy to have you come under my roof! 7 That is why I did not presume to come to you. Instead, say the word, and my servant must be healed. 8 For I too am a man set under authority, with soldiers under me. I say to this one, 'Go!' and he goes, and to another, 'Come!' and he comes, and to my slave, 'Do this!' and he does it." 9 When Jesus heard this, he was amazed at him. He turned and said to the crowd that followed him, "I tell you, not even in Israel have I found such faith!" 10 So when those who had been sent returned to the house, they found the slave well.

11 Soon afterward Jesus went to a town called Nain, and his disciples and a large crowd went with him. 12 As he approached the town gate, a man who had died was being carried out, the only son of his mother (who was a widow), and a large crowd from the town was with her. 13 When the Lord saw her, he had compassion for her and said to her, "Do not weep." 14 Then he came up and touched the bier, and those who carried it stood still. He said, "Young man, I say to you, get up!" 15 So the dead man sat up and began to speak, and Jesus gave him back to his mother. 16 Fear seized them all, and they began to glorify God, saying, "A great prophet has appeared among us!" and "God has come to help his people!" 17 This report

about Jesus circulated throughout Judea and all the surrounding country.

18 John's disciples informed him about all these things. So John called two of his disciples 19 and sent them to Jesus to ask, "Are you the one who is to come, or should we look for another?" 20 When the men came to Jesus, they said, "John the Baptist has sent us to you to ask, 'Are you the one who is to come, or should we look for another?'" 21 At that very time Jesus cured many people of diseases, sicknesses, and evil spirits, and granted sight to many who were blind. 22 So he answered them, "Go tell John what you have seen and heard: The blind see, the lame walk, lepers are cleansed, the deaf hear, the dead are raised, the poor have good news proclaimed to them. 23 Blessed is anyone who takes no offense at me."

24 When John's messengers had gone, Jesus began to speak to the crowds about John: "What did you go out into the wilderness to see? A reed shaken by the wind? 25 What did you go out to see? A man dressed in soft clothing? Look, those who wear soft clothing and live in luxury are in the royal palaces! 26 What did you go out to see? A prophet? Yes, I tell you, and more than a prophet. 27 This is the one about whom it is written, 'Look, I am sending my messenger ahead of you, who will prepare your way before you.' 28 I tell you, among those born of women no one is greater than John. Yet the one who is least in the kingdom of God is greater than he is." 29 (Now all the people who heard this, even the tax collectors, acknowledged God's justice because they had been baptized with John's baptism. 30 However, the Pharisees and the experts in religious law rejected God's purpose for themselves because they had not been baptized by John.)

31 "To what then should I compare the people of this generation, and what are they like? 32 They are like children sitting in the marketplace and calling out to one another,

"'We played the flute for you, yet you did not dance;
we wailed in mourning, yet you did not weep.'

33 For John the Baptist has come eating no bread and drinking no wine, and you say, 'He has a demon!' 34 The Son of Man has come eating and drinking, and you say, 'Look at him, a glutton and a drunk, a friend of tax collectors and sinners!' 35 But wisdom is vindicated by all her children."

36 Now one of the Pharisees asked Jesus to have dinner with him, so he went into the Pharisee's house and took his place at the table. 37 Then when a woman of that town, who was a sinner,

learned that Jesus was dining at the Pharisee's house, she brought an alabaster jar of perfumed oil. 38 As she stood behind him at his feet, weeping, she began to wet his feet with her tears. She wiped them with her hair, kissed them, and anointed them with the perfumed oil. 39 Now when the Pharisee who had invited him saw this, he said to himself, "If this man were a prophet, he would know who and what kind of woman this is who is touching him, that she is a sinner." 40 So Jesus answered him, "Simon, I have something to say to you." He replied, "Say it, Teacher." 41 "A certain creditor had two debtors; one owed him 500 silver coins, and the other 50. 42 When they could not pay, he canceled the debts of both. Now which of them will love him more?" 43 Simon answered, "I suppose the one who had the bigger debt canceled." Jesus said to him, "You have judged rightly." 44 Then, turning toward the woman, he said to Simon, "Do you see this woman? I entered your house. You gave me no water for my feet, but she has wet my feet with her tears and wiped them with her hair. 45 You gave me no kiss of greeting, but from the time I entered she has not stopped kissing my feet. 46 You did not anoint my head with oil, but she has anointed my feet with perfumed oil. 47 Therefore I tell you, her sins, which were many, are forgiven, thus she loved much; but the one who is forgiven little loves little." 48 Then Jesus said to her, "Your sins are forgiven." 49 But those who were at the table with him began to say among themselves, "Who is this, who even forgives sins?" 50 He said to the woman, "Your faith has saved you; go in peace."

8:1 Sometime afterward he went on through towns and villages, preaching and proclaiming the good news of the kingdom of God. The twelve were with him, 2 and also some women who had been healed of evil spirits and disabilities: Mary (called Magdalene), from whom seven demons had gone out, 3 and Joanna the wife of Cuza (Herod's household manager), Susanna, and many others who provided for them out of their own resources.

4 While a large crowd was gathering and people were coming to Jesus from one town after another, he spoke to them in a parable: 5 "A sower went out to sow his seed. And as he sowed, some fell along the path and was trampled on, and the wild birds devoured it. 6 Other seed fell on rock, and when it came up, it withered because it had no moisture. 7 Other seed fell among the thorns, and they grew up with it and choked it. 8 But other seed fell on good soil and grew, and it produced a hundred times as much grain." As he said this, he called out, "The one who has ears to hear had better listen!"

9 Then his disciples asked him what this parable meant. 10 He said, "You have been given the opportunity to know the secrets of

the kingdom of God, but for others they are in parables, so that although they see they may not see, and although they hear they may not understand.

11 "Now the parable means this: The seed is the word of God. 12 Those along the path are the ones who have heard; then the devil comes and takes away the word from their hearts, so that they may not believe and be saved. 13 Those on the rock are the ones who receive the word with joy when they hear it, but they have|no root. They believe for a while, but in a time of testing fall away. 14 As for the seed that fell among thorns, these are the ones who hear, but as they go on their way they are choked by the worries and riches and pleasures of life, and their fruit does not mature. 15 But as for the seed that landed on good soil, these are the ones who, after hearing the word, cling to it with an honest and good heart, and bear fruit with steadfast endurance.

16 "No one lights a lamp and then covers it with a jar or puts it under a bed, but puts it on a lampstand so that those who come in can see the light. 17 For nothing is hidden that will not be revealed, and nothing concealed that will not be made known and brought to light. 18 So listen carefully, for whoever has will be given more, but whoever does not have, even what he thinks he has will be taken from him."

19 Now Jesus' mother and his brothers came to him, but they could not get near him because of the crowd. 20 So he was told, "Your mother and your brothers are standing outside, wanting to see you." 21 But he replied to them, "My mother and my brothers are those who hear the word of God and do it."

22 One day Jesus got into a boat with his disciples and said to them, "Let's go across to the other side of the lake." So they set out, 23 and as they sailed he fell asleep. Now a violent windstorm came down on the lake, and the boat started filling up with water, and they were in danger. 24 They came and woke him, saying, "Master, Master, we are about to die!" So he got up and rebuked the wind and the raging waves; they died down, and it was calm. 25 Then he said to them, "Where is your faith?" But they were afraid and amazed, saying to one another, "Who then is this? He commands even the winds and the water, and they obey him!"

26 So they sailed over to the region of the Gerasenes, which is opposite Galilee. 27 As Jesus stepped ashore, a certain man from the town met him who was possessed by demons. For a long time this man had worn no clothes and had not lived in a house, but among the tombs. 28 When he saw Jesus, he cried out, fell down before him, and shouted with a loud voice, "Leave me alone, Jesus, Son of the Most High God! I beg you, do not torment me!" 29 For Jesus had

started commanding the evil spirit to come out of the man. (For it had seized him many times, so he would be bound with chains and shackles and kept under guard. But he would break the restraints and be driven by the demon into deserted places.) 30 Jesus then asked him, "What is your name?" He said, "Legion," because many demons had entered him. 31 And they began to beg him not to order them to depart into the abyss. 32 Now a large herd of pigs was feeding there on the hillside, and the demonic spirits begged Jesus to let them go into them. He gave them permission. 33 So the demons came out of the man and went into the pigs, and the herd of pigs rushed down the steep slope into the lake and drowned. 34 When the herdsmen saw what had happened, they ran off and spread the news in the town and countryside. 35 So the people went out to see what had happened, and they came to Jesus. They found the man from whom the demons had gone out, sitting at Jesus' feet, clothed and in his right mind, and they were afraid. 36 Those who had seen it told them how the man who had been demon-possessed had been healed. 37 Then all the people of the Gerasenes and the surrounding region asked Jesus to leave them alone, for they were seized with great fear. So he got into the boat and left. 38 The man from whom the demons had gone out begged to go with him, but Jesus sent him away, saying, 39 "Return to your home, and declare what God has done for you." So he went away, proclaiming throughout the whole town what Jesus had done for him.

40 Now when Jesus returned, the crowd welcomed him because they were all waiting for him. 41 Then a man named Jairus, who was a leader of the synagogue, came up. Falling at Jesus' feet, he pleaded with him to come to his house, 42 because he had an only daughter, about twelve years old, and she was dying.

As Jesus was on his way, the crowds pressed around him. 43 Now a woman was there who had been suffering from a hemorrhage for twelve years but could not be healed by anyone. 44 She came up behind Jesus and touched the edge of his cloak, and at once the bleeding stopped. 45 Then Jesus asked, "Who was it who touched me?" When they all denied it, Peter said, "Master, the crowds are surrounding you and pressing against you!" 46 But Jesus said, "Someone touched me, for I know that power has gone out from me." 47 When the woman saw that she could not escape notice, she came trembling and fell down before him. In the presence of all the people, she explained why she had touched him and how she had been immediately healed. 48 Then he said to her, "Daughter, your faith has made you well. Go in peace."

49 While he was still speaking, someone from the synagogue leader's house came and said, "Your daughter is dead; do not

trouble the teacher any longer." 50 But when Jesus heard this, he told him, "Do not be afraid; just believe, and she will be healed." 51 Now when he came to the house, Jesus did not let anyone go in with him except Peter, John, and James, and the child's father and mother. 52 Now they were all wailing and mourning for her, but he said, "Stop your weeping; she is not dead but asleep!" 53 And they began making fun of him because they knew that she was dead. 54 But Jesus gently took her by the hand and said, "Child, get up." 55 Her spirit returned, and she got up immediately. Then he told them to give her something to eat. 56 Her parents were astonished, but he ordered them to tell no one what had happened.

9:1 After Jesus called the twelve together, he gave them power and authority over all demons and to cure diseases, 2 and he sent them out to proclaim the kingdom of God and to heal the sick. 3 He said to them, "Take nothing for your journey—no staff, no bag, no bread, no money, and do not take an extra tunic. 4 Whatever house you enter, stay there until you leave the area. 5 Wherever they do not receive you, as you leave that town, shake the dust off your feet as a testimony against them." 6 Then they departed and went throughout the villages, proclaiming the good news and healing people everywhere.

7 Now Herod the tetrarch heard about everything that was happening, and he was thoroughly perplexed because some people were saying that John had been raised from the dead, 8 while others were saying that Elijah had appeared, and still others that one of the prophets of long ago had risen. 9 Herod said, "I had John beheaded, but who is this about whom I hear such things?" So Herod wanted to learn about Jesus.

10 When the apostles returned, they told Jesus everything they had done. Then he took them with him and they withdrew privately to a town called Bethsaida. 11 But when the crowds found out, they followed him. He welcomed them, spoke to them about the kingdom of God, and cured those who needed healing. 12 Now the day began to draw to a close, so the twelve came and said to Jesus, "Send the crowd away, so they can go into the surrounding villages and countryside and find lodging and food because we are in an isolated place." 13 But he said to them, "You give them something to eat." They replied, "We have no more than five loaves and two fish—unless we go and buy food for all these people." 14 (Now about 5,000 men were there.) Then he said to his disciples, "Have them sit down in groups of about fifty each." 15 So they did as Jesus directed, and the people all sat down.

16 Then he took the five loaves and the two fish, and looking up to heaven he gave thanks and broke them. He gave them to the

disciples to set before the crowd. 17 They all ate and were satisfied, and what was left over was picked up—twelve baskets of broken pieces.

18 Once when Jesus was praying by himself and his disciples were nearby, he asked them, "Who do the crowds say that I am?" 19 They answered, "John the Baptist; others say Elijah; and still others that one of the prophets of long ago has risen." 20 Then he said to them, "But who do you say that I am?" Peter answered, "The Christ of God." 21 But he forcefully commanded them not to tell this to anyone, 22 saying, "The Son of Man must suffer many things and be rejected by the elders, chief priests, and experts in the law, and be killed, and on the third day be raised."

23 Then he said to them all, "If anyone wants to become my follower, he must deny himself, take up his cross daily, and follow me. 24 For whoever wants to save his life will lose it, but whoever loses his life because of me will save it. 25 For what does it benefit a person if he gains the whole world but loses or forfeits himself? 26 For whoever is ashamed of me and my words, the Son of Man will be ashamed of that person when he comes in his glory and in the glory of the Father and of the holy angels. 27 But I tell you most certainly, there are some standing here who will not experience death before they see the kingdom of God."

28 Now about eight days after these sayings, Jesus took with him Peter, John, and James, and went up the mountain to pray. 29 As he was praying, the appearance of his face was transformed, and his clothes became very bright, a brilliant white. 30 Then two men, Moses and Elijah, began talking with him. 31 They appeared in glorious splendor and spoke about his departure that he was about to carry out at Jerusalem. 32 Now Peter and those with him were quite sleepy, but as they became fully awake, they saw his glory and the two men standing with him. 33 Then as the men were starting to leave, Peter said to Jesus, "Master, it is good for us to be here. Let us make three shelters, one for you and one for Moses and one for Elijah"—not knowing what he was saying. 34 As he was saying this, a cloud came and overshadowed them, and they were afraid as they entered the cloud. 35 Then a voice came from the cloud, saying, "This is my Son, my Chosen One. Listen to him!" 36 After the voice had spoken, Jesus was found alone. So they kept silent and told no one at that time anything of what they had seen.

37 Now on the next day, when they had come down from the mountain, a large crowd met him. 38 Then a man from the crowd cried out, "Teacher, I beg you to look at my son—he is my only child! 39 A spirit seizes him, and he suddenly screams; it throws him into

convulsions and causes him to foam at the mouth. It hardly ever leaves him alone, torturing him severely. 40 I begged your disciples to cast it out, but they could not do so." 41 Jesus answered, "You unbelieving and perverse generation! How much longer must I be with you and endure you? Bring your son here." 42 As the boy was approaching, the demon threw him to the ground and shook him with convulsions. But Jesus rebuked the unclean spirit, healed the boy, and gave him back to his father. 43 Then they were all astonished at the mighty power of God.

But while the entire crowd was amazed at everything Jesus was doing, he said to his disciples, 44 "Take these words to heart, for the Son of Man is going to be betrayed into the hands of men." 45 But they did not understand this statement; its meaning had been concealed from them, so that they could not grasp it. Yet they were afraid to ask him about this statement.

46 Now an argument started among the disciples as to which of them might be the greatest. 47 But when Jesus discerned their innermost thoughts, he took a child, had him stand by his side, 48 and said to them, "Whoever welcomes this child in my name welcomes me, and whoever welcomes me welcomes the one who sent me, for the one who is least among you all is the one who is great."

49 John answered, "Master, we saw someone casting out demons in your name, and we tried to stop him because he is not a disciple along with us." 50 But Jesus said to him, "Do not stop him, for whoever is not against you is for you."

51 Now when the days drew near for him to be taken up, Jesus set out resolutely to go to Jerusalem. 52 He sent messengers on ahead of him. As they went along, they entered a Samaritan village to make things ready in advance for him, 53 but the villagers refused to welcome him because he was determined to go to Jerusalem. 54 Now when his disciples James and John saw this, they said, "Lord, do you want us to call fire to come down from heaven and consume them?" 55 But Jesus turned and rebuked them, 56 and they went on to another village.

57 As they were walking along the road, someone said to him, "I will follow you wherever you go." 58 Jesus said to him, "Foxes have dens and the birds in the sky have nests, but the Son of Man has no place to lay his head." 59 Jesus said to another, "Follow me." But he replied, "Lord, first let me go and bury my father." 60 But Jesus said to him, "Let the dead bury their own dead, but as for you, go and proclaim the kingdom of God." 61 Yet another said, "I will follow you, Lord, but first let me say goodbye to my family." 62 Jesus said to him, "No one who puts his hand to the plow and looks back is fit for the kingdom of God."

2. Look back at your notations. Most genealogies at the time of Luke's writing did not include women. What women did you find in Jesus's genealogy?

____

____

3. What does it reveal about Jesus that he can cure the sick, cast out demons, and has power over death?

____

____

4. How does your answer to #3 affect how you view him and relate to him personally?

____

____

Wednesday: Jesus, Lord of the Natural and the Supernatural

1. Pray for insight and read or listen to Luke 10–14. Circle references to women, and underline references to Jesus's power over the supernatural world.

> 10:1 After this the Lord appointed seventy-two others and sent them on ahead of him two by two into every town and place where he himself was about to go. 2 He said to them, "The harvest is plentiful, but the workers are few. Therefore ask the Lord of the harvest to send out workers into his harvest. 3 Go! I am sending you out like lambs surrounded by wolves. 4 Do not carry a money bag, a traveler's bag, or sandals, and greet no one on the road. 5 Whenever you enter a house, first say, 'May peace be on this house!' 6 And if a peace-loving person is there, your peace will remain on him, but if not, it will return to you. 7 Stay in that same house, eating and drinking what they give you, for the worker deserves his pay.

Do not move around from house to house. 8 Whenever you enter a town and the people welcome you, eat what is set before you. 9 Heal the sick in that town and say to them, 'The kingdom of God has come upon you!' 10 But whenever you enter a town and the people do not welcome you, go into its streets and say, 11 'Even the dust of your town that clings to our feet we wipe off against you. Nevertheless know this: The kingdom of God has come.' 12 I tell you, it will be more bearable on that day for Sodom than for that town!

13 "Woe to you, Chorazin! Woe to you, Bethsaida! For if the miracles done in you had been done in Tyre and Sidon, they would have repented long ago, sitting in sackcloth and ashes. 14 But it will be more bearable for Tyre and Sidon in the judgment than for you! 15 And you, Capernaum, will you be exalted to heaven? No, you will be thrown down to Hades!

16 "The one who listens to you listens to me, and the one who rejects you rejects me, and the one who rejects me rejects the one who sent me."

17 Then the seventy-two returned with joy, saying, "Lord, even the demons submit to us in your name!" 18 So he said to them, "I saw Satan fall like lightning from heaven. 19 Look, I have given you authority to tread on snakes and scorpions and on the full force of the enemy, and nothing will hurt you. 20 Nevertheless, do not rejoice that the spirits submit to you, but rejoice that your names stand written in heaven."

21 On that same occasion Jesus rejoiced in the Holy Spirit and said, "I praise you, Father, Lord of heaven and earth, because you have hidden these things from the wise and intelligent and revealed them to little children. Yes, Father, for this was your gracious will. 22 All things have been given to me by my Father. No one knows who the Son is except the Father, or who the Father is except the Son and anyone to whom the Son decides to reveal him."

23 Then Jesus turned to his disciples and said privately, "Blessed are the eyes that see what you see! 24 For I tell you that many prophets and kings longed to see what you see but did not see it, and to hear what you hear but did not hear it."

25 Now an expert in religious law stood up to test Jesus, saying, "Teacher, what must I do to inherit eternal life?" 26 He said to him, "What is written in the law? How do you understand it?" 27 The expert answered, "Love the Lord your God with all your heart, with all your soul, with all your strength, and with all your mind, and love your neighbor as yourself." 28 Jesus said to him, "You have answered correctly; do this, and you will live."

29 But the expert, wanting to justify himself, said to Jesus, "And who is my neighbor?" 30 Jesus replied, "A man was going down from Jerusalem to Jericho, and fell into the hands of robbers, who stripped him, beat him up, and went off, leaving him half dead. 31 Now by chance a priest was going down that road, but when he saw the injured man, he passed by on the other side. 32 So too a Levite, when he came up to the place and saw him, passed by on the other side. 33 But a Samaritan who was traveling came to where the injured man was, and when he saw him, he felt compassion for him. 34 He went up to him and bandaged his wounds, pouring olive oil and wine on them. Then he put him on his own animal, brought him to an inn, and took care of him. 35 The next day he took out two silver coins and gave them to the innkeeper, saying, 'Take care of him, and whatever else you spend, I will repay you when I come back this way.' 36 Which of these three do you think became a neighbor to the man who fell into the hands of the robbers?" 37 The expert in religious law said, "The one who showed mercy to him." So Jesus said to him, "Go and do the same."

38 Now as they went on their way, Jesus entered a certain village where a woman named Martha welcomed him as a guest. 39 She had a sister named Mary, who sat at the Lord's feet and listened to what he said. 40 But Martha was distracted with all the preparations she had to make, so she came up to him and said, "Lord, don't you care that my sister has left me to do all the work alone? Tell her to help me." 41 But the Lord answered her, "Martha, Martha, you are worried and troubled about many things, 42 but one thing is needed. Mary has chosen the best part; it will not be taken away from her."

11:1 Now Jesus was praying in a certain place. When he stopped, one of his disciples said to him, "Lord, teach us to pray, just as John taught his disciples." 2 So he said to them, "When you pray, say:

"'Father, may your name be honored;
may your kingdom come.
3 Give us each day our daily bread,
4 and forgive us our sins,
for we also forgive everyone who sins against us.
And do not lead us into temptation.'"

5 Then he said to them, "Suppose one of you has a friend, and you go to him at midnight and say to him, 'Friend, lend me three loaves of bread, 6 because a friend of mine has stopped here while on a journey, and I have nothing to set before him.' 7 Then he will reply from inside, 'Do not bother me. The door is already shut, and

my children and I are in bed. I cannot get up and give you anything.' 8 I tell you, even though the man inside will not get up and give him anything because he is his friend, yet because of the first man's sheer persistence he will get up and give him whatever he needs.

9 "So I tell you: Ask, and it will be given to you; seek, and you will find; knock, and the door will be opened for you. 10 For everyone who asks receives, and the one who seeks finds, and to the one who knocks, the door will be opened. 11 What father among you, if your son asks for a fish, will give him a snake instead of a fish? 12 Or if he asks for an egg, will give him a scorpion? 13 If you then, although you are evil, know how to give good gifts to your children, how much more will the heavenly Father give the Holy Spirit to those who ask him!"

14 Now he was casting out a demon that was mute. When the demon had gone out, the man who had been mute began to speak, and the crowds were amazed. 15 But some of them said, "By the power of Beelzebul, the ruler of demons, he casts out demons!" 16 Others, to test him, began asking for a sign from heaven. 17 But Jesus, realizing their thoughts, said to them, "Every kingdom divided against itself is destroyed, and a divided household falls. 18 So if Satan too is divided against himself, how will his kingdom stand? I ask you this because you claim that I cast out demons by Beelzebul. 19 Now if I cast out demons by Beelzebul, by whom do your sons cast them out? Therefore they will be your judges. 20 But if I cast out demons by the finger of God, then the kingdom of God has already overtaken you. 21 When a strong man, fully armed, guards his own palace, his possessions are safe. 22 But when a stronger man attacks and conquers him, he takes away the first man's armor on which the man relied and divides up his plunder. 23 Whoever is not with me is against me, and whoever does not gather with me scatters.

24 "When an unclean spirit goes out of a person, it passes through waterless places looking for rest but not finding any. Then it says, 'I will return to the home I left.' 25 When it returns, it finds the house swept clean and put in order. 26 Then it goes and brings seven other spirits more evil than itself, and they go in and live there, so the last state of that person is worse than the first."

27 As he said these things, a woman in the crowd spoke out to him, "Blessed is the womb that bore you and the breasts at which you nursed!" 28 But he replied, "Blessed rather are those who hear the word of God and obey it!"

29 As the crowds were increasing, Jesus began to say, "This generation is a wicked generation; it looks for a sign, but no sign will be given to it except the sign of Jonah. 30 For just as Jonah

became a sign to the people of Nineveh, so the Son of Man will be a sign to this generation. 31 The queen of the South will rise up at the judgment with the people of this generation and condemn them, because she came from the ends of the earth to hear the wisdom of Solomon—and now, something greater than Solomon is here! 32 The people of Nineveh will stand up at the judgment with this generation and condemn it, because they repented when Jonah preached to them—and now, something greater than Jonah is here!

33 "No one after lighting a lamp puts it in a hidden place or under a basket, but on a lampstand, so that those who come in can see the light. 34 Your eye is the lamp of your body. When your eye is healthy, your whole body is full of light, but when it is diseased, your body is full of darkness. 35 Therefore see to it that the light in you is not darkness. 36 If then your whole body is full of light, with no part in the dark, it will be as full of light as when the light of a lamp shines on you."

37 As he spoke, a Pharisee invited Jesus to have a meal with him, so he went in and took his place at the table. 38 The Pharisee was astonished when he saw that Jesus did not first wash his hands before the meal. 39 But the Lord said to him, "Now you Pharisees clean the outside of the cup and the plate, but inside you are full of greed and wickedness. 40 You fools! Didn't the one who made the outside make the inside as well? 41 But give from your heart to those in need, and then everything will be clean for you.

42 "But woe to you Pharisees! You give a tenth of your mint, rue, and every herb, yet you neglect justice and love for God! But you should have done these things without neglecting the others. 43 Woe to you Pharisees! You love the best seats in the synagogues and elaborate greetings in the marketplaces! 44 Woe to you! You are like unmarked graves, and people walk over them without realizing it!"

45 One of the experts in religious law answered him, "Teacher, when you say these things, you insult us too." 46 But Jesus replied, "Woe to you experts in religious law as well! You load people down with burdens difficult to bear, yet you yourselves refuse to touch the burdens with even one of your fingers! 47 Woe to you! You build the tombs of the prophets whom your ancestors killed. 48 So you testify that you approve of the deeds of your ancestors because they killed the prophets and you build their tombs! 49 For this reason also the wisdom of God said, 'I will send them prophets and apostles, some of whom they will kill and persecute,' 50 so that this generation may be held accountable for the blood of all the prophets that has been shed since the beginning of the world, 51 from the

blood of Abel to the blood of Zechariah, who was killed between the altar and the sanctuary. Yes, I tell you, it will be charged against this generation. 52 Woe to you experts in religious law! You have taken away the key to knowledge! You did not go in yourselves, and you hindered those who were going in."

53 When he went out from there, the experts in the law and the Pharisees began to oppose him bitterly and to ask him hostile questions about many things, 54 plotting against him to catch him in something he might say.

12:1 Meanwhile, when many thousands of the crowd had gathered so that they were trampling on one another, Jesus began to speak first to his disciples, "Be on your guard against the yeast of the Pharisees, which is hypocrisy. 2 Nothing is hidden that will not be revealed, and nothing is secret that will not be made known. 3 So then whatever you have said in the dark will be heard in the light, and what you have whispered in private rooms will be proclaimed from the housetops.

4 "I tell you, my friends, do not be afraid of those who kill the body, and after that have nothing more they can do. 5 But I will warn you whom you should fear: Fear the one who, after the killing, has authority to throw you into hell. Yes, I tell you, fear him! 6 Aren't five sparrows sold for two pennies? Yet not one of them is forgotten before God. 7 In fact, even the hairs on your head are all numbered. Do not be afraid; you are more valuable than many sparrows.

8 "I tell you, whoever acknowledges me before men, the Son of Man will also acknowledge before God's angels. 9 But the one who denies me before men will be denied before God's angels. 10 And everyone who speaks a word against the Son of Man will be forgiven, but the person who blasphemes against the Holy Spirit will not be forgiven. 11 But when they bring you before the synagogues, the rulers, and the authorities, do not worry about how you should make your defense or what you should say, 12 for the Holy Spirit will teach you at that moment what you must say."

13 Then someone from the crowd said to him, "Teacher, tell my brother to divide the inheritance with me." 14 But Jesus said to him, "Man, who made me a judge or arbitrator between you two?" 15 Then he said to them, "Watch out and guard yourself from all types of greed because one's life does not consist in the abundance of his possessions." 16 He then told them a parable: "The land of a certain rich man produced an abundant crop, 17 so he thought to himself, 'What should I do, for I have nowhere to store my crops?' 18 Then he said, 'I will do this: I will tear down my barns and build bigger ones, and there I will store all my grain and my

goods. 19 And I will say to myself, "You have plenty of goods stored up for many years; relax, eat, drink, celebrate!"' 20 But God said to him, 'You fool! This very night your life will be demanded back from you, but who will get what you have prepared for yourself?' 21 So it is with the one who stores up riches for himself, but is not rich toward God."

22 Then Jesus said to his disciples, "Therefore I tell you, do not worry about your life, what you will eat, or about your body, what you will wear. 23 For there is more to life than food, and more to the body than clothing. 24 Consider the ravens: They do not sow or reap, they have no storeroom or barn, yet God feeds them. How much more valuable are you than the birds! 25 And which of you by worrying can add an hour to his life? 26 So if you cannot do such a very little thing as this, why do you worry about the rest? 27 Consider how the flowers grow; they do not work or spin. Yet I tell you, not even Solomon in all his glory was clothed like one of these! 28 And if this is how God clothes the wild grass, which is here today and tomorrow is tossed into the fire to heat the oven, how much more will he clothe you, you people of little faith! 29 So do not be overly concerned about what you will eat and what you will drink, and do not worry about such things. 30 For all the nations of the world pursue these things, and your Father knows that you need them. 31 Instead, pursue his kingdom, and these things will be given to you as well.

32 "Do not be afraid, little flock, for your Father is well pleased to give you the kingdom. 33 Sell your possessions and give to the poor. Provide yourselves purses that do not wear out—a treasure in heaven that never decreases, where no thief approaches and no moth destroys. 34 For where your treasure is, there your heart will be also.

35 "Get dressed for service and keep your lamps burning; 36 be like people waiting for their master to come back from the wedding celebration, so that when he comes and knocks, they can immediately open the door for him. 37 Blessed are those slaves whom their master finds alert when he returns! I tell you the truth, he will dress himself to serve, have them take their place at the table, and will come and wait on them! 38 Even if he comes in the second or third watch of the night and finds them alert, blessed are those slaves! 39 But understand this: If the owner of the house had known at what hour the thief was coming, he would not have let his house be broken into. 40 You also must be ready because the Son of Man will come at an hour when you do not expect him."

41 Then Peter said, "Lord, are you telling this parable for us or for everyone?" 42 The Lord replied, "Who then is the faithful and

wise manager, whom the master puts in charge of his household servants, to give them their allowance of food at the proper time? 43 Blessed is that slave whom his master finds at work when he returns. 44 I tell you the truth, the master will put him in charge of all his possessions. 45 But if that slave should say to himself, 'My master is delayed in returning,' and he begins to beat the other slaves, both men and women, and to eat, drink, and get drunk, 46 then the master of that slave will come on a day when he does not expect him and at an hour he does not foresee, and will cut him in two, and assign him a place with the unfaithful. 47 That servant who knew his master's will but did not get ready or do what his master asked will receive a severe beating. 48 But the one who did not know his master's will and did things worthy of punishment will receive a light beating. From everyone who has been given much, much will be required, and from the one who has been entrusted with much, even more will be asked.

49 "I have come to bring fire on the earth—and how I wish it were already kindled! 50 I have a baptism to undergo, and how distressed I am until it is finished! 51 Do you think I have come to bring peace on earth? No, I tell you, but rather division! 52 For from now on there will be five in one household divided, three against two and two against three. 53 They will be divided, father against son and son against father, mother against daughter and daughter against mother, mother-in-law against her daughter-in-law and daughter-in-law against mother-in-law."

54 Jesus also said to the crowds, "When you see a cloud rising in the west, you say at once, 'A rainstorm is coming,' and it does. 55 And when you see the south wind blowing, you say, 'There will be scorching heat,' and there is. 56 You hypocrites! You know how to interpret the appearance of the earth and the sky, but how can you not know how to interpret the present time?

57 "And why don't you judge for yourselves what is right? 58 As you are going with your accuser before the magistrate, make an effort to settle with him on the way, so that he will not drag you before the judge, and the judge hand you over to the officer, and the officer throw you into prison. 59 I tell you, you will never get out of there until you have paid the very last cent!"

2. What common themes did you notice in Jesus's teachings?

____

____

3. In what areas of your life do you need to trust that Jesus has power over the natural and supernatural worlds?

---

4. Pray, asking him to help you trust and yield to him.

Thursday: Jesus the Greatest Teacher

1. Pray for the Spirit to speak through the Word. Then read Luke 15–19. If possible, read the text aloud or listen to it read. If you read it for yourself, put a star by words of Jesus's teaching.

> 15:1 Now all the tax collectors and sinners were coming to hear him. 2 But the Pharisees and the experts in the law were complaining, "This man welcomes sinners and eats with them."
>
> 3 So Jesus told them this parable: 4 "Which one of you, if he has a hundred sheep and loses one of them, would not leave the ninety-nine in the open pasture and go look for the one that is lost until he finds it? 5 Then when he has found it, he aces it on his shoulders, rejoicing. 6 Returning home, he calls together his friends and neighbors, telling them, 'Rejoice with me because I have found my sheep that was lost.' 7 I tell you, in the same way there will be more joy in heaven over one sinner who repents than over ninety-nine righteous people who have no need to repent.
>
> 8 "Or what woman, if she has ten silver coins and loses one of them, does not light a lamp, sweep the house, and search thoroughly until she finds it? 9 Then when she has found it, she calls together her friends and neighbors, saying, 'Rejoice with me, for I have found the coin that I had lost.' 10 In the same way, I tell you, there is joy in the presence of God's angels over one sinner who repents."
>
> 11 Then Jesus said, "A man had two sons. 12 The younger of them said to his father, 'Father, give me the share of the estate that will belong to me.' So he divided his assets between them. 13 After a few days, the younger son gathered together all he had and left on a journey to a distant country, and there he squandered his wealth with a wild lifestyle. 14 Then after he had spent everything, a severe famine took place in that country, and he began to be in need. 15 So he went and worked for one of the citizens of that

country, who sent him to his fields to feed pigs. 16 He was longing to eat the carob pods the pigs were eating, but no one gave him anything. 17 But when he came to his senses, he said, 'How many of my father's hired workers have food enough to spare, but here I am dying from hunger! 18 I will get up and go to my father and say to him, "Father, I have sinned against heaven and against you. 19 I am no longer worthy to be called your son; treat me like one of your hired workers."' 20 So he got up and went to his father. But while he was still a long way from home his father saw him, and his heart went out to him; he ran and hugged his son and kissed him. 21 Then his son said to him, 'Father, I have sinned against heaven and against you; I am no longer worthy to be called your son.' 22 But the father said to his slaves, 'Hurry! Bring the best robe, and put it on him! Put a ring on his finger and sandals on his feet! 23 Bring the fattened calf and kill it! Let us eat and celebrate, 24 because this son of mine was dead, and is alive again—he was lost and is found!' So they began to celebrate.

25 "Now his older son was in the field. As he came and approached the house, he heard music and dancing. 26 So he called one of the slaves and asked what was happening. 27 The slave replied, 'Your brother has returned, and your father has killed the fattened calf because he got his son back safe and sound.' 28 But the older son became angry and refused to go in. His father came out and appealed to him, 29 but he answered his father, 'Look! These many years I have worked like a slave for you, and I never disobeyed your commands. Yet you never gave me even a goat so that I could celebrate with my friends! 30 But when this son of yours came back, who has devoured your assets with prostitutes, you killed the fattened calf for him!' 31 Then the father said to him, 'Son, you are always with me, and everything that belongs to me is yours. 32 It was appropriate to celebrate and be glad, for your brother was dead, and is alive; he was lost and is found.'"

16:1 Jesus also said to the disciples, "There was a rich man who was informed of accusations that his manager was wasting his assets. 2 So he called the manager in and said to him, 'What is this I hear about you? Turn in the account of your administration, because you can no longer be my manager.' 3 Then the manager said to himself, 'What should I do, since my master is taking my position away from me? I'm not strong enough to dig, and I'm too ashamed to beg. 4 I know what to do so that when I am put out of management, people will welcome me into their homes.' 5 So he contacted his master's debtors one by one. He asked the first, 'How much do you owe my master?' 6 The man replied, '100 measures of olive oil.' The manager said to him, 'Take your bill, sit down quickly, and write 50.' 7 Then he said to another, 'And how much do you owe?' The second man replied, '100 measures of wheat.' The manager said to him, 'Take your bill, and write 80.' 8 The master commended the dishonest manager because he acted shrewdly. For the people of this world are more shrewd in dealing with their contemporaries than the people of light. 9 And I tell you, make friends for yourselves by how you use worldly wealth, so that when it runs out, you will be welcomed into the eternal homes.

10 "The one who is faithful in a very little is also faithful in much, and the one who is dishonest in a very little is also dishonest in much. 11 If then you haven't been trustworthy in handling worldly wealth, who will entrust you with the true riches? 12 And if you haven't been trustworthy with someone else's property, who will give you your own? 13 No servant can serve two masters, for either he will hate the one and love the other, or he will be devoted to the one and despise the other. You cannot serve God and money."

14 The Pharisees (who loved money) heard all this and ridiculed him. 15 But Jesus said to them, "You are the ones who justify yourselves in men's eyes, but God knows your hearts. For what is highly prized among men is utterly detestable in God's sight.

16 "The law and the prophets were in force until John; since then, the good news of the kingdom of God has been proclaimed, and everyone is urged to enter it. 17 But it is easier for heaven and earth to pass away than for one tiny stroke of a letter in the law to become void.

18 "Everyone who divorces his wife and marries someone else commits adultery, and the one who marries a woman divorced from her husband commits adultery.

19 "There was a rich man who dressed in purple and fine linen and who feasted sumptuously every day. 20 But at his gate lay a poor man named Lazarus whose body was covered with sores, 21 who longed to eat what fell from the rich man's table. In addition, the dogs came and licked his sores.

22 "Now the poor man died and was carried by the angels to Abraham's side. The rich man also died and was buried. 23 And in Hades, as he was in torment, he looked up and saw Abraham far off with Lazarus at his side. 24 So he called out, 'Father Abraham, have mercy on me, and send Lazarus to dip the tip of his finger in water and cool my tongue because I am in anguish in this fire.' 25 But Abraham said, 'Child, remember that in your lifetime you received your good things and Lazarus likewise bad things, but now he is comforted here and you are in anguish. 26 Besides all this, a great chasm has been fixed between us, so that those who want to cross over from

here to you cannot do so, and no one can cross from there to us.' 27 So the rich man said, 'Then I beg you, father—send Lazarus to my father's house 28 (for I have five brothers) to warn them so that they don't come into this place of torment.' 29 But Abraham said, 'They have Moses and the prophets; they must respond to them.' 30 Then the rich man said, 'No, father Abraham, but if someone from the dead goes to them, they will repent.' 31 He replied to him, 'If they do not respond to Moses and the prophets, they will not be convinced even if someone rises from the dead.'"

17:1 Jesus said to his disciples, "Stumbling blocks are sure to come, but woe to the one through whom they come! 2 It would be better for him to have a millstone tied around his neck and be thrown into the sea than for him to cause one of these little ones to sin. 3 Watch yourselves! If your brother sins, rebuke him. If he repents, forgive him. 4 Even if he sins against you seven times in a day, and seven times returns to you saying, 'I repent,' you must forgive him."

5 The apostles said to the Lord, "Increase our faith!" 6 So the Lord replied, "If you had faith the size of a mustard seed, you could say to this black mulberry tree, 'Be pulled out by the roots and planted in the sea,' and it would obey you.

7 "Would any one of you say to your slave who comes in from the field after plowing or shepherding sheep, 'Come at once and sit down for a meal'? 8 Won't the master instead say to him, 'Get my dinner ready, and make yourself ready to serve me while I eat and drink. Then you may eat and drink'? 9 He won't thank the slave because he did what he was told, will he? 10 So you too, when you have done everything you were commanded to do, should say, 'We are slaves undeserving of special praise; we have only done what was our duty.'"

11 Now on the way to Jerusalem, Jesus was passing along between Samaria and Galilee. 12 As he was entering a village, ten men with leprosy met him. They stood at a distance, 13 raised their voices and said, "Jesus, Master, have mercy on us." 14 When he saw them he said, "Go and show yourselves to the priests." And as they went along, they were cleansed. 15 Then one of them, when he saw he was healed, turned back, praising God with a loud voice. 16 He fell with his face to the ground at Jesus' feet and thanked him. (Now he was a Samaritan.) 17 Then Jesus said, "Were not ten cleansed? Where are the other nine? 18 Was no one found to turn back and give praise to God except this foreigner?" 19 Then he said to the man, "Get up and go your way. Your faith has made you well."

20 Now at one point the Pharisees asked Jesus when the kingdom of God was coming, so he answered, "The kingdom of God is not coming with signs to be observed, 21 nor will they say, 'Look, here it is!' or 'There!' For indeed, the kingdom of God is in your midst."

22 Then he said to the disciples, "The days are coming when you will desire to see one of the days of the Son of Man, and you will not see it. 23 Then people will say to you, 'Look, there he is!' or 'Look, here he is!' Do not go out or chase after them. 24 For just like the lightning flashes and lights up the sky from one side to the other, so will the Son of Man be in his day. 25 But first he must suffer many things and be rejected by this generation. 26 Just as it was in the days of Noah, so too it will be in the days of the Son of Man. 27 People were eating, they were drinking, they were marrying, they were being given in marriage—right up to the day Noah entered the ark. Then the flood came and destroyed them all. 28 Likewise, just as it was in the days of Lot, people were eating, drinking, buying, selling, planting, building; 29 but on the day Lot went out from Sodom, fire and sulfur rained down from heaven and destroyed them all. 30 It will be the same on the day the Son of Man is revealed. 31 On that day, anyone who is on the roof, with his goods in the house, must not come down to take them away, and likewise the person in the field must not turn back. 32 Remember Lot's wife! 33 Whoever tries to keep his life will lose it, but whoever loses his life will preserve it. 34 I tell you, in that night there will be two people in one bed; one will be taken and the other left. 35 There will be two women grinding grain together; one will be taken and the other left."

37 Then the disciples said to him, "Where, Lord?" He replied to them, "Where the dead body is, there the vultures will gather."

18:1 Then Jesus told them a parable to show them they should always pray and not lose heart. 2 He said, "In a certain city there was a judge who neither feared God nor respected people. 3 There was also a widow in that city who kept coming to him and saying, 'Give me justice against my adversary.' 4 For a while he refused, but later on he said to himself, 'Though I neither fear God nor have regard for people, 5 yet because this widow keeps on bothering me, I will give her justice, or in the end she will wear me out by her unending pleas.'" 6 And the Lord said, "Listen to what the unrighteous judge says! 7 Won't God give justice to his chosen ones, who cry out to him day and night? Will he delay long to help them? 8 I tell you, he will give them justice speedily. Nevertheless, when the Son of Man comes, will he find faith on earth?"

9 Jesus also told this parable to some who were confident that they were righteous and looked down on everyone else. 10 "Two men went up to the temple to pray, one a Pharisee and the other a tax collector. 11 The Pharisee stood and prayed about himself like this: 'God, I thank you that I am not like other people: extortionists, unrighteous people, adulterers—or even like this tax collector. 12 I fast twice a week; I give a tenth of everything I get.' 13 The tax collector,

however, stood far off and would not even look up to heaven, but beat his breast and said, 'God, be merciful to me, sinner that I am!' 14 I tell you that this man went down to his home justified rather than the Pharisee. For everyone who exalts himself will be humbled, but he who humbles himself will be exalted."

15 Now people were even bringing their babies to him for him to touch. But when the disciples saw it, they began to scold those who brought them. 16 But Jesus called for the children, saying, "Let the little children come to me and do not try to stop them, for the kingdom of God belongs to such as these. 17 I tell you the truth, whoever does not receive the kingdom of God like a child will never enter it."

18 Now a certain leader asked him, "Good teacher, what must I do to inherit eternal life?" 19 Jesus said to him, "Why do you call me good? No one is good except God alone. 20 You know the commandments: 'Do not commit adultery, do not murder, do not steal, do not give false testimony, honor your father and mother.'" 21 The man replied, "I have wholeheartedly obeyed all these laws since my youth." 22 When Jesus heard this, he said to him, "One thing you still lack. Sell all that you have and give the money to the poor, and you will have treasure in heaven. Then come, follow me." 23 But when the man heard this, he became very sad, for he was extremely wealthy. 24 When Jesus noticed this, he said, "How hard it is for the rich to enter the kingdom of God! 25 In fact, it is easier for a camel to go through the eye of a needle than for a rich person to enter the kingdom of God." 26 Those who heard this said, "Then who can be saved?" 27 He replied, "What is impossible for mere humans is possible for God." 28 And Peter said, "Look, we have left everything we own to follow you! 29 Then Jesus said to them, "I tell you the truth, there is no one who has left home or wife or brothers or parents or children for the sake of God's kingdom 30 who will not receive many times more in this age—and in the age to come, eternal life."

31 Then Jesus took the twelve aside and said to them, "Look, we are going up to Jerusalem, and everything that is written about the Son of Man by the prophets will be accomplished. 32 For he will be handed over to the Gentiles; he will be mocked, mistreated, and spat on. 33 They will flog him severely and kill him. Yet on the third day he will rise again." 34 But the twelve understood none of these things. This saying was hidden from them, and they did not grasp what Jesus meant.

35 As Jesus approached Jericho, a blind man was sitting by the road begging. 36 When he heard a crowd going by, he asked what was going on. 37 They told him, "Jesus the Nazarene is passing by." 38 So he called out, "Jesus, Son of David, have mercy on me!" 39 And

those who were in front scolded him to get him to be quiet, but he shouted even more, "Son of David, have mercy on me!" 40 So Jesus stopped and ordered the beggar to be brought to him. When the man came near, Jesus asked him, 41 "What do you want me to do for you?" He replied, "Lord, let me see again." 42 Jesus said to him, "Receive your sight; your faith has healed you." 43 And immediately he regained his sight and followed Jesus, praising God. When all the people saw it, they too gave praise to God.

19:1 Jesus entered Jericho and was passing through it. 2 Now a man named Zacchaeus was there; he was a chief tax collector and was rich. 3 He was trying to get a look at Jesus, but being a short man he could not see over the crowd. 4 So he ran on ahead and climbed up into a sycamore tree to see him because Jesus was going to pass that way. 5 And when Jesus came to that place, he looked up and said to him, "Zacchaeus, come down quickly because I must stay at your house today." 6 So he came down quickly and welcomed Jesus joyfully. 7 And when the people saw it, they all complained, "He has gone in to be the guest of a man who is a sinner." 8 But Zacchaeus stopped and said to the Lord, "Look, Lord, half of my possessions I now give to the poor, and if I have cheated anyone of anything, I am paying back four times as much!" 9 Then Jesus said to him, "Today salvation has come to this household because he too is a son of Abraham! 10 For the Son of Man came to seek and to save the lost."

11 While the people were listening to these things, Jesus proceeded to tell a parable because he was near to Jerusalem, and because they thought that the kingdom of God was going to appear immediately. 12 Therefore he said, "A nobleman went to a distant country to receive for himself a kingdom and then return. 13 And he summoned ten of his slaves, gave them ten minas, and said to them, 'Do business with these until I come back.' 14 But his citizens hated him and sent a delegation after him, saying, 'We do not want this man to be king over us!' 15 When he returned after receiving the kingdom, he summoned these slaves to whom he had given the money. He wanted to know how much they had earned by trading. 16 So the first one came before him and said, 'Sir, your mina has made ten minas more.' 17 And the king said to him, 'Well done, good slave! Because you have been faithful in a very small matter, you will have authority over ten cities.' 18 Then the second one came and said, 'Sir, your mina has made five minas.' 19 So the king said to him, 'And you are to be over five cities.' 20 Then another slave came and said, 'Sir, here is your mina that I put away for safekeeping in a piece of cloth. 21 For I was afraid of you because you are a severe man. You withdraw what you did not deposit and reap what you did

not sow.' 22 The king said to him, 'I will judge you by your own words, you wicked slave! So you knew, did you, that I was a severe man, withdrawing what I didn't deposit and reaping what I didn't sow? 23 Why then didn't you put my money in the bank, so that when I returned I could have collected it with interest?' 24 And he said to his attendants, 'Take the mina from him, and give it to the one who has ten.' 25 But they said to him, 'Sir, he has ten minas already!' 26 'I tell you that everyone who has will be given more, but from the one who does not have, even what he has will be taken away. 27 But as for these enemies of mine who did not want me to be their king, bring them here and slaughter them in front of me!'"

28 After Jesus had said this, he continued on ahead, going up to Jerusalem. 29 Now when he approached Bethphage and Bethany, at the place called the Mount of Olives, he sent two of the disciples, 30 telling them, "Go to the village ahead of you. When you enter it, you will find a colt tied there that has never been ridden. Untie it and bring it here. 31 If anyone asks you, 'Why are you untying it?' just say, 'The Lord needs it.'" 32 So those who were sent ahead found it exactly as he had told them. 33 As they were untying the colt, its owners asked them, "Why are you untying that colt?" 34 They replied, "The Lord needs it." 35 Then they brought it to Jesus, threw their cloaks on the colt, and had Jesus get on it. 36 As he rode along, they spread their cloaks on the road. 37 As he approached the road leading down from the Mount of Olives, the whole crowd of his disciples began to rejoice and praise God with a loud voice for all the mighty works they had seen: 38 "Blessed is the king who comes in the name of the Lord! Peace in heaven and glory in the highest!" 39 But some of the Pharisees in the crowd said to him, "Teacher, rebuke your disciples." 40 He answered, "I tell you, if they keep silent, the very stones will cry out!"

41 Now when Jesus approached and saw the city, he wept over it, 42 saying, "If you had only known on this day, even you, the things that make for peace! But now they are hidden from your eyes. 43 For the days will come upon you when your enemies will build an embankment against you and surround you and close in on you from every side. 44 They will demolish you—you and your children within your walls—and they will not leave within you one stone on top of another because you did not recognize the time of your visitation from God."

45 Then Jesus entered the temple courts and began to drive out those who were selling things there, 46 saying to them, "It is written, 'My house will be a house of prayer,' but you have turned it into a den of robbers!"

47 Jesus was teaching daily in the temple courts. The chief priests and the experts in the law and the prominent leaders among the people were seeking to assassinate him, 48 but they could not find a way to do it, for all the people hung on his words.

2. Look at your notations. What does Jesus seem to emphasize a lot in his teaching?

____

____

____

____

3. Jesus is a wonderful teacher. What of his teachings in this section do you need to allow to change you?

____

____

Friday: Jesus Lord over Death and Life

1. Pray for insight and read Luke 20–24. Underline what women are doing in these chapters. Circle references to life, death, and Jesus's power.

20:1 Now one day, as Jesus was teaching the people in the temple courts and proclaiming the gospel, the chief priests and the experts in the law with the elders came up 2 and said to him, "Tell us: By what authority are you doing these things? Or who is it who gave you this authority?" 3 He answered them, "I will also ask you a question, and you tell me: 4 John's baptism—was it from heaven or from people?" 5 So they discussed it with one another, saying, "If we say, 'From heaven,' he will say, 'Why did you not believe him?' 6 But if we say, 'From people,' all the people will stone us because they are convinced that John was a prophet." 7 So they replied that they did not know where it came from. 8 Then Jesus said to them, "Neither will I tell you by whose authority I do these things."

9 Then he began to tell the people this parable: "A man planted a vineyard, leased it to tenant farmers, and went on a journey for a long time. 10 When harvest time came, he sent a slave to the tenants so that they would give him his portion of the crop. However, the tenants beat his slave and sent him away empty-handed. 11 So he sent another slave. They beat this one too, treated him outrageously, and sent him away empty-handed. 12 So he sent still a third. They even wounded this one and threw him out. 13 Then the owner of the vineyard said, 'What should I do? I will send my one dear son; perhaps they will respect him.' 14 But when the tenants saw him, they said to one another, 'This is the heir; let's kill him so the inheritance will be ours!' 15 So they threw him out of the vineyard and killed him. What then will the owner of the vineyard do to them? 16 He will come and destroy those tenants and give the vineyard to others." When the people heard this, they said, "May this never happen!" 17 But Jesus looked straight at them and said, "Then what is the meaning of that which is written: 'The stone the builders rejected has become the cornerstone'? 18 Everyone who falls on this stone will be broken to pieces, and the one on whom it falls will be crushed." 19 Then the experts in the law and the chief priests wanted to arrest him that very hour because they realized he had told this parable against them. But they were afraid of the people.

20 Then they watched him carefully and sent spies who pretended to be sincere. They wanted to take advantage of what he might say so that they could deliver him up to the authority and jurisdiction of the governor. 21 Thus they asked him, "Teacher, we know that you speak and teach correctly, and show no partiality, but teach the way of God in accordance with the truth. 22 Is it right for us to pay the tribute tax to Caesar or not?" 23 But Jesus perceived their deceit and said to them, 24 "Show me a denarius. Whose image and inscription are on it?" They said, "Caesar's." 25 So he said to them, "Then give to Caesar the things that are Caesar's, and to God the things that are God's." 26 Thus they were unable in the presence of the people to trap him with his own words. And stunned by his answer, they fell silent.

27 Now some Sadducees (who contend that there is no resurrection) came to him. 28 They asked him, "Teacher, Moses wrote for us that if a man's brother dies leaving a wife but no children, that man must marry the widow and father children for his brother. 29 Now there were seven brothers. The first one married a woman and died without children. 30 The second 31 and then the third married her, and in this same way all seven died, leaving no children.

32 Finally the woman died too. 33 In the resurrection, therefore, whose wife will the woman be? For all seven had married her."

34 So Jesus said to them, "The people of this age marry and are given in marriage. 35 But those who are regarded as worthy to share in that age and in the resurrection from the dead neither marry nor are given in marriage. 36 In fact, they can no longer die because they are equal to angels and are sons of God, since they are sons of the resurrection. 37 But even Moses revealed that the dead are raised in the passage about the bush, where he calls the Lord the God of Abraham and the God of Isaac and the God of Jacob. 38 Now he is not God of the dead, but of the living, for all live before him." 39 Then some of the experts in the law answered, "Teacher, you have spoken well!" 40 For they did not dare any longer to ask him anything.

41 But he said to them, "How is it that they say that the Christ is David's son? 42 For David himself says in the book of Psalms,

'The Lord said to my lord,
"Sit at my right hand,
43 until I make your enemies a footstool for your feet."'

44 If David then calls him 'Lord,' how can he be his son?"

45 As all the people were listening, Jesus said to his disciples, 46 "Beware of the experts in the law. They like walking around in long robes, and they love elaborate greetings in the marketplaces and the best seats in the synagogues and the places of honor at banquets. 47 They devour widows' property, and as a show make long prayers. They will receive a more severe punishment."

21:1 Jesus looked up and saw the rich putting their gifts into the offering box. 2 He also saw a poor widow put in two small copper coins. 3 He said, "I tell you the truth, this poor widow has put in more than all of them. 4 For they all offered their gifts out of their wealth. But she, out of her poverty, put in everything she had to live on."

5 Now while some were speaking about the temple, how it was adorned with beautiful stones and offerings, Jesus said, 6 "As for these things that you are gazing at, the days will come when not one stone will be left on another. All will be torn down!" 7 So they asked him, "Teacher, when will these things happen? And what will be the sign that these things are about to take place?" 8 He said, "Watch out that you are not misled. For many will come in my name, saying, 'I am he,' and, 'The time is near.' Do not follow them! 9 And when you hear of wars and rebellions, do not be afraid. For these things must happen first, but the end will not come at once."

10 Then he said to them, "Nation will rise up in arms against nation, and kingdom against kingdom. 11 There will be great earthquakes, and famines and plagues in various places, and there will be terrifying sights and great signs from heaven. 12 But before all this, they will seize you and persecute you, handing you over to the synagogues and prisons. You will be brought before kings and governors because of my name. 13 This will be a time for you to serve as witnesses. 14 Therefore be resolved not to rehearse ahead of time how to make your defense. 15 For I will give you the words along with the wisdom that none of your adversaries will be able to withstand or contradict. 16 You will be betrayed even by parents, brothers, relatives, and friends, and they will have some of you put to death. 17 You will be hated by everyone because of my name. 18 Yet not a hair of your head will perish. 19 By your endurance you will gain your lives.

20 "But when you see Jerusalem surrounded by armies, then know that its desolation has come near. 21 Then those who are in Judea must flee to the mountains. Those who are inside the city must depart. Those who are out in the country must not enter it, 22 because these are days of vengeance, to fulfill all that is written. 23 Woe to those who are pregnant and to those who are nursing their babies in those days! For there will be great distress on the earth and wrath against this people. 24 They will fall by the edge of the sword and be led away as captives among all nations. Jerusalem will be trampled down by the Gentiles until the times of the Gentiles are fulfilled.

25 "And there will be signs in the sun and moon and stars, and on the earth nations will be in distress, anxious over the roaring of the sea and the surging waves. 26 People will be fainting from fear and from the expectation of what is coming on the world, for the powers of the heavens will be shaken. 27 Then they will see the Son of Man arriving in a cloud with power and great glory. 28 But when these things begin to happen, stand up and raise your heads because your redemption is drawing near."

29 Then he told them a parable: "Look at the fig tree and all the other trees. 30 When they sprout leaves, you see for yourselves and know that summer is now near. 31 So also you, when you see these things happening, know that the kingdom of God is near. 32 I tell you the truth, this generation will not pass away until all these things take place. 33 Heaven and earth will pass away, but my words will never pass away.

34 "But be on your guard so that your hearts are not weighed down with dissipation and drunkenness and the worries of this life, and that day close down upon you suddenly like a trap. 35 For it

will overtake all who live on the face of the whole earth. 36 But stay alert at all times, praying that you may have strength to escape all these things that must happen, and to stand before the Son of Man."

37 So every day Jesus was teaching in the temple courts, but at night he went and stayed on the Mount of Olives. 38 And all the people came to him early in the morning to listen to him in the temple courts.

22:1 Now the Feast of Unleavened Bread, which is called the Passover, was approaching. 2 The chief priests and the experts in the law were trying to find some way to execute Jesus, for they were afraid of the people.

3 Then Satan entered Judas, the one called Iscariot, who was one of the twelve. 4 He went away and discussed with the chief priests and officers of the temple guard how he might betray Jesus, handing him over to them. 5 They were delighted and arranged to give him money. 6 So Judas agreed and began looking for an opportunity to betray Jesus when no crowd was present.

7 Then the day for the feast of Unleavened Bread came, on which the Passover lamb had to be sacrificed. 8 Jesus sent Peter and John, saying, "Go and prepare the Passover for us to eat." 9 They said to him, "Where do you want us to prepare it?" 10 He said to them, "Listen, when you have entered the city, a man carrying a jar of water will meet you. Follow him into the house that he enters, 11 and tell the owner of the house, 'The Teacher says to you, "Where is the guest room where I may eat the Passover with my disciples?"' 12 Then he will show you a large furnished room upstairs. Make preparations there." 13 So they went and found things just as he had told them, and they prepared the Passover.

14 Now when the hour came, Jesus took his place at the table and the apostles joined him. 15 And he said to them, "I have earnestly desired to eat this Passover with you before I suffer. 16 For I tell you, I will not eat it again until it is fulfilled in the kingdom of God." 17 Then he took a cup, and after giving thanks he said, "Take this and divide it among yourselves. 18 For I tell you that from now on I will not drink of the fruit of the vine until the kingdom of God comes." 19 Then he took bread, and after giving thanks he broke it and gave it to them, saying, "This is my body which is given for you. Do this in remembrance of me." 20 And in the same way he took the cup after they had eaten, saying, "This cup that is poured out for you is the new covenant in my blood.

21 "But look, the hand of the one who betrays me is with me on the table. 22 For the Son of Man is to go just as it has been

determined, but woe to that man by whom he is betrayed!" 23 So they began to question one another as to which of them it could possibly be who would do this.

24 A dispute also started among them over which of them was to be regarded as the greatest. 25 So Jesus said to them, "The kings of the Gentiles lord it over them, and those in authority over them are called 'benefactors.' 26 Not so with you; instead the one who is greatest among you must become like the youngest, and the leader like the one who serves. 27 For who is greater, the one who is seated at the table, or the one who serves? Is it not the one who is seated at the table? But I am among you as one who serves.

28 "You are the ones who have remained with me in my trials. 29 Thus I grant to you a kingdom, just as my Father granted to me, 30 that you may eat and drink at my table in my kingdom, and you will sit on thrones judging the twelve tribes of Israel.

31 "Simon, Simon, pay attention! Satan has demanded to have you all, to sift you like wheat, 32 but I have prayed for you, Simon, that your faith may not fail. When you have turned back, strengthen your brothers." 33 But Peter said to him, "Lord, I am ready to go with you both to prison and to death!" 34 Jesus replied, "I tell you, Peter, the rooster will not crow today until you have denied three times that you know me."

35 Then Jesus said to them, "When I sent you out with no money bag, or traveler's bag, or sandals, you didn't lack anything, did you?" They replied, "Nothing." 36 He said to them, "But now, the one who has a money bag must take it, and likewise a traveler's bag too. And the one who has no sword must sell his cloak and buy one. 37 For I tell you that this scripture must be fulfilled in me, 'And he was counted with the transgressors.' For what is written about me is being fulfilled." 38 So they said, "Look, Lord, here are two swords." Then he told them, "It is enough."

39 Then Jesus went out and made his way, as he customarily did, to the Mount of Olives, and the disciples followed him.

40 When he came to the place, he said to them, "Pray that you will not fall into temptation." 41 He went away from them about a stone's throw, knelt down, and prayed, 42 "Father, if you are willing, take this cup away from me. Yet not my will but yours be done." [43 Then an angel from heaven appeared to him and strengthened him. 44 And in his anguish he prayed more earnestly, and his sweat was like drops of blood falling to the ground.] 45 When he got up from prayer, he came to the disciples and found them sleeping, exhausted from grief. 46 So he said to them, "Why are you sleeping? Get up and pray that you will not fall into temptation!"

47 While he was still speaking, suddenly a crowd appeared, and the man named Judas, one of the twelve, was leading them. He walked up to Jesus to kiss him. 48 But Jesus said to him, "Judas, would you betray the Son of Man with a kiss?" 49 When those who were around him saw what was about to happen, they said, "Lord, should we use our swords?" 50 Then one of them struck the high priest's slave, cutting off his right ear. 51 But Jesus said, "Enough of this!" And he touched the man's ear and healed him. 52 Then Jesus said to the chief priests, the officers of the temple guard, and the elders who had come out to get him, "Have you come out with swords and clubs like you would against an outlaw? 53 Day after day when I was with you in the temple courts, you did not arrest me. But this is your hour, and that of the power of darkness!"

54 Then they arrested Jesus, led him away, and brought him into the high priest's house. But Peter was following at a distance. 55 When they had made a fire in the middle of the courtyard and sat down together, Peter sat down among them. 56 Then a slave girl, seeing him as he sat in the firelight, stared at him and said, "This man was with him too!" 57 But Peter denied it: "Woman, I don't know him!" 58 Then a little later someone else saw him and said, "You are one of them too." But Peter said, "Man, I am not!" 59 And after about an hour still another insisted, "Certainly this man was with him because he too is a Galilean." 60 But Peter said, "Man, I don't know what you're talking about!" At that moment, while he was still speaking, a rooster crowed. 61 Then the Lord turned and looked straight at Peter, and Peter remembered the word of the Lord, how he had said to him, "Before a rooster crows today, you will deny me three times." 62 And he went outside and wept bitterly.

63 Now the men who were holding Jesus under guard began to mock him and beat him. 64 They blindfolded him and asked him repeatedly, "Prophesy! Who hit you?" 65 They also said many other things against him, reviling him.

66 When day came, the council of the elders of the people gathered together, both the chief priests and the experts in the law. Then they led Jesus away to their council 67 and said, "If you are the Christ, tell us." But he said to them, "If I tell you, you will not believe, 68 and if I ask you, you will not answer. 69 But from now on the Son of Man will be seated at the right hand of the power of God." 70 So they all said, "Are you the Son of God, then?" He answered them, "You say that I am." 71 Then they said, "Why do we need further testimony? We have heard it ourselves from his own lips!"

23:1 Then the whole group of them rose up and brought Jesus before Pilate. 2 They began to accuse him, saying, "We found this man subverting our nation, forbidding us to pay the tribute tax to Caesar and claiming that he himself is Christ, a king." 3 So Pilate asked Jesus, "Are you the king of the Jews?" He replied, "You say so." 4 Then Pilate said to the chief priests and the crowds, "I find no basis for an accusation against this man." 5 But they persisted in saying, "He incites the people by teaching throughout all Judea. It started in Galilee and ended up here!"

6 Now when Pilate heard this, he asked whether the man was a Galilean. 7 When he learned that he was from Herod's jurisdiction, he sent him over to Herod, who also happened to be in Jerusalem at that time. 8 When Herod saw Jesus, he was very glad, for he had long desired to see him because he had heard about him and was hoping to see him perform some miraculous sign. 9 So Herod questioned him at considerable length; Jesus gave him no answer. 10 The chief priests and the experts in the law were there, vehemently accusing him. 11 Even Herod with his soldiers treated him with contempt and mocked him. Then, dressing him in elegant clothes, Herod sent him back to Pilate. 12 That very day Herod and Pilate became friends with each other, for prior to this they had been enemies.

13 Then Pilate called together the chief priests, the leaders, and the people, 14 and said to them, "You brought me this man as one who was misleading the people. When I examined him before you, I did not find this man guilty of anything you accused him of doing. 15 Neither did Herod, for he sent him back to us. Look, he has done nothing deserving death. 16 I will therefore have him flogged and release him."

18 But they all shouted out together, "Take this man away! Release Barabbas for us!" 19 (This was a man who had been thrown into prison for an insurrection started in the city, and for murder.) 20 Pilate addressed them once again because he wanted to release Jesus. 21 But they kept on shouting, "Crucify, crucify him!" 22 A third time he said to them, "Why? What wrong has he done? I have found him guilty of no crime deserving death. I will therefore flog him and release him." 23 But they were insistent, demanding with loud shouts that he be crucified. And their shouts prevailed. 24 So Pilate decided that their demand should be granted. 25 He released the man they asked for, who had been thrown in prison for insurrection and murder. But he handed Jesus over to their will.

26 As they led him away, they seized Simon of Cyrene, who was coming in from the country. They placed the cross on his back

and made him carry it behind Jesus. 27 A great number of the people followed him, among them women who were mourning and wailing for him. 28 But Jesus turned to them and said, "Daughters of Jerusalem, do not weep for me, but weep for yourselves and for your children. 29 For this is certain: The days are coming when they will say, 'Blessed are the barren, the wombs that never bore children, and the breasts that never nursed!' 30 Then they will begin to say to the mountains, 'Fall on us!' and to the hills, 'Cover us!' 31 For if such things are done when the wood is green, what will happen when it is dry?"

32 Two other criminals were also led away to be executed with him. 33 So when they came to the place that is called "The Skull," they crucified him there, along with the criminals, one on his right and one on his left. 34 [But Jesus said, "Father, forgive them, for they don't know what they are doing."] Then they threw dice to divide his clothes. 35 The people also stood there watching, but the leaders ridiculed him, saying, "He saved others. Let him save himself if he is the Christ of God, his chosen one!" 36 The soldiers also mocked him, coming up and offering him sour wine, 37 and saying, "If you are the king of the Jews, save yourself!" 38 There was also an inscription over him, "This is the king of the Jews."

39 One of the criminals who was hanging there railed at him, saying, "Aren't you the Christ? Save yourself and us!" 40 But the other rebuked him, saying, "Don't you fear God, since you are under the same sentence of condemnation? 41 And we rightly so, for we are getting what we deserve for what we did, but this man has done nothing wrong." 42 Then he said, "Jesus, remember me when you come in your kingdom." 43 And Jesus said to him, "I tell you the truth, today you will be with me in paradise."

44 It was now about noon, and darkness came over the whole land until three in the afternoon, 45 because the sun's light failed. The temple curtain was torn in two. 46 Then Jesus, calling out with a loud voice, said, "Father, into your hands I commit my spirit!" And after he said this he breathed his last.

47 Now when the centurion saw what had happened, he praised God and said, "Certainly this man was innocent!" 48 And all the crowds that had assembled for this spectacle, when they saw what had taken place, returned home beating their breasts. 49 And all those who knew Jesus stood at a distance, and the women who had followed him from Galilee saw these things.

50 Now there was a man named Joseph who was a member of the council, a good and righteous man. 51 (He had not consented to their plan and action.) He was from the Judean town of

Arimathea, and was looking forward to the kingdom of God. 52 He went to Pilate and asked for the body of Jesus. 53 Then he took it down, wrapped it in a linen cloth, and placed it in a tomb cut out of the rock, where no one had yet been buried. 54 It was the day of preparation, and the Sabbath was beginning. 55 The women who had accompanied Jesus from Galilee followed, and they saw the tomb and how his body was laid in it. 56 Then they returned and prepared aromatic spices and perfumes.

On the Sabbath they rested according to the commandment.

24:1 Now on the first day of the week, at early dawn, the women went to the tomb, taking the aromatic spices they had prepared. 2 They found that the stone had been rolled away from the tomb, 3 but when they went in, they did not find the body of the Lord Jesus. 4 While they were perplexed about this, suddenly two men stood beside them in dazzling attire. 5 The women were terribly frightened and bowed their faces to the ground, but the men said to them, "Why do you look for the living among the dead? 6 He is not here, but has been raised! Remember how he told you, while he was still in Galilee, 7 that the Son of Man must be delivered into the hands of sinful men, and be crucified, and on the third day rise again." 8 Then the women remembered his words, 9 and when they returned from the tomb, they told all these things to the eleven and to all the rest. 10 Now it was Mary Magdalene, Joanna, Mary the mother of James, and the other women with them who told these things to the apostles. 11 But these words seemed like pure nonsense to them, and they did not believe them. 12 But Peter got up and ran to the tomb. He bent down and saw only the strips of linen cloth; then he went home, wondering what had happened.

13 Now that very day two of them were on their way to a village called Emmaus, about seven miles from Jerusalem. 14 They were talking to each other about all the things that had happened. 15 While they were talking and debating these things, Jesus himself approached and began to accompany them 16 (but their eyes were kept from recognizing him). 17 Then he said to them, "What are these matters you are discussing so intently as you walk along?" And they stood still, looking sad. 18 Then one of them, named Cleopas, answered him, "Are you the only visitor to Jerusalem who doesn't know the things that have happened there in these days?" 19 He said to them, "What things?" "The things concerning Jesus the Nazarene," they replied, "a man who, with his powerful deeds and words, proved to be a prophet before God and all the people; 20 and how our chief priests and leaders handed him over to be condemned to death, and crucified him. 21 But we had hoped that he was the one who was going to redeem Israel. Not only this, but

it is now the third day since these things happened. 22 Furthermore, some women of our group amazed us. They were at the tomb early this morning, 23 and when they did not find his body, they came back and said they had seen a vision of angels, who said he was alive. 24 Then some of those who were with us went to the tomb and found it just as the women had said, but they did not see him." 25 So he said to them, "You foolish people—how slow of heart to believe all that the prophets have spoken! 26 Wasn't it necessary for the Christ to suffer these things and enter into his glory?" 27 Then beginning with Moses and all the prophets, he interpreted to them the things written about himself in all the scriptures.

28 So they approached the village where they were going. He acted as though he wanted to go farther, 29 but they urged him, "Stay with us because it is getting toward evening and the day is almost done." So he went in to stay with them.

30 When he had taken his place at the table with them, he took the bread, blessed and broke it, and gave it to them. 31 At this point their eyes were opened and they recognized him. Then he vanished out of their sight. 32 They said to each other, "Didn't our hearts burn within us while he was speaking with us on the road, while he was explaining the scriptures to us?" 33 So they got up that very hour and returned to Jerusalem. They found the eleven and those with them gathered together 34 and saying, "The Lord has really risen and has appeared to Simon!" 35 Then they told what had happened on the road, and how they recognized him when he broke the bread.

36 While they were saying these things, Jesus himself stood among them and said to them, "Peace be with you." 37 But they were startled and terrified, thinking they saw a ghost. 38 Then he said to them, "Why are you frightened, and why do doubts arise in your hearts? 39 Look at my hands and my feet; it's me! Touch me and see; a ghost does not have flesh and bones like you see I have." 40 When he had said this, he showed them his hands and his feet. 41 And while they still could not believe it (because of their joy) and were amazed, he said to them, "Do you have anything here to eat?" 42 So they gave him a piece of broiled fish, 43 and he took it and ate it in front of them.

44 Then he said to them, "These are my words that I spoke to you while I was still with you, that everything written about me in the law of Moses and the prophets and the psalms must be fulfilled." 45 Then he opened their minds so they could understand the scriptures, 46 and said to them, "Thus it stands written that the Christ would suffer and would rise from the dead on the third day,

> 47 and repentance for the forgiveness of sins would be proclaimed in his name to all nations, beginning from Jerusalem. 48 You are witnesses of these things. 49 And look, I am sending you what my Father promised. But stay in the city until you have been clothed with power from on high."
>
> 50 Then Jesus led them out as far as Bethany, and lifting up his hands, he blessed them. 51 Now during the blessing he departed and was taken up into heaven. 52 So they worshiped him and returned to Jerusalem with great joy, 53 and were continually in the temple courts blessing God.

Look back at your notations. What kinds of things do you see women doing as they follow Jesus?

____

____

What are some of your favorite things about Jesus as Luke presents his story?

____

____

What in today's reading reveals that Jesus is lord of life and death?

____

____

If Jesus is lord over your life and death, in what areas of your life do you need to yield control/surrender?

____

____

Saturday: May It Be As You Have Spoken

Scripture: "So Mary said, 'Yes, I am a servant of the Lord; let this happen to me according to your word' (Luke 1:38).

"Conceived by the Holy Spirit, born of the Virgin Mary..." This line describes Jesus. It comes from the Apostles' Creed, written in the early centuries of the church.

Jesus Christ was born of a Virgin—often called the Virgin Mary. As someone who has spent years attending women's Bible studies, I've completed my share of Bible studies on women in the Bible. But ironically, not one of them has included Mary, mother of Jesus. Considering that our Savior was the offspring of her womb, that she is the only parent of Jesus named in the stories about the magi, or wise men, (Matt. 2:11), and that no other humans besides Jesus, Mary, and Pontius Pilate are named in the Apostle's Creed, that omission seems like a big oversight.

Luke in his Gospel mentions Jesus's mother twelve times. She also appears five times in Matthew, once in Mark, once in John, and once in the Book of Acts. After Jesus, Paul, and Peter, the fourth most described person in the New Testament is Jesus's mother, Mary.

When the angel appears to her, Mary is probably a teen. When Mary and Joseph take Jesus to the temple to dedicate him, they take a dove as an offering (Luke 2:24), which suggests they are poor. They also belong to an ethnic group that's under the thumb of oppressive governments—both of Herod and of Rome. Picture a young, poor, powerless adolescent. And a female.

When the angel appeared and told Mary she would bear a son, although Mary had known no man, she believed. She was a woman of divine favor and faith, believing God would do the impossible.

In her last week of pregnancy, this living tabernacle carrying our Lord, walked about eighty miles from Nazareth to Bethlehem because of a census. She gave birth in a strange, noisy, crowded, unsanitary town without pain meds or friends to help. Mary was the primary witness of the incarnation—the arrival of the God-man to earth as a human baby. And she had to place her newborn in a smelly place where animals slobber.

Mary was there when the shepherds rushed in to proclaim the angels' glad tidings. And later in a house, Mary witnessed the worship of the magi and received God's provision through their gifts. Then suddenly, while still nursing her infant, she had to flee with Joseph for about two hundred miles. On foot. Because an evil ruler wanted to slaughter her baby. How terrifying!

Luke's account holds up Mary as a positive example of a response to God's pronouncement: "Let this happen to me according to your word," Mary said (1:38). Greek has more than one term for "word," and Luke cites Mary as referring to that which was spoken aloud.

Mary knew Scripture by heart. Even though no woman in history had ever conceived without a man, Mary didn't even need to think it over. "Let these words happen," she said. "I'm your servant."

Luke contrasts her amazing response with that of Zechariah. Zechariah and Elizabeth were old and infertile, yet the angel told Zechariah they would have a baby through a miracle of a different kind. Had an old couple ever, in salvation history, conceived a child? Yes, indeed—Sarah and Abraham. Did Zechariah as a priest have all kinds of access to Scripture? He sure did. Was he, as a spiritual leader, supposed to model faith? Absolutely. But did Zechariah believe? No.

In contrast, had a girl who'd never known—in the biblical sense—a man ever conceived a child? Never. She had no precedent to assure her it would happen. But did Mary believe anyway? Yes.

By pointing this out, Luke is not suggesting women are more spiritual than men. In the next chapter he holds up both the aged Simeon and Anna as models of faith. Yet in the pairing of Mary and Zechariah's appearances from angels, Luke contrasts the response of a powerless unknown girl with that of the religious expert who had access to the Holy Place. Throughout his Gospel, Luke will make similar pairings of those whom one expects to be "spiritual" vs. those who actually are.

Mary shows an astonishing grasp of scripture. Her hymn of praise—often referred to as The Magnificat (as "Magnificat" is Latin for "[My soul] magnifies [the Lord]") demonstrates a knowledge of her nation's history, echoing the hymn of Hannah (see 1 Sam. 1). Mary's response to Gabriel is such an evidence of scriptural literacy, in fact, that many Medieval painters depict Mary reading a book. The Fitzwilliam Museum in Cambridge even has a Book of Hours with a nativity scene in which a literate Mary reads in bed (with animals nearby) while Joseph cradles Baby Jesus.

Here is Mary's speech as Luke records it:

> "My soul exalts the Lord,
> and my spirit has begun to rejoice in God my Savior,
> because he has looked upon the humble state of his servant.

For from now on all generations will call me blessed,

because he who is mighty has done great things for me, and holy is his name;

from generation to generation he is merciful to those who fear him.

He has demonstrated power with his arm; he has scattered those whose pride wells up from the sheer arrogance of their hearts.

He has brought down the mighty from their thrones, and has lifted up those of lowly position;

he has filled the hungry with good things, and has sent the rich away empty.

He has helped his servant Israel, remembering his mercy,

as he promised to our ancestors, to Abraham and to his descendants forever" (Luke 1:46–55).

Did you notice the part about all generations calling her blessed? That includes us.

Let us rise, then, with our own generation to marvel at the grace of God shown to this lowly woman. Although we are often more like Zechariah in how much more access we have to knowing about God and the redemption story, let us like Mary respond with trusting obedience. May we declare God's mercy, power, might, and faithfulness, joining our voices with hers to exalt the Lord born from her womb—the one who has ascended into heaven and who sits at the right hand of God, the Father Almighty, Maker of heaven and earth.

For memorization: So Mary said, "Yes, I am a servant of the Lord; let this happen to me according to your [spoken] word." (Luke 1:38).

Prayer: *Heavenly Father, thank you for choosing a humble, powerless girl to be the human mother of our Lord and Savior, Jesus Christ. Thank you for her obedience; help me to be like her in her absolute trust in you, even when lacking understanding of your ways. Thank you for sending your dear Son to earth. Thank you for His life and death and resurrection. Thank you that through your Spirit we can believe in Jesus Christ as Your only Son, our Lord. Please take control of our lives and mold us to be like Him, even when we don't understand. In His name and through the power of the Spirit we ask these things, Amen.*

Week 2 of 7

Jesus: The Son of Man: Luke 1–4

Sunday: The Voice Crying in the Wilderness

Scripture: "As for me, I baptize you with water for repentance, but He who is coming after me is mightier than I, and I am not fit to remove His sandals; He will baptize you with the Holy Spirit and fire" (John the Baptist, Luke 3:16)

About four hundred years before Christ, the prophet Malachi (fifth century BC) predicted that the prophet Elijah (who had lived in the ninth century BC) would one day return and herald the arrival of the Messiah (Mal. 4:5). In John the Baptist's day, many Jewish people expected the literal Elijah to return from the dead as Messiah's forerunner. Elijah himself had raised a dead person, so there was some precedent for coming back from the dead. The announcement of Elizabeth and Zechariah's son, John, identified their baby as the fulfillment of Malachi's prophecy; he would come in the "spirit and power" of Elijah (Luke 1:17, 76).

When asked if he was Elijah, John said, "I am not" (John 1:21).

Yet, Jesus identified John as Elijah (Matt. 11:14; 17:11–13; Mark 9:12–13).

So, which is true? Was John Elijah or not Elijah?

Well...both.

John was not literally Elijah reincarnated or resurrected. Consequently, when asked about his identity, John told the truth in denying he was the actual prophet Elijah. John was John, not Elijah.

Yet Jesus, in accordance with the angel's announcement of John's birth, identified John as his messianic forerunner, Elijah, because John fulfilled the role of forerunner assigned to Elijah. In the words of theologian Fleming Rutledge, "When we read the description of John the Baptist in Mark and realize it is the same as the description of Elijah in 2 Kings 1:8 [hairy with a leather belt around his waist], we begin to understand what is going on here. John the Baptist is the new Elijah."

One spring when my husband and I visited Jordan, we stood at the site where pilgrims throughout church history have commemorated John's baptism of Jesus. I realized once again that what we sometimes miss when reading the Bible can become clearer when we travel to an actual site: events that happened centuries apart often shared the same location. In the case of John the Baptist, the wilderness where he ate locusts is the same location where Elijah ate locusts. As we drove away from the river where John baptized Jesus and the dove ascended on our Lord, we passed the hill from which Elijah was transported.

When people in John's day went out to the desert to see him, they were heading toward the ancient abode of Elijah. John literally inhabited Elijah's space. John dressed like Elijah, wore his hair like Elijah, ate desert food like Elijah, and hung out in "Elijah" territory. With that in mind, pay attention to how Matthew records the events (Matt. 3:1–11; the parts in all-caps are quotes from the Old Testament):

> Now in those days John the Baptist came, preaching in the wilderness of Judea, saying, "Repent, for the kingdom of heaven is at hand." For this is the one referred to by Isaiah the prophet when he said, "THE VOICE OF ONE CRYING IN THE WILDERNESS, 'MAKE READY THE WAY OF THE LORD, MAKE HIS PATHS STRAIGHT!'" Now John himself had a garment of camel's hair and a leather belt around his waist; and his food was locusts and wild honey. Then Jerusalem was going out to him, and all Judea and all the district around the Jordan; and they were being baptized by him in the Jordan River, as they confessed their sins. But when he saw many of the Pharisees and Sadducees coming for baptism, he said to them, "You brood of vipers, who warned you to flee from the wrath to come? Therefore bear fruit in keeping with repentance; and do not suppose that you can say to

> yourselves, 'We have Abraham for our father'; for I say to you that from these stones God is able to raise up children to Abraham. The axe is already laid at the root of the trees; therefore every tree that does not bear good fruit is cut down and thrown into the fire. As for me, I baptize you with water for repentance, but He who is coming after me is mightier than I, and I am not fit to remove His sandals; He will baptize you with the Holy Spirit and fire."

John told these spiritual leaders (in no uncertain terms) that the way to prepare for the King's coming was to repent. That is still true for us today.

Also while in Jordan, my husband and I passed below the ruins of Machaerus, Herod's fortified hilltop palace overlooking the Dead Sea. Beneath that royal abode, according to Flavius Josephus, John the Baptist sat in a dungeon till Herod ordered him beheaded. All that's left of the fortress today are some marble floors and a few walls and pillars. But significantly, the snake-infested cave-pits used as prisons remain. In one of these, below the fortress, John would have sat rotting in the dark, fighting off literal serpents, and wondering why the new kingdom of God looked nothing like the glory days he'd envisioned.

Yet despite his bewilderment, John remained faithful to death. He feared only God, not the king. Nor the wife of the king. Nor her dancing daughter who asked for his head. Nor the religious leaders. John didn't hide his fearless loyalty. He ultimately forfeited his life rather than allow any power besides God to own him.

John emphasized one thing: "Repent!" And repentance shows fruit.

How does our own fruit look? Do we heed the words and example of John? Or are we like the priests of his day letting power make us deaf to the cries of the spiritually abused? Do we teach a prosperity gospel, saying that most of the poor got there by their own laziness? Or do we care for Jesus Christ in the face of the hungry, the unsheltered, the resident alien, the widow threatened with losing her orphans? Do we use critiques of Critical Race Theory as excuses to oppose efforts to fight racism? Or do we push past analysis-paralysis to use whatever forms of privilege we have for good? Do we resist true justice, paralyzed by the fear that it might have the word "social" attached to it, or do we actually do justice? Do we cling so loyally to our favorite nation or political party that we overlook its sins? Do we harbor bitterness and speak evil of others, or do we forgive, even when it's hard to love sacrificially? Do we pride ourselves in loathing the killing of fetuses while dishonoring other people's lives, from conception to old age? Do we demonstrate humility, or are we ruled by selfish ambition? Do we really believe we must decrease, but Jesus must increase? How well John knows God's people when he says, "Your fruit must be in keeping with repentance."

Luke begins his Gospel with the remarkable story of John the Baptist's birth and ministry. In Jesus's first coming, the forerunner preached repentance. The first time Jesus came to earth, he came as a servant to seek and save the lost.

But when he returns, he will come in glory. Will he find us asleep? Or will he find us ready, bearing fruit?

For memorization:

And you, my child, will be called a prophet of the Most High;
for you will go on before the Lord to prepare the way for him,
to give his people the knowledge of salvation
through the forgiveness of their sins,
because of the tender mercy of our God,
by which the rising sun will come to us from heaven
to shine on those living in darkness
and in the shadow of death,
to guide our feet into the path of peace" —Zechariah (Luke 1:76–79).

Prayer: (Adapted from a Puritan prayer in *The Valley of Vision*): *Creator of the ends of the earth, Governor of the universe, Judge of all humans, Head of the church, Savior of sinners: Your greatness is unsearchable, Your goodness infinite, Your compassions unfailing, Your providence boundless, Your mercies ever new. We bless you for the words of salvation. How important, suitable, encouraging are the doctrines, promises, and invitations of the gospel of peace! We were lost, but in our lostness you presented to us a full, free and eternal salvation; weak, but here we learn that help is found in One that is mighty; poor, but in him we discover unsearchable riches; blind, but we find he has treasures of wisdom and knowledge. We thank you for your unspeakable gift. Father, Your Son is our only refuge, foundation, hope, confidence; we depend upon his death, rest in his righteousness, desire to bear his image. May his glory fill our minds, his love reign in our affections, his cross inflame us with ardor. Let us as Christians fill our various situations in life, escape the snares to which they expose us, discharge the duties that arise from our circumstances, enjoy with moderation their advantages, improve with* *diligence their usefulness. And may every place and company we are in be benefited by us. In Jesus's name we pray. Amen*

MONDAY: JESUS, FULLY HUMAN

1. Pray for the Spirit's insight. Then read Luke 1 (below). Circle references to humility and low social status.

1:1 Now many have undertaken to compile an account of the things that have been fulfilled among us, 2 like the accounts passed on to us by those who were eyewitnesses and servants of the word from the beginning. 3 So it seemed good to me as well, because I have followed all things carefully from the beginning, to write an orderly account for you, most excellent Theophilus, 4 so that you may know for certain the things you were taught.

5 During the reign of Herod king of Judea, there lived a priest named Zechariah who belonged to the priestly division of Abijah, and he had a wife named Elizabeth, who was a descendant of Aaron. 6 They were both righteous in the sight of God, following all the commandments and ordinances of the Lord blamelessly. 7 But they did not have a child because Elizabeth was barren, and they were both very old.

8 Now while Zechariah was serving as priest before God when his division was on duty, 9 he was chosen by lot, according to the custom of the priesthood, to enter the Holy Place of the Lord and burn incense. 10 Now the whole crowd of people were praying outside at the hour of the incense offering. 11 An angel of the Lord, standing on the right side of the altar of incense, appeared to him. 12 And Zechariah, visibly shaken when he saw the angel, was seized with fear. 13 But the angel said to him, "Do not be afraid, Zechariah, for your prayer has been heard, and your wife Elizabeth will bear you a son; you will name him John. 14 Joy and gladness will come to you, and many will rejoice at his birth, 15 for he will be great in the sight of the Lord. He must never drink wine or strong drink, and he will be filled with the Holy Spirit, even before his birth. 16 He will turn many of the people of Israel to the Lord their God. 17 And he will go as forerunner before the Lord in the spirit and power of Elijah, to turn the hearts of the fathers back to their children and the disobedient to the wisdom of the just, to make ready for the Lord a people prepared for him."

18 Zechariah said to the angel, "How can I be sure of this? For I am an old man, and my wife is old as well." 19 The angel answered

him, "I am Gabriel, who stands in the presence of God, and I was sent to speak to you and to bring you this good news. 20 And now because you did not believe my words, which will be fulfilled in their time, you will be silent, unable to speak, until the day these things take place."

21 Now the people were waiting for Zechariah, and they began to wonder why he was delayed in the Holy Place. 22 When he came out, he was not able to speak to them. They realized that he had seen a vision in the Holy Place because he was making signs to them and remained unable to speak. 23 When his time of service was over, he went to his home.

24 After some time his wife Elizabeth became pregnant, and for five months she kept herself in seclusion. She said, 25 "This is what the Lord has done for me at the time when he has been gracious to me, to take away my disgrace among people."

26 In the sixth month of Elizabeth's pregnancy, the angel Gabriel was sent by God to a town of Galilee called Nazareth, 27 to a virgin engaged to a man whose name was Joseph, a descendant of David, and the virgin's name was Mary. 28 The angel came to her and said, "Greetings, favored one, the Lord is with you!" 29 But she was greatly troubled by his words and began to wonder about the meaning of this greeting. 30 So the angel said to her, "Do not be afraid, Mary, for you have found favor with God! 31 Listen: You will become pregnant and give birth to a son, and you will name him Jesus. 32 He will be great and will be called the Son of the Most High, and the Lord God will give him the throne of his father David. 33 He will reign over the house of Jacob forever, and his kingdom will never end." 34 Mary said to the angel, "How will this be, since I have not been intimate with a man?" 35 The angel replied, "The Holy Spirit will come upon you, and the power of the Most High will overshadow you. Therefore the child to be born will be holy; he will be called the Son of God.

36 "And look, your relative Elizabeth has also become pregnant with a son in her old age—although she was called barren, she is now in her sixth month! 37 For nothing will be impossible with God." 38 So Mary said, "Yes, I am a servant of the Lord; let this happen to me according to your word." Then the angel departed from her.

39 In those days Mary got up and went hurriedly into the hill country, to a town of Judah, 40 and entered Zechariah's house and greeted Elizabeth. 41 When Elizabeth heard Mary's greeting, the baby leaped in her womb, and Elizabeth was filled with the Holy Spirit. 42 She exclaimed with a loud voice, "Blessed are you among

women, and blessed is the child in your womb! 43 And who am I that the mother of my Lord should come and visit me? 44 For the instant the sound of your greeting reached my ears, the baby in my womb leaped for joy. 45 And blessed is she who believed that what was spoken to her by the Lord would be fulfilled."

46 And Mary said,

"My soul exalts the Lord,

47 and my spirit has begun to rejoice in God my Savior,

48 because he has looked upon the humble state of his servant.

For from now on all generations will call me blessed,

49 because he who is mighty has done great things for me, and holy is his name;

50 from generation to generation he is merciful to those who fear him.

51 He has demonstrated power with his arm; he has scattered those whose pride wells up from the sheer arrogance of their hearts.

52 He has brought down the mighty from their thrones, and has lifted up those of lowly position;

53 he has filled the hungry with good things, and has sent the rich away empty.

54 He has helped his servant Israel, remembering his mercy,

55 as he promised to our ancestors, to Abraham and to his descendants forever."

56 So Mary stayed with Elizabeth about three months and then returned to her home.

57 Now the time came for Elizabeth to have her baby, and she gave birth to a son. 58 Her neighbors and relatives heard that the Lord had shown great mercy to her, and they rejoiced with her. 59 On the eighth day they came to circumcise the child, and they wanted to name him Zechariah after his father. 60 But his mother replied, "No! He must be named John." 61 They said to her, "But none of your relatives bears this name." 62 So they made signs to the baby's father, inquiring what he wanted to name his son. 63 He asked for a writing tablet and wrote, "His name is John." And they were all amazed. 64 Immediately Zechariah's mouth was opened and his tongue released, and he spoke, blessing God. 65 All their neighbors were filled with fear, and throughout the entire hill country of Judea all these things were talked about. 66 All who heard these things kept them in their hearts, saying, "What then will this child be?" For the Lord's hand was indeed with him.

67 Then his father Zechariah was filled with the Holy Spirit and prophesied,

68 "Blessed be the Lord God of Israel,

because he has come to help and has redeemed his people.

69 For he has raised up a horn of salvation for us in the house of his servant David,

70 as he spoke through the mouth of his holy prophets from long ago,

71 that we should be saved from our enemies

and from the hand of all who hate us.

72 He has done this to show mercy to our ancestors,

and to remember his holy covenant—

73 the oath that he swore to our ancestor Abraham.

This oath grants 74 that we, being rescued from the hand of our enemies, may serve him without fear,

75 in holiness and righteousness before him for as long as we live.

76 And you, child, will be called the prophet of the Most High.

For you will go before the Lord to prepare his ways,

77 to give his people knowledge of salvation through the forgiveness of their sins.

78 Because of our God's tender mercy,

the dawn will break upon us from on high

79 to give light to those who sit in darkness and in the shadow of death,

to guide our feet into the way of peace."

80 And the child kept growing and becoming strong in spirit, and he was in the wilderness until the day he was revealed to Israel.

2. Why do you think the God of the universe came to earth via a family of low social status rather than in earthly majesty? What does this reveal about his character?

____

____

"An account of the things that have been fulfilled among us" (v. 1) – Fulfillment of prophecy is a major theme in Luke's Gospel.

3. Who does Luke identify as his sources of information (v. 2)?

____

____

4. What sort of account does Luke set out to write, for whom, and why (vv. 3–4)? Give thanks for this story.

____

____

____

5. Study the chart showing Gabriel's appearances to Daniel, Zechariah, and Mary. What similarities in the appearances of the angel do you see?

____

____

Gabriel's Appearances to Daniel, Zechariah, and Mary

To whom Gabriel appeared	When Gabriel appears	Human fear	Sent from God	Mute	Greeting denotes favor with God	Words preserved
Daniel	At the time of sacrifice and prayer (Dan 9:21)	"Do not be afraid, Daniel" (Dan 10:12)	"I have come in response to your words" (Dan. 10:12)	Daniel struck mute at the angel's words (Dan 10:15)	"Hail, O highly esteemed" (Dan. 10:11)	Daniel preserves a word in his heart (Dan. 7:28)
Zechariah	At the time of sacrifice and prayer (Luke 1:10)	"Do not be afraid, Zechariah" (Luke 1:13)	"I was sent to speak to you" (Luke 1:19)	Zechariah told he will become mute (Luke 1:20)		
Mary		"Do not be afraid, Mary" (Luke 1:30)	Gabriel "was sent by God" (Luke 1:26)		"Hail, favored one!" (Luke 1:28)	"Mary preserved these words in her heart" (Luke 2:51)

Three times the Scriptures record an appearance from Gabriel the archangel—to the prophet Daniel; to the priest Zechariah, father of John the Baptist; and to Mary, mother of Jesus. A careful look at the texts reveals how much the narrators' wording seems designed to align the stories in Luke 2, 19, and 21 with Daniel 7:28.

1. Pray for the Holy Spirit to grant insight and read the following excerpt from Luke 1. As you read, circle the names of all the people mentioned and underline the emotions you see mentioned.

> 1:1 Now many have undertaken to compile an account of the things that have been fulfilled among us, 2 like the accounts passed on to us by those who were eyewitnesses and servants of the word from the beginning. 3 So it seemed good to me as well, because I have followed all things carefully from the beginning, to write an orderly account for you, most excellent Theophilus, 4 so that you may know for certain the things you were taught.
>
> 5 During the reign of Herod king of Judea, there lived a priest named Zechariah who belonged to the priestly division of Abijah, and he had a wife named Elizabeth, who was a descendant of Aaron. 6 They were both righteous in the sight of God, following all the commandments and ordinances of the Lord blamelessly. 7 But they did not have a child because Elizabeth was barren, and they were both very old.
>
> 8 Now while Zechariah was serving as priest before God when his division was on duty, 9 he was chosen by lot, according to the custom of the priesthood, to enter the Holy Place of the Lord and burn incense. 10 Now the whole crowd of people were praying outside at the hour of the incense offering. 11 An angel of the Lord, standing on the right side of the altar of incense, appeared to him. 12 And Zechariah, visibly shaken when he saw the angel, was seized with fear. 13 But the angel said to him, "Do not be afraid, Zechariah, for your prayer has been heard, and your wife Elizabeth will bear you a son; you will name him John. 14 Joy and gladness will come to you, and many will rejoice at his birth, 15 for he will be great in the sight of the Lord. He must never drink wine or strong drink, and he will be filled with the Holy Spirit, even before his birth. 16 He will turn many of the people of Israel to the Lord their God. 17 And he will go as forerunner before the Lord in the spirit and power of Elijah, to turn the hearts of the fathers back to their children and the disobedient to the wisdom of the just, to make ready for the Lord a people prepared for him."
>
> 18 Zechariah said to the angel, "How can I be sure of this? For I am an old man, and my wife is old as well." 19 The angel answered

him, "I am Gabriel, who stands in the presence of God, and I was sent to speak to you and to bring you this good news. 20 And now because you did not believe my words, which will be fulfilled in their time, you will be silent, unable to speak, until the day these things take place."

21 Now the people were waiting for Zechariah, and they began to wonder why he was delayed in the Holy Place. 22 When he came out, he was not able to speak to them. They realized that he had seen a vision in the Holy Place because he was making signs to them and remained unable to speak. 23 When his time of service was over, he went to his home.

24 After some time his wife Elizabeth became pregnant, and for five months she kept herself in seclusion. She said, 25 "This is what the Lord has done for me at the time when he has been gracious to me, to take away my disgrace among people."

2. What person in this story did you find it easiest to imagine? What emotions do you think this person felt as a participant in the events?

The Religious Setting of the Gospel of Luke:
Before the coming of Christ, four hundred years had passed since the last recorded word from God through Malachi. And God had continued to work. For example, the feast of Hanukkah, which Jesus attended (the Feast of Lights mentioned in John 10), commemorated a miracle that happened during this so-called silent period. Nevertheless, prophecy was rare, making this time period in Israel's history among the worst of times, especially when you combine the lack of divine prophecy with wave after wave of foreign military occupation.

The Political Setting
"During the reign of Herod king of Judea" (1:5)—Christianity's key events are rooted in real times and places. Herod, king of Judea, was the one whom historians call "Herod the Great." A descendant of Abraham through Ishmael, this pro-Rome (the occupier) king undertook massive building projects, including the fortress at Masada and the expansion of the Temple Mount in Jerusalem. Herod had a reputation for paranoia and cruelty, evidenced by his executing his own family members, including his second wife, Mariamne, and their two

sons, whom he had strangled. Herod had other relatives killed as well: Mariamne's brother, her grandfather, and her mother. This is the same ruler who, as recorded in Matthew's Gospel, ordered "The Slaughter of the Innocents" after the magi departed from his presence. Because of Herod's actions, an angel of the Lord warned Joseph in a dream to take Mary and Jesus and flee to Egypt. It was in the time of such a ruler that Messiah came to rescue his people from their sin.

"A priest named Zechariah who belonged to the priestly division of Abijah (v. 5)—Before King David died, he and others organized priests into groups by birth. To even out the groups' sizes, leaders cast lots to create a more balanced number of members. The author of 1 Chronicles lists Abjiah as belonging to this priestly class that descended from the tribe of Levi through Aaron (1 Chr. 24:6–10). The man described here is John the Baptist's father.

"And he [Zechariah] had a wife named Elizabeth, who was a descendant of Aaron" (v. 5). Like her husband, Elizabeth came from a priest-class family. Aaron, brother of Moses, lived a thousand years before the events Luke records. Although Luke is probably a Gentile, he establishes the key characters' Jewish and religious credentials. By this time, according to some estimates, the Jewish priestly class numbered about eighteen thousand members.

"They were both righteous in the sight of God, following all the commandments and ordinances of the Lord blamelessly. But they did not have a child because Elizabeth was barren, and they were both very old" (vv. 6–7). Barrenness and fertility on a national level is a motif we see in the Old Testament, often relating to the people's sin and obedience (see Deut. 7). Luke makes it clear, however, that Elizabeth's inability to conceive has nothing to do with lack of character. Often in God's redemption story when the Almighty is about to do something great, we see a miraculous conception. Elizabeth and Mary, whose stories we read in this chapter, join a long line of women in Israel's history with remarkable conception stories—women such as Sarah, Rebecca, Rachel, Samson's mother, and Hannah. Among these is even Ruth the Moabite (outsider) woman, who conceived Boaz's child after her ten-year childless marriage ended in her husband's death, setting the stage for her to marry a descendant in the Messiah's lineage.

"Chosen by lot, according to the custom of the priesthood, to enter the Holy Place of the Lord and burn incense" (v. 9; Zechariah was probably experiencing a once-in-a-lifetime event.

"Whole crowd of people were praying outside at the hour of the incense offering" (v. 10). The time was probably at 9 a.m. Incense in the Scriptures is often associated with the prayers of the people, and we see that connection here. The people of God had a set time and place for daily prayers. Prayer is major theme in the Gospel of Luke.

Once a year on the Day of Atonement, the high priest would enter the holy of holies in the temple to sprinkle blood and burn incense. Outside the curtain dividing the holy of holies from the holy place stood a lampstand, the table for the bread of the Presence, and the altar of incense. In this area priests would offer incense daily. This space was where Zechariah stood, expecting to be alone, when "an angel of the Lord, standing on the right side of the altar of incense, appeared to him" (v. 11).

3. Do you have a set time and place for daily prayer? When do you gather with others for prayer?

____

____

____

4. How can you build strong habits of prayer?

____

____

5. Imagine a supernatural being suddenly appearing to you. What might you think and feel? Describe what you might experience as the physical effects on your body.

____

____

____

____

6. What two reasons does the angel give Zechariah for telling him to "fear not" (v. 13)?

____

____

7. List the events the angel says will happen (vv. 13–17).

____

____

8. What reason (beyond the miracle of a baby following infertility) is given for joy, gladness, and people rejoicing at John's birth (v. 15)?

____

____

9. What is Zechariah's response to the angel's word (v. 18)?

____

____

10. Notice Gabriel's rebuke (v. 19). Why do you think Gabriel finds Zechariah's response so offensive?

____

____

11. Notice Elizabeth's words five months into her pregnancy: "This is what the Lord has done for me at the time when he has been gracious to me, to take away my disgrace among people" (v. 25). In whose eyes had she actually been disgraced? Why do you think that was so?

____

____

Wednesday: The Annunciation

1. Pray for insight from the Spirit and read the wonderful story from Luke 1:26–38. Notice the faith in Mary's response. Underline all the miracles you find. And circle references to "wait" and "waiting."

> 26 In the sixth month of Elizabeth's pregnancy, the angel Gabriel was sent by God to a town of Galilee called Nazareth, 27 to a virgin engaged to a man whose name was Joseph, a descendant of David, and the virgin's name was Mary. 28 The angel came to her and said, "Greetings, favored one, the Lord is with you!"
>
> 29 But she was greatly troubled by his words and began to wonder about the meaning of this greeting.
>
> 30 So the angel said to her, "Do not be afraid, Mary, for you have found favor with God! 31 Listen: You will become pregnant and give birth to a son, and you will name him Jesus. 32 He will be great and will be called the Son of the Most High, and the Lord God will give him the throne of his father David. 33 He will reign over the house of Jacob forever, and his kingdom will never end."
>
> 34 Mary said to the angel, "How will this be, since I have not been intimate with a man?"
>
> 35 The angel replied, "The Holy Spirit will come upon you, and the power of the Most High will overshadow you. Therefore the child to be born will be holy; he will be called the Son of God. 36 "And look, your relative Elizabeth has also become pregnant with a son in her old age—although she was called barren, she is now in her sixth month! 37 For nothing will be impossible with God."
>
> 38 So Mary said, "Yes, I am a servant of the Lord; let this happen to me according to your word." Then the angel departed from her.

The angel Gabriel was sent by God (v. 26). Gabriel was the angel who appeared to Zechariah (Luke 1:19). In the supernatural world, many fallen angels (demons) and good angels exist. But only two good angels are named in the Bible—Michael and Gabriel. The Hebrew Bible records that the prophet Daniel received a visit from Gabriel, who came to explain Daniel's visions (Dan. 8:15–26, 9:21–27). Here, Gabriel also appears to Joseph, to whom Mary was betrothed (cf. Matt. 1:20–21). But being sent by God to tell Mary what is about to happen has to be Gabriel's most amazing assignment ever. Zechariah asked, "How will I know?" but Mary asked, "How will it happen?"

Prophecy Fulfilled in the First Two Chapters of Luke

"Fulfillment" of prophesy is a recurring theme throughout the Gospel of Luke. Elizabeth says of Mary, "Blessed is she who believed that what was spoken to her by the Lord would be fulfilled" (Luke 1:45). Here's a sampling of "fulfillment" as seen in only the first few stories:

Chapter 1

Zechariah's wife Elizabeth will bear him a son (v. 13).

They will name their son John (v. 13).

Joy and gladness will come to Elizabeth and Zechariah, and many will rejoice at their son's birth (vv. 14, 58).

Their son will be great in the sight of the Lord. He will be filled with the Holy Spirit, even before his birth (v. 15).

John will turn many of the people of Israel to the Lord their God (v. 16).

John will go as a forerunner before the Lord in the spirit and power of Elijah (v. 17).

Zechariah will be silent, unable to speak, until the angel's predictions take place (v. 20).

Chapter 2

Mary will become pregnant and give birth to a son (v. 31).

She will name him "Jesus" (v. 31).

Jesus will be great and will be called "Son of the Most High" (v. 32)

Mary will conceive and bear a child without knowing a man (v. 35).

Generations after Mary will call her blessed (v. 49).

God helped Israel, remembering his mercy, as he promised to Abraham and to his descendants forever (v. 55).

2. Look at yesterday's Luke text to see how Gabriel responds to Zechariah's question (1:19). Contrast Gabriel's response to Mary's question (v. 35). How do they differ?

____

____

"To a virgin engaged to a man" (v. 27). Both before Mary's conception and throughout her pregnancy, she remained a virgin (see Matt. 1:25). This detail removes any doubt that the child she bore had a biologically human father. Jesus had a human mother but no human father. Incidentally, this is one reason the appearance of God on earth required Messiah to be male. If a female had given birth to a female, male humanity would have been excluded altogether in the incarnation. But in Jesus's incarnation, both female (his mother) and male (Jesus) humanity are fully represented. In addition to saying Mary is a virgin, the text adds that Mary is engaged, which at the time is a legally binding act, requiring divorce to break the engagement.

3. Take a moment to marvel and give thanks that God enrobed himself in human flesh and came as a servant.

"Greetings, favored one, the Lord is with you!" (v. 28). The original language here suggests God is showing Mary favor or "grace" (the literal word). The Vulgate (Latin translation from the Greek), which renders this phrase as "Mary, full of grace" has been read as suggesting Mary already has rather than receives grace. But that's backwards. God has chosen to bestow grace—both on her, and through her to us. "Grace" is an important word in this passage. We will see it again.

4. What does the angel predict about the son who will be born to Mary (vv. 31–35)?

____

____

"And look, your relative Elizabeth..." (v. 36). In some English translations the word "relative" is rendered as "cousin," but it does not have to mean a relation that specific. Elizabeth could have been Mary's aunt.

5. Write out Luke 1:37 in the space provided.

____

____

6. In what area of your life do you need to believe God is able to do the impossible?

____

____

Today's reading is longer than usual; Luke 1 is the longest chapter in the New Testament, and it is filled with important details that give us the miraculous background stories about both John the forerunner and Jesus Christ, the Promised One. God set all these events in motion. He knows all things. He keeps his promises. With him all things are possible! Put a star by the speeches:

39 In those days Mary got up and went hurriedly into the hill country, to a town of Judah, 40 and entered Zechariah's house and greeted Elizabeth.

41 When Elizabeth heard Mary's greeting, the baby leaped in her womb, and Elizabeth was filled with the Holy Spirit. 42 She exclaimed with a loud voice, "Blessed are you among women, and blessed is the child in your womb! 43 And who am I that the mother of my Lord should come and visit me? 44 For the instant the sound of your greeting reached my ears, the baby in my womb leaped for joy. 45 And blessed is she who believed that what was spoken to her by the Lord would be fulfilled."

46 And Mary said,

"My soul exalts the Lord,

47 and my spirit has begun to rejoice in God my Savior,

48 because he has looked upon the humble state of his servant.

For from now on all generations will call me blessed,

49 because he who is mighty has done great things for me, and holy is his name;

50 from generation to generation he is merciful to those who fear him.

51 He has demonstrated power with his arm; he has scattered those whose pride wells up from the sheer arrogance of their hearts.

52 He has brought down the mighty from their thrones, and has lifted up those of lowly position;

53 he has filled the hungry with good things, and has sent the rich away empty.

54 He has helped his servant Israel, remembering his mercy,

55 as he promised to our ancestors, to Abraham and to his descendants forever."

56 So Mary stayed with Elizabeth about three months and then returned to her home.

57 Now the time came for Elizabeth to have her baby, and she gave birth to a son. 58 Her neighbors and relatives heard that the Lord had shown great mercy to her, and they rejoiced with her.

59 On the eighth day they came to circumcise the child, and they wanted to name him Zechariah after his father.

60 But his mother replied, "No! He must be named John."

61 They said to her, "But none of your relatives bears this name." 62 So they made signs to the baby's father, inquiring what he wanted to name his son.

63 He asked for a writing tablet and wrote, "His name is John." And they were all amazed. 64 Immediately Zechariah's mouth was opened and his tongue released, and he spoke, blessing God.

65 All their neighbors were filled with fear, and throughout the entire hill country of Judea all these things were talked about. 66 All who heard these things kept them in their hearts, saying, "What then will this child be?" For the Lord's hand was indeed with him.

67 Then his father Zechariah was filled with the Holy Spirit and prophesied,

68 "Blessed be the Lord God of Israel,

because he has come to help and has redeemed his people.

69 For he has raised up a horn of salvation for us in the house of his servant David,

70 as he spoke through the mouth of his holy prophets from long ago,

71 that we should be saved from our enemies

and from the hand of all who hate us.

72 He has done this to show mercy to our ancestors,

and to remember his holy covenant—

73 the oath that he swore to our ancestor Abraham.

This oath grants 74 that we, being rescued from the hand of our enemies,

may serve him without fear,

75 in holiness and righteousness before him for as long as we live.

76 And you, child, will be called the prophet of the Most High.

For you will go before the Lord to prepare his ways,

77 to give his people knowledge of salvation through the forgiveness of their sins.

78 Because of our God's tender mercy,

the dawn will break upon us from on high

79 to give light to those who sit in darkness and in the shadow of death,

to guide our feet into the way of peace."

80 And the child kept growing and becoming strong in spirit, and he was in the wilderness until the day he was revealed to Israel.

7. After Mary responds with total belief, she hurries off to the hill country to see Elizabeth. When Mary arrives, before she says a word, what hints does the text give that supernatural events are continuing to happen (vv. 41–44)?

____

____

8. Elizabeth speaks prophetically with supernatural knowledge about an event she did not witness. What does she say about how Mary responded to the angel's pronouncement (v. 45)?

____

____

Mary also speaks prophetically. What she says in response to Elizabeth is often compared with the prayer of Hannah, an event that happened about eleven centuries earlier. (This is one reason Mary is said to have been biblically literate.) Hannah and her husband were infertile, and she miraculously conceived a son. That son grew up to became the prophet Samuel, who anointed David as king. Here is Hannah's prayer from 1 Samuel 2:

> 1 "My heart has rejoiced in the Lord;
> my horn has been raised high because of the Lord.
> I have loudly denounced my enemies.
> Indeed I rejoice in your deliverance.
> 2 No one is holy like the Lord!
> There is no one other than you!
> There is no rock like our God!
> 3 Don't keep speaking so arrogantly.
> Proud talk should not come out of your mouth,
> for the Lord is a God who knows;
> he evaluates what people do.
> 4 The bows of warriors are shattered,
> but those who stumbled have taken on strength.
> 5 The well fed hire themselves out to earn food,
> but the hungry no longer lack.
> Even the barren woman has given birth to seven,

but the one with many children has declined.
6 The Lord both kills and gives life;
he brings down to the grave and raises up.
7 The Lord impoverishes and makes wealthy;
he humbles and he exalts.
8 He lifts the weak from the dust;
he raises the poor from the ash heap
to seat them with princes–
he bestows on them an honored position.
The foundations of the earth belong to the Lord–
he placed the world on them.
9 He watches over his holy ones,
but the wicked are made speechless in the darkness,
for it is not by one's own strength that one prevails.
10 The Lord shatters his adversaries;
he thunders against them from the heavens.
The Lord executes judgment to the ends of the earth.
He will strengthen his king
and exalt the power of his anointed one" (1 Sam. 2:1–10).

And here is Mary's prayer again, as recorded in Luke 1:

46 And Mary said,
"My soul exalts the Lord,
47 and my spirit has begun to rejoice in God my Savior,
48 because he has looked upon the humble state of his servant.
For from now on all generations will call me blessed,

49 because he who is mighty has done great things for me, and holy is his name;

50 from generation to generation he is merciful to those who fear him.

51 He has demonstrated power with his arm; he has scattered those whose pride wells up from the sheer arrogance of their hearts.

52 He has brought down the mighty from their thrones, and has lifted up those of lowly position;

53 he has filled the hungry with good things, and has sent the rich away empty.

54 He has helped his servant Israel, remembering his mercy,

55 as he promised to our ancestors, to Abraham and to his descendants forever" (Luke 1:46–55).

9. What similarities do you see between the two women's pronouncements?

Elizabeth is six months pregnant when Mary arrives (1:26). And Mary stays with her about three months (v. 56). But apparently Mary returns home shortly before Elizabeth delivers a son. At that time, friends and family rejoice with the old woman in God's mercy. The time comes to circumcise the baby on the eighth day, and the people assume the couple will name their son after a relative, according to custom. But Elizabeth insists on a different name: John—which means "God is gracious" or "graced by God."

10. Up to this point, Zechariah has been mute. And when the people ask him what he wants to name his son, how does he respond, and what is the result (vv. 63–66)?

---

11. Circle all references to salvation, redemption, and promise-keeping in Zechariah's Spirit-filled prophecy:

> 68 "Blessed be the Lord God of Israel,
> because he has come to help and has redeemed his people.
> 69 For he has raised up a horn of salvation for us in the house of his servant David,
> 70 as he spoke through the mouth of his holy prophets from long ago,
> 71 that we should be saved from our enemies
> and from the hand of all who hate us.
> 72 He has done this to show mercy to our ancestors,
> and to remember his holy covenant—
> 73 the oath that he swore to our ancestor Abraham.
> This oath grants 74 that we, being rescued from the hand of our enemies,
> may serve him without fear,
> 75 in holiness and righteousness before him for as long as we live.

12. Zechariah turns to speak specifically to his child. List what Zechariah says the child will do and why (vv. 76–79).

____

____

The dawn will break upon us from on high (v. 78)—Through the prophet Malachi, God had predicted that "the sun of vindication will rise with healing wings" (Mal. 4:2), which many understood as a reference to the Messiah. It is possible that Zechariah sees the fulfillment of this prediction happening before his eyes.

Four hundred years earlier, when God spoke through the prophet Malachi, he announced, "I will send my messenger, who will prepare the way before me" (Mal. 3:1). John the Baptizer became that messenger—in the Spirit and power of Elijah. And John lived in the wilderness where Elijah had ministered.

13. What do all these events reveal about the faithfulness of God?

____

____

Thursday: Jesus's Nativity and Dedication

1. Pray for insight and read Luke 2. Underline supernatural events and all references to Jews and Gentiles.

> 2:1 Now in those days a decree went out from Caesar Augustus to register all the empire for taxes. 2 This was the first registration, taken when Quirinius was governor of Syria. 3 Everyone went to his own town to be registered. 4 So Joseph also went up from the town of Nazareth in Galilee to Judea, to the city of David called Bethlehem, because he was of the house and family line of David. 5 He went to be registered with Mary, who was promised in marriage to him, and who was expecting a child. 6 While they were there, the time came for her to deliver her child. 7 And she gave birth to her firstborn son and wrapped him in strips of cloth and laid him in a manger, because there was no place for them in the inn.

8 Now there were shepherds nearby living out in the field, keeping guard over their flock at night. 9 An angel of the Lord appeared to them, and the glory of the Lord shone around them, and they were absolutely terrified. 10 But the angel said to them, "Do not be afraid! Listen carefully, for I proclaim to you good news that brings great joy to all the people: 11 Today your Savior is born in the city of David. He is Christ the Lord. 12 This will be a sign for you: You will find a baby wrapped in strips of cloth and lying in a manger." 13 Suddenly a vast, heavenly army appeared with the angel, praising God and saying,

14 "Glory to God in the highest,
and on earth peace among people with whom he is pleased!"

15 When the angels left them and went back to heaven, the shepherds said to one another, "Let us go over to Bethlehem and see this thing that has taken place, that the Lord has made known to us." 16 So they hurried off and located Mary and Joseph, and found the baby lying in a manger. 17 When they saw him, they related what they had been told about this child, 18 and all who heard it were astonished at what the shepherds said. 19 But Mary treasured up all these words, pondering in her heart what they might mean. 20 So the shepherds returned, glorifying and praising God for all they had heard and seen; everything was just as they had been told.

21 At the end of eight days, when he was circumcised, he was named Jesus, the name given by the angel before he was conceived in the womb.

22 Now when the time came for their purification according to the law of Moses, Joseph and Mary brought Jesus up to Jerusalem to present him to the Lord 23 (just as it is written in the law of the Lord, "Every firstborn male will be set apart to the Lord"), 24 and to offer a sacrifice according to what is specified in the law of the Lord, a pair of doves or two young pigeons.

25 Now there was a man in Jerusalem named Simeon who was righteous and devout, looking for the restoration of Israel, and the Holy Spirit was upon him. 26 It had been revealed to him by the Holy Spirit that he would not die before he had seen the Lord's Christ. 27 So Simeon, directed by the Spirit, came into the temple courts, and when the parents brought in the child Jesus to do for him what was customary according to the law, 28 Simeon took him in his arms and blessed God, saying,

29 "Now, according to your word, Sovereign Lord,
permit your servant to depart in peace.
30 For my eyes have seen your salvation
31 that you have prepared in the presence of all peoples:

32 a light,
for revelation to the Gentiles
and for glory to your people Israel."

33 So the child's father and mother were amazed at what was said about him. 34 Then Simeon blessed them and said to his mother Mary, "Listen carefully: This child is destined to be the cause of the falling and rising of many in Israel and to be a sign that will be rejected. 35 Indeed, as a result of him the thoughts of many hearts will be revealed—and a sword will pierce your own soul as well!"

36 There was also a prophetess, Anna the daughter of Phanuel, of the tribe of Asher. She was very old, having been married to her husband for seven years until his death. 37 She had lived as a widow since then for eighty-four years. She never left the temple, worshiping with fasting and prayer night and day. 38 At that moment, she came up to them and began to give thanks to God and to speak about the child to all who were waiting for the redemption of Jerusalem.

39 So when Joseph and Mary had performed everything according to the law of the Lord, they returned to Galilee, to their own town of Nazareth. 40 And the child grew and became strong, filled with wisdom, and the favor of God was upon him.

41 Now Jesus' parents went to Jerusalem every year for the Feast of the Passover. 42 When he was twelve years old, they went up according to custom. 43 But when the feast was over, as they were returning home, the boy Jesus stayed behind in Jerusalem. His parents did not know it, 44 but (because they assumed that he was in their group of travelers) they went a day's journey. Then they began to look for him among their relatives and acquaintances. 45 When they did not find him, they returned to Jerusalem to look for him. 46 After three days they found him in the temple courts, sitting among the teachers, listening to them and asking them questions. 47 And all who heard Jesus were astonished at his understanding and his answers. 48 When his parents saw him, they were overwhelmed. His mother said to him, "Child, why have you treated us like this? Look, your father and I have been looking for you anxiously." 49 But he replied, "Why were you looking for me? Didn't you know that I must be in my Father's house?" 50 Yet his parents did not understand the remark he made to them. 51 Then he went down with them and came to Nazareth, and was obedient to them. But his mother kept all these things in her heart.

52 And Jesus increased in wisdom and in stature and in favor with God and with people.

"A decree went out from Caesar Augustus to register all the empire for taxes. This was the first registration, taken when Quirinius was governor of Syria" (Luke 2:1–2). Herod was the local magistrate; Caesar Augustus reigned over the entire Roman empire. History tells us the latter reigned from 31 BC to AD 14. The most reasonable date for the census event is 6 BC or in early 5 BC. Contrary to what many think, Jesus was not born in the year "zero." Based on descriptions in the New Testament such as this one and the account of the slaughter of children after the magi's visit, historians calculate that Jesus was born between 6 and 4 BC. These precise dates are one reason some in academic arenas typically refer to the eras by using "BCE" (Before the Common Era) and "CE" (Common Era)—instead of assuming a date of birth/the lordship of Christ with BC ("before Christ") and AD (Anno Domini, Latin for "in the year of our Lord"). The point is historical precision and religious neutrality, not necessarily to undermine the validity of the story. If no notation appears, the time after Jesus's birth is assumed (whether AD or CE). The "BC/AD" dating system, devised by a monk in 525, was not widely used until the ninth century. Of greater significance to us is the observation that the events of Jesus's birth are grounded in historical events.

Joseph also went up from the town of Nazareth in Galilee to Judea, to the city of David called Bethlehem, because he was of the house and family line of David (vv. 3–4). King David was born in Bethlehem, and Joseph, Mary's betrothed, was one of David's descendants. Because of the census, Joseph had to take his fiancée and return to his ancestral town to be registered. That's a ninety-mile trek, ascending to a mile-high town that takes about thirty-three hours to walk from Nazareth when someone is not nine months pregnant. Micah made this prediction about Bethlehem four hundred years before Jesus:

> "As for you, Bethlehem Ephrathah, seemingly insignificant among the clans of Judah—from you a king will emerge who will rule over Israel on my behalf, one whose origins are in the distant past" (Micah 5:1)

2. What does fulfilled prophecy suggest about the attributes and character of God?

____

____

3. What was the shepherds' response to the angels' appearances and announcements (vv. 8–20)?

____

____

4. What hints do you get that Mary and Joseph were religiously observant Jews (vv. 21–24, 41)?

____

____

"He was named Jesus" (v. 21)—The Greek name, *Iesous*, is the equivalent to the Hebrew Yeshua, or Joshua. It means "Yahweh saves" or "The Lord saves."

"To offer a sacrifice according to what is specified in the law of the Lord, a pair of doves or two young pigeons" (v. 24). Joseph and Mary were religiously observant. Leviticus says, "This is the law of the one who bears a child, for the male or the female child. If she cannot afford a sheep, then she must take two turtledoves or two young pigeons, one for a burnt offering and one for a sin offering, and the priest is to make atonement on her behalf, and she will be clean" (Lev. 12:8).

5. What is significant about naming their son "the Lord saves"? And what does their offering reveal about Jesus's parents' socio-economic status?

____

____

"Looking for the restoration of Israel..." (v. 25)—"The restoration" could be translated "the comfort" or "the consolation." The elderly Simeon was looking for God to keep his promise to rescue his people. The New Testament is full of such people. Notice that the prophet Anna spoke in the temple to all who were "waiting for the redemption of Jerusalem" (v. 38).

6. How does the text describe Simeon (vv. 25–26)?

____

____

7. What did God promise Simeon, and how do you think he knew when to go to the temple to hold the long-awaited child (vv. 26, 27)?

____

____

8. What subtle hint does the text give about how Simeon felt when all this happened (vv. 26–29)?

____

____

9. What hints do you find in Simeon's prayer that this child has come for both Jew and Gentile (vv. 30–32)? And how do Mary and Joseph respond?

____

____

10. The mighty will fall; the humble will rise. The holy family is in the middle of this wonderful, joy-filled, supernatural moment when Simeon delivers a sobering prediction (vv. 34–35). Use your imagination. What do you think Mary felt when she heard his words? How was her life filled with a pierced soul?

____

____

11. The prophet Anna is identified by her tribal identity—of Asher. For the bride, assume an average age of fourteen years on her wedding day.

Anna became a widow after seven years of marriage (v. 37; so, assume widowhood at 21) and lived as a widow for eighty-four years (v. 38). What do you calculate is her age when she sees the infant Jesus? Who is her audience? What is her message?

The child grew and became strong, filled with wisdom, and the favor of God was upon him (v. 40). Luke gives further evidence of Jesus's humanity. The child grew as any human would grow—in body, soul, and spirit. Jesus also continually experienced God's "grace" or "favor." Compare this with how the chapter ends: "And Jesus increased in wisdom and in stature and in favor with God and with people" (v. 52). He grows socially as well, and contines to receive God's favor.

"(Because they assumed that he was in their group of travelers) they went a day's journey" [v. 44]**).** Jerusalem is about a thirty-mile walk from Nazareth, and Jesus's family had walked there for Passover, the first day of the seven-day Feast of Unleavened Bread. People likely traveled in groups with friends, neighbors, and family, so it's not unusual that on the return, Mary and Joseph assume Jesus is with the group. They are a full day's distance from Jerusalem when they realize Jesus is not with them. Imagine the panic, the rush back over miles, and the three-day hunt in Jerusalem for their pre-teen! Tradition suggests that Mary herself is the source of this story for Luke. And Luke is quick to note Jesus was submissive to his parents (v. 51). Luke's point is not the panic or the search.

12. What do Jesus's parents find him doing (vv. 46–47)?

---

13. What hint do 12-year-old Jesus's words ("I must") and actions ("be in the temple") suggest about his identity (vv. 46–49)?

---

14. How does Jesus perceive himself in relation to God (v. 49)?

____

____

FRIDAY: THE BAPTISM OF JESUS

1. Pray for the Spirit's help in understanding. Then read Luke chapters 3 and 4. Circle all fulfilled prophesies; and in the section on Jesus's genealogy, underline the references in chapters 3 and 4 to Jesus as God's Son or the phrase "the son of God."

3:1 In the fifteenth year of the reign of Tiberius Caesar, when Pontius Pilate was governor of Judea, and Herod was tetrarch of Galilee, and his brother Philip was tetrarch of the region of Iturea and Trachonitis, and Lysanias was tetrarch of Abilene, 2 during the high priesthood of Annas and Caiaphas, the word of God came to John the son of Zechariah in the wilderness. 3 He went into all the region around the Jordan River, preaching a baptism of repentance for the forgiveness of sins.

4 As it is written in the book of the words of the prophet Isaiah,
"The voice of one shouting in the wilderness:
'Prepare the way for the Lord,
make his paths straight.
5 Every valley will be filled,
and every mountain and hill will be brought low,
and the crooked will be made straight,
and the rough ways will be made smooth,
6 and all humanity will see the salvation of God.'"

7 So John said to the crowds that came out to be baptized by him, "You offspring of vipers! Who warned you to flee from the coming wrath? 8 Therefore produce fruit that proves your repentance, and don't begin to say to yourselves, 'We have Abraham as our father.' For I tell you that God can raise up children for Abraham from these stones! 9 Even now the ax is laid at the root of the trees, and every tree that does not produce good fruit will be cut down and thrown into the fire."

10 So the crowds were asking him, "What then should we do?" 11 John answered them, "The person who has two tunics must share with the person who has none, and the person who has food

must do likewise." 12 Tax collectors also came to be baptized, and they said to him, "Teacher, what should we do?" 13 He told them, "Collect no more than you are required to." 14 Then some soldiers also asked him, "And as for us—what should we do?" He told them, "Take money from no one by violence or by false accusation, and be content with your pay."

15 While the people were filled with anticipation and they all wondered whether perhaps John could be the Christ, 16 John answered them all, "I baptize you with water, but one more powerful than I am is coming—I am not worthy to untie the strap of his sandals. He will baptize you with the Holy Spirit and fire. 17 His winnowing fork is in his hand to clean out his threshing floor and to gather the wheat into his storehouse, but the chaff he will burn up with inextinguishable fire."

18 And in this way, with many other exhortations, John proclaimed good news to the people. 19 But when John rebuked Herod the tetrarch because of Herodias, his brother's wife, and because of all the evil deeds that he had done, 20 Herod added this to them all: He locked up John in prison.

21 Now when all the people were baptized, Jesus also was baptized. And while he was praying, the heavens opened, 22 and the Holy Spirit descended on him in bodily form like a dove. And a voice came from heaven, "You are my one dear Son; in you I take great delight."

23 So Jesus, when he began his ministry, was about thirty years old. He was the son (as was supposed) of Joseph, the son of Heli, 24 the son of Matthat, the son of Levi, the son of Melchi, the son of Jannai, the son of Joseph, 25 the son of Mattathias, the son of Amos, the son of Nahum, the son of Esli, the son of Naggai, 26 the son of Maath, the son of Mattathias, the son of Semein, the son of Josech, the son of Joda, 27 the son of Joanan, the son of Rhesa, the son of Zerubbabel, the son of Shealtiel, the son of Neri, 28 the son of Melchi, the son of Addi, the son of Cosam, the son of Elmadam, the son of Er, 29 the son of Joshua, the son of Eliezer, the son of Jorim, the son of Matthat, the son of Levi, 30 the son of Simeon, the son of Judah, the son of Joseph, the son of Jonam, the son of Eliakim, 31 the son of Melea, the son of Menna, the son of Mattatha, the son of Nathan, the son of David, 32 the son of Jesse, the son of Obed, the son of Boaz, the son of Sala, the son of Nahshon, 33 the son of Amminadab, the son of Admin, the son of Arni, the son of Hezron, the son of Perez, the son of Judah, 34 the son of Jacob, the son of Isaac, the son of Abraham, the son of Terah, the son of Nahor, 35 the son of Serug, the son of Reu, the son of Peleg, the son of Eber, the son of Shelah, 36 the son of Cainan,

the son of Arphaxad, the son of Shem, the son of Noah, the son of Lamech, 37 the son of Methuselah, the son of Enoch, the son of Jared, the son of Mahalalel, the son of Kenan, 38 the son of Enosh, the son of Seth, the son of Adam, the son of God.

4:1 Then Jesus, full of the Holy Spirit, returned from the Jordan River and was led by the Spirit in the wilderness, 2 where for forty days he endured temptations from the devil. He ate nothing during those days, and when they were completed, he was famished. 3 The devil said to him, "If you are the Son of God, command this stone to become bread." 4 Jesus answered him, "It is written, 'Man does not live by bread alone.'"

5 Then the devil led him up to a high place and showed him in a flash all the kingdoms of the world. 6 And he said to him, "To you I will grant this whole realm—and the glory that goes along with it, for it has been relinquished to me, and I can give it to anyone I wish. 7 So then, if you will worship me, all this will be yours." 8 Jesus answered him, "It is written, 'You are to worship the Lord your God and serve only him.'"

9 Then the devil brought him to Jerusalem, had him stand on the highest point of the temple, and said to him, "If you are the Son of God, throw yourself down from here, 10 for it is written, 'He will command his angels concerning you, to protect you,' 11 and 'with their hands they will lift you up, so that you will not strike your foot against a stone.'" 12 Jesus answered him, "It is said, 'You are not to put the Lord your God to the test.'" 13 So when the devil had completed every temptation, he departed from him until a more opportune time.

14 Then Jesus, in the power of the Spirit, returned to Galilee, and news about him spread throughout the surrounding countryside. 15 He began to teach in their synagogues and was praised by all.

16 Now Jesus came to Nazareth, where he had been brought up, and went into the synagogue on the Sabbath day, as was his custom. He stood up to read, 17 and the scroll of the prophet Isaiah was given to him. He unrolled the scroll and found the place where it was written,

> 18 *"The Spirit of the Lord is upon me,*
> *because he has anointed me to proclaim good news to the poor.*
> *He has sent me to proclaim release to the captives*
> *and the regaining of sight to the blind,*
> *to set free those who are oppressed,*
> *19 to proclaim the year of the Lord's favor."*

20 Then he rolled up the scroll, gave it back to the attendant, and sat down. The eyes of everyone in the synagogue were fixed on

him. 21 Then he began to tell them, "Today this scripture has been fulfilled even as you heard it being read." 22 All were speaking well of him, and were amazed at the gracious words coming out of his mouth. They said, "Isn't this Joseph's son?" 23 Jesus said to them, "No doubt you will quote to me the proverb, 'Physician, heal yourself!' and say, 'What we have heard that you did in Capernaum, do here in your hometown too.'" 24 And he added, "I tell you the truth, no prophet is acceptable in his hometown. 25 But in truth I tell you, there were many widows in Israel in Elijah's days, when the sky was shut up three and a half years and there was a great famine over all the land. 26 Yet Elijah was sent to none of them, but only to a woman who was a widow at Zarephath in Sidon. 27 And there were many lepers in Israel in the time of the prophet Elisha, yet none of them was cleansed except Naaman the Syrian." 28 When they heard this, all the people in the synagogue were filled with rage. 29 They got up, forced him out of the town, and brought him to the brow of the hill on which their town was built, so that they could throw him down the cliff. 30 But he passed through the crowd and went on his way.

31 So he went down to Capernaum, a town in Galilee, and on the Sabbath he began to teach the people. 32 They were amazed at his teaching because he spoke with authority.

33 Now in the synagogue there was a man who had the spirit of an unclean demon, and he cried out with a loud voice, 34 "Ha! Leave us alone, Jesus the Nazarene! Have you come to destroy us? I know who you are—the Holy One of God." 35 But Jesus rebuked him: "Silence! Come out of him!" Then, after the demon threw the man down in their midst, he came out of him without hurting him. 36 They were all amazed and began to say to one another, "What's happening here? For with authority and power he commands the unclean spirits, and they come out!" 37 So the news about him spread into all areas of the region.

38 After Jesus left the synagogue, he entered Simon's house. Now Simon's mother-in-law was suffering from a high fever, and they asked Jesus to help her. 39 So he stood over her, commanded the fever, and it left her. Immediately she got up and began to serve them.

40 As the sun was setting, all those who had any relatives sick with various diseases brought them to Jesus. He placed his hands on every one of them and healed them. 41 Demons also came out of many, crying out, "You are the Son of God!" But he rebuked them and would not allow them to speak because they knew that he was the Christ.

42 The next morning Jesus departed and went to a deserted place. Yet the crowds were seeking him, and they came to him and tried to keep him from leaving them. 43 But Jesus said to them, "I must proclaim the good news of the kingdom of God to the other towns too, for that is what I was sent to do." 44 So he continued to preach in the synagogues of Judea.

"Herod was tetrarch of Galilee" (3:1)—Herod Antipas had a long reign of forty-two years. He was the half-Samaritan, half-Idumean son of Herod the Great. Historians say the identification of rulers makes the year here AD 29, plus or minus a year. Luke is concerned for historical accuracy, which is confirmed by historical records outside of the Bible.

"During the high priesthood of Annas and Caiaphas" (v. 2)—Caiaphas, who served from AD 18–36, was the high priest in actual service at this time. Annas served previously but retained the title.

"The word of God came to John the son of Zechariah in the wilderness" (v. 2). Luke makes clear the source of John's prophetic ministry: God.

2. John is preaching to his own people—the descendants of Abraham through Jacob. What is John's message to them (vv. 3, 7, 8)?

____

____

3. What does John say are the evidences of true repentance (vv. 11–14)?

____

____

"Tax collectors also came to be baptized" (v. 12)—Tax collectors were notorious for abusing their power to line their own pockets (see also Luke 15:1–2; 19:8). In modern terms, think of corrupt government officials, those who accept bribes for bids and those who run Ponzi schemes. Note that Jesus does not tell them to quit collecting taxes, but to show their repentance by bringing honesty to their occupations. The same is true for the Roman soldiers, known for extorting, threatening, and making false accusations (v. 14). The goal is not for most to leave their jobs and enter vocational ministry, but to live righteously in their current occupations.

"He will baptize you with the Holy Spirit and with fire" (v. 16). This is probably a prophecy about the Day of Pentecost, when the Spirit descends like tongues of fire, and men, women, slave and free, young and old from many nations prophesy as a sign of the Spirit.

"His winnowing fork is in his hand to clean out his threshing floor and to gather the wheat into his storehouse...chaff will burn with inextinguishable fire" (v. 17)—A winnowing fork is a pitchfork made of wood and used to throw chaff—husks, shells, sheaths, the unusable parts—and grain into the air to separate them. The grain is heavy, but the chaff flies away in the breeze. Chaff is gathered and burned; wheat gets gathered and stored for future use. When all is burned or stored, the threshing floor is clean. Notice that in both verses 16 and 17, John mentions fire. Either people will experience the good fire when the Spirit descends, or they will be burned like chaff. The solution? Repent. Have a change of heart. And show it by works.

4. What does John believe about Jesus (vv. 16–18)?

____

____

Jesus also was baptized (v. 21). Why did Jesus need to be baptized? Certainly not because Jesus needed to be "saved" or because baptism saves anyone—he didn't, and it doesn't. Some believe Jesus was simply setting an example for his followers. Some see Jesus's baptism as an opportunity to show his affirmation from God, as the Father said, "This is my beloved Son." Some see it as the Trinity marking the official beginning of Jesus's public ministry. Some see it as a covenant act in which Jesus identifies with his spiritual community. Some see it as an act of ritual purity and consecration before the Spirit descends on Him. Some see the reason(s) as part or all of these.

5. Father, Son, and Holy Spirit are all revealed as present at Jesus's baptism. How is each seen in this event?

____

____

6. Luke traces Jesus's legal genealogy through his adoptive father (v. 23) back to Adam (v. 38). What do verses 22 and 38 have in common? What point do you think Luke is making by placing the genealogy here?

"Led by the Spirit in the wilderness, where for forty days he endured temptations from the devil" (4:1–2)—"Wilderness" and "forty" call to mind the nation of Israel, which wandered in the desert for forty years. They did so because of disobedience. But Jesus is led by the Spirit.

7. Each time Jesus is tempted to receive something to which he has every right—as the Son of God—to do, what does he quote and obey (vv. 4, 8, 12)? What does this suggest about how those who follow Jesus are to defeat the accuser's attacks and temptations?

"Now Jesus came to Nazareth, where he had been brought up" (v. 16). Notice that Jesus begins his ministry in his own hometown.

"[He] went into the synagogue on the Sabbath day, as was his custom" (v. 16). Jesus was in the habit of gathering with his spiritual community regularly. Literary evidence says they sang, read set readings, heard a homily, and received a blessing.

"Today this scripture has been fulfilled even as you heard it being read" (v. 21). Jesus finds and reads Isaiah 61:1 and part of v. 2; but he also quotes Isaiah 58:6. By saying the text is about himself, he claims to have the Spirit of the Lord; to be anointed ["Messiah" means "anointed one"] by God; to preach good news to the poor; to proclaim release to captives; to heal the blind; to free the oppressed; to proclaim the good news of God's favor (vv. 18–19). Without stating it outright, He is claiming to be the promised Messiah for whom they have been waiting.

"Good news to the poor" (v. 18) – In Jesus's preaching elsewhere he refers to those who are poor in spirit. But he does not add "in spirit" here. In his ministry he will literally feed hungry people.

"Release to the captives" (v. 18)—In the Old Testament, this phrase referred to people enslaved in exile; in Luke-Acts the author uses the term to refer to forgiveness of sins.

8. How did the people initially respond to Jesus, and how does Luke describe the words coming from Jesus's mouth (v. 22)?

____

____

"Isn't this Joseph's son?" (v. 22)—Apparently the people did not refer to Jesus as "Mary's son" nor think of him as illegitimate. The idea that Mary experienced public shame for her "unplanned pregnancy" does not actually have support from the text. The point of this detail, though, is not Jesus's heredity. The people wonder how their local guy could actually be the Messiah. It's often hard to see exceptional gifts in those we encounter daily. Thus, we have the oft-quoted observation that "a prophet is without honor in his own country."

Jesus backs up his observation about a prophet with two examples in which, when Israel rejected God's prophets, God turned from his people and sent prophets to Gentiles:

"Many widows in Israel...Elijah...a widow at Zarephath in Sidon" (vv. 24–26)—We find the story Jesus is referencing in 1 Kings 17. During a three-year famine, the prophet and, being the youngest boy, Elijah had multiple opportunities to minister to widows in Israel, but he was sent (presumably by God) to only one widow in a territory that Israel considered "wicked."

"Many lepers in Israel...Elisha...none of them cleansed except Naaman the Syrian" (vv. 26–27) – We find the story of Elisha and Naaman in 2 Kings 5. The prophet Elisha has had multiple opportunities to minister to lepers in Israel, but he cleanses only Naaman, a Syrian—an outsider.

10. What do the people think about Jesus's statement, illustrated by two stories from scripture (vv. 28–30)? What actions result? How does their behavior support his observation in v. 24? It had been going so well. Why do you think Jesus would stir things up so much?

____

____

11. Jesus goes to another synagogue on the Sabbath—this time in Capernaum, about thirty miles from Nazareth. What amazes the people about his teaching (vv. 31–32) and his healing (v. 36)?

12. Who do demons say Jesus is (vv. 34, 41)?

"But he rebuked them and would not allow them to speak because they knew that he was the Christ" (v. 41). Although Jesus himself has claimed to be the Anointed One, he also wants to remain somewhat incognito. But why? Many scholars think it's because people expected the Messiah to wrest political power from Rome, and in Jesus's first advent he had a more important mission than becoming Israel's literal king. Huge crowds would have impeded that mission.

13. What power does Jesus demonstrate in healing a demon-possessed man and Simon's mother-in-law?

14. What does Jesus insist is his own message and mission (v. 43)?

15. What is Jesus's initial strategy for accomplishing this mission (v. 44)?

____

____

Saturday: Shepherd Like a Girl

Scripture: Now there were shepherds nearby living out in the field, keeping guard over their flock at night. An angel of the Lord appeared to them, and the glory of the Lord shone around them, and they were absolutely terrified. But the angel said to them, "Do not be afraid! Listen carefully, for I proclaim to you good news that brings great joy to all the people: Today your Savior is born in the city of David. He is Christ the Lord. This will be a sign for you: You will find a baby wrapped in strips of cloth and lying in a manger" (Luke 2:8–13).

My understanding of shepherds shifted radically when I traveled with my husband and daughter to Kenya's Rift Valley. My husband is a U.S.-based missionary serving national leaders there. While we were in Kenya, his ministry partner, Joseph, a Maasai warrior, introduced us to some friends.

The Maasai are pastoral people—shepherds. Like our partner, Joseph, they live in individual huts inside bomas—enclosures made of brambles encircling huts made by women out of mud, sticks, grass, and cow dung. The boma serves as a livestock pen.

The girls usually shepherd goats and sheep, sometimes with their moms or a grandparent, while boys shepherd the larger livestock or attend school. If a family has no girls—or not enough of them—the youngest son or sons also get assigned to sheep/goat duty. The pecking order is usually men, animals, women, children. For these pastoral peoples, livestock are their pantries, 401(k) plans, Meals on Wheels, and bank accounts. Often the shepherd-girls lack education, because someone has to guard the assets, and boys' educations have typically taken priority.

This setup or a similar one has been true for many shepherding tribes and peoples across time and geography. Consider that David, son of Jesse, had multiple brothers—at least three in the army—and, being the youngest boy, was the shepherd among Jesse's eight sons.

The Maasai, like some of the Bedouins my husband and I met on a trip to Jordan, live—or abide—in the field, and that is exactly how Luke describes what the shepherds in Jesus's birth narrative are doing. They are abiding, or living in the field—not just "hanging out" temporarily as part of their work. They are living there and watching their flock (singular). The shepherds to whom the angel choir appears are probably not a bunch of unrelated guys from different families watching multiple flocks on an open hillside. More likely, they're from one extended family unit that consists of male, female, old, and young.

A highlight of my time with the Maasai in 2008 was watching the "Jesus" film with them. We threw a bedsheet over the top of a hut, hooked up a generator and, voila! The best part was hearing their gasps of joy when the angels appeared to shepherds saying, in Naa—their own language— "Fear not! For I bring you good news of great joy for all the people!"

This experience led me to ask some questions of the people who live much closer to the world of the text. And here's what I learned:

Vocational shepherds are not outcasts. They smell a lot like a typical cowboy. Animal pens stink, but humans who keep the animals don't walk around with dung clinging to themselves if they can help it.

Nevertheless, ***shepherds don't inhabit halls of power.*** My shepherd friends were overjoyed that in the film, instead of appearing to leaders in palaces or temples, the angels' announcement came for "*all* the people"—from the highest to the lowest. Shepherds are not necessarily the lowest of the low. But they are not the highest, either.

Girls were likely to have been present when the announcement was made about the good news being for all. Rachel was a shepherd in the ancient Near East (Gen. 29:9). And if the shepherds (plural) in Luke's account were part of a family unit, males and females witnessed the angels' appearance.

As is true today, ***sheep in Jesus's time were probably not wandering around on the hillside at night, but gathered into the sheepfold*** (see John 10). Shepherds guarded one entrance. I corresponded with a Maasai brother about this, and he told me that in his world, after the animals go into their pen for the night, the whole extended family gathers around the fire for stories. It seems reasonable for us, then, to envision an extended family warming themselves around a fire in the dark near a pen when suddenly—floodlights!

Some think the sheep being watched in the Bible story were those specially destined for sacrifice. The source of this information was a rabbinic Jewish scholar who converted to Christianity, but his idea has been further vetted, and it now seems unlikely. Nevertheless, the child who was born, the Good Shepherd, was indeed the lamb who was slain.

What are some spiritual ramifications?

Women shepherd people. As mentioned, "Rachel came with her father's sheep, for she was a shepherd" (Gen. 29:9). The woman in Song of Songs is grazing her goats (Song of Songs 1:8). If we want to read biblical texts about shepherding as the original readers would have understood them, we will envision both males and females. The metaphor of a shepherd is that of one entrusted with the care of the vulnerable. Who needs your shepherding care?

We benefit by reading the Bible in community with Christians whose lives are closer to the world of the text than those who have central heating and bank accounts with passwords. That means taking the posture of a learner in the presence of those who can see what many of us cannot. Whose voice do you need to hear, either through reading or conversation?

Representation matters. When I mentioned on Twitter the possibility that females might have witnessed the pronouncement of "good news for all the people," some responded with tears and joy. For the first time they saw themselves in the story. In a quick search for Christmas Bible art, I found Mary to be the only female in any of the multiple scenes. The biggest demographic leaving the church is young females. Why do you think that might that be? How can we better show that women were key witnesses to the events of Jesus's birth, death, and resurrection?

God loves the lowly, and so must we. Although shepherds are not the lowest of the low (as they are sometimes described), they themselves still acknowledge that they're also not the rich or powerful of this world. The heavenly choice to make the announcement to those outside of the usual power structures reveals something about the heart of God and inclusiveness of the good news. How can we be like him?

What does Luke tell us these manger-visitors did? After seeing the swaddled child, they spread the word, and they glorified God. Like them, let us do the same—Go, tell it on the mountain! Jesus Christ is born!

For memorization: "From generation to generation he is merciful to those who fear him" (Luke 2:50).

Prayer: *Thank you, Lord, for the gift of your Son. Please grant that we might serve him without fear, in holiness and righteousness all our days. Thank you for bringing to us the knowledge of salvation, through the forgiveness of sins because of your tender mercy. Thank you that the rising sun has come from heaven and he has shined light in the darkness to guide our feet in the path of peace. May your will be done on earth as it is in heaven, through Jesus Christ and the power of the Spirit, Amen.*

Week 3 of 7

Jesus: Conqueror of Sin and Death: Luke 5–8

Sunday: "This Is My Beloved Son"

Scripture: And the Holy Spirit descended on him in bodily form like a dove. And a voice came from heaven, "You are my one dear Son; in you I take great delight" (Luke 3:22).

Many Bible Lands trips from North America include an optional excursion from Israel into Petra, an amazing UNESCO site in Jordan famous for its rose-colored, rock-cut architecture. The place has been made all the more famous by Indiana Jones. But strangely, such excursions often leave out one of the holiest sites in the world—Bethany Beyond the Jordan.

Not to be confused with the Bethany near Jerusalem where Lazarus and his sisters, Mary and Martha lived, Bethany Beyond the Jordan is the site of not one, but numerous miracles recorded in the Bible. Sitting across the river and nine miles east of Jericho, this Bethany is where the children of Israel crossed the Jordan on dry ground as they entered the Promised Land (Josh. 1–5); where Elijah the Tishbite went from Jericho, and a whirlwind took him (2 Kings 2); and where John the Baptizer came in the spirit and strength of Elijah and lived among reeds—still present—swaying in the wind, ate honey, and made people wonder if he was Elijah himself (Luke 1:17). Best of all—when Jesus approached John in this location, his relative prophesied about the Lamb of God who takes away the sin of the world (John 1:29). And there John baptized Jesus. The Father spoke of His Son, and the Holy Spirit descended like a dove: Father, Son, Spirit.

It's no wonder that early Christians revered this place. In the fourth century, Queen Helen—mother of Constantine—was baptized at Bethany Beyond the Jordan. Pilgrims wrote of visiting here. In nearby Madaba, visitors can still view a multi-million-stone mosaic map of the Holy Land commissioned in the sixth century that tags this Bethany as a pilgrimage site.

The mosaic marking this place does so with a lion chasing a gazelle. Some believe the animals depict the savage nature of the wilderness. But others think these animals symbolize Herod Antipas attacking John the Baptist. The label "Bet Abara," or "house of crossing" also marks the spot on the map, along with two fish. Although these could represent the last inhabitable water on the way to the Dead Sea, fish were also symbols of ancient Christianity.

When I was on this spot some years earlier on a press junket, I met an Armenian Christian who served as Bethany Beyond the Jordan's commission director. As he walked with our group, he said, "I am a tool who would like to experience the site with you." He insisted that he learned something new there every day.

He told us how USAID gave $6 million to build the infrastructure, and Jordan signed a peace treaty in 1994, which allowed access. It then took four years to de-mine the river's east banks. In the process of digging, archaeologists made many discoveries—of monasteries, baptism pools, and churches. Open only since 1998, the site was "still a baby," he said. He noted that the Jordan River was not even a "river" as we perceive such waterways. It did look more like a brown creek. "Yet it is the holiest of all [rivers] in the world," our guide reminded us.

A number of sources outside of the Bible affirm the location's identification. Why else would people have built eight ancient churches in this wilderness? "I truly believe these Christians would never have built here unless it were the spot [where John baptized Jesus]," the commissioner said. "And how else to account for the fact that so many early Christian pilgrims describe this as a destination they visited on their way to Mt. Nebo?"—today a fifteen-minute drive away.

To reach the river required us to walk on a path through high reeds and tamarisk trees. Once we stood at the waters' edge, our guide spoke with passion: "I love it!" he said. "It is a blessing from God to be working in a place as holy as this. Part of my job is to look at sources. So I started reading the Bible more and more." He told of how doing so changed him, and now he now reads the Scriptures every day. "I love doing what I'm doing… I want to appeal to the heart, and not here." He pointed to his head.

As we turned to depart, he took off his archaeologist's hat and donned his pastoral one. With a raised brow and a twinkle in his eye, he asked, "Why was Jesus baptized at the lowest point on earth?"

For memorization: John answered them all, "I baptize you with water, but one more powerful than I am is coming—I am not worthy to untie the strap of his sandals. He will baptize you with the Holy Spirit and fire. (Luke 2:16)

Prayer: *Almighty and everlasting God, who, when Christ had been baptized in the River Jordan and as the Holy Spirit descended upon him, declared him solemnly to be your beloved Son, grant that we, your children by adoption, reborn of water and the Holy Spirit, may be well pleasing to you. Thank you for the gift of your Son—that he stooped to the lowest point on earth in order to raise us up with him to the highest heaven in newness of life. Through our Lord Jesus Christ, your Son, who lives and reigns with you in the unity of the Holy Spirit for ever and ever. Amen.*

Monday: Jesus, The Fish Whisperer

1. Pray for insight and read Luke 5. Circle all references to "Simon" and "Peter." Notice whom Jesus calls and what he has power over.

> 5:1 Now Jesus was standing by the Lake of Gennesaret, and the crowd was pressing around him to hear the word of God. 2 He saw two boats by the lake, but the fishermen had gotten out of them and were washing their nets. 3 He got into one of the boats, which was Simon's, and asked him to put out a little way from the shore. Then Jesus sat down and taught the crowds from the boat. 4 When he had finished speaking, he said to Simon, "Put out into the deep water and lower your nets for a catch." 5 Simon answered, "Master,

we worked hard all night and caught nothing! But at your word I will lower the nets." 6 When they had done this, they caught so many fish that their nets started to tear. 7 So they motioned to their partners in the other boat to come and help them. And they came and filled both boats, so that they were about to sink. 8 But when Simon Peter saw it, he fell down at Jesus' knees, saying, "Go away from me, Lord, for I am a sinful man!" 9 For Peter and all who were with him were astonished at the catch of fish that they had taken, 10 and so were James and John, Zebedee's sons, who were Simon's business partners. Then Jesus said to Simon, "Do not be afraid; from now on you will be catching people!" 11 So when they had brought their boats to shore, they left everything and followed him.

12 While Jesus was in one of the towns, a man came to him who was covered with leprosy. When he saw Jesus, he bowed down with his face to the ground and begged him, "Lord, if you are willing, you can make me clean." 13 So he stretched out his hand and touched him, saying, "I am willing. Be clean!" And immediately the leprosy left him. 14 Then he ordered the man to tell no one, but commanded him, "Go and show yourself to a priest, and bring the offering for your cleansing, as Moses commanded, as a testimony to them." 15 But the news about him spread even more, and large crowds were gathering together to hear him and to be healed of their illnesses. 16 Yet Jesus himself frequently withdrew to the wilderness and prayed.

17 Now on one of those days, while he was teaching, there were Pharisees and teachers of the law sitting nearby (who had come from every village of Galilee and Judea and from Jerusalem), and the power of the Lord was with him to heal. 18 Just then some men showed up, carrying a paralyzed man on a stretcher. They were trying to bring him in and place him before Jesus. 19 But since they found no way to carry him in because of the crowd, they went up on the roof and let him down on the stretcher through the roof tiles right in front of Jesus. 20 When Jesus saw their faith, he said, "Friend, your sins are forgiven." 21 Then the experts in the law and the Pharisees began to think to themselves, "Who is this man who is uttering blasphemies? Who can forgive sins but God alone?" 22 When Jesus perceived their hostile thoughts, he said to them, "Why are you raising objections within yourselves? 23 Which is easier, to say, 'Your sins are forgiven,' or to say, 'Stand up and walk'? 24 But so that you may know that the Son of Man has authority on earth to forgive sins"—he said to the paralyzed man—"I tell you, stand up, take your stretcher and go home." 25 Immediately he stood up before them, picked up the stretcher he had been lying on,

and went home, glorifying God. 26 Then astonishment seized them all, and they glorified God. They were filled with awe, saying, "We have seen incredible things today."

27 After this, Jesus went out and saw a tax collector named Levi sitting at the tax booth. "Follow me," he said to him. 28 And he got up and followed him, leaving everything behind.

29 Then Levi gave a great banquet in his house for Jesus, and there was a large crowd of tax collectors and others sitting at the table with them. 30 But the Pharisees and their experts in the law complained to his disciples, saying, "Why do you eat and drink with tax collectors and sinners?" 31 Jesus answered them, "Those who are well don't need a physician, but those who are sick do. 32 I have not come to call the righteous, but sinners to repentance."

33 Then they said to him, "John's disciples frequently fast and pray, and so do the disciples of the Pharisees, but yours continue to eat and drink." 34 So Jesus said to them, "You cannot make the wedding guests fast while the bridegroom is with them, can you? 35 But those days are coming, and when the bridegroom is taken from them, at that time they will fast." 36 He also told them a parable: "No one tears a patch from a new garment and sews it on an old garment. If he does, he will have torn the new, and the piece from the new will not match the old. 37 And no one pours new wine into old wineskins. If he does, the new wine will burst the skins and will be spilled, and the skins will be destroyed. 38 Instead new wine must be poured into new wineskins. 39 No one after drinking old wine wants the new, for he says, 'The old is good enough.'"

2. Whom does Jesus call? What does he have power over?

____

____

"By the Lake of Gennesaret" (5:1) – i.e., the Sea of Galilee. This lake is also called Lake Tiberias.

"Pressing around him to hear the word of God" (v. 1) – Notice what Jesus is preaching.

3. In the miracle of the fish (vv. 2–11), what does Jesus demonstrate about who he is and what he has the authority to do?

____

____

"Master..." (v. 5) – Initially, Simon uses a different term from the usual word for "master" or "lord." An *epistates* in ancient Greece was a superintendent or overseer serving as a ruler's representative. He typically exercised control and collected taxes.

Simon Peter, a pro fisherman, is willing to do what he's told, but he warns respectfully that doing so will be useless. Why does he think lowering the net will be a waste of time and effort (v. 5)?

Luke uses the names "Simon" and "Peter" interchangeably in this chapter. He refers to Simon as "Simon Peter" for the first time here (5:8). Notice Simon Peter's response to Jesus's miracle (vv. 8–9). What title does Peter use of Jesus now (v. 8)?

"He fell down at Jesus' knees, saying, 'Go away from me, Lord, for I am a sinful man!'" (v. 9)—Instead of gawking and rejoicing at Jesus's miracle-working ability, like one might expect a person to do after seeing something amazing, Simon Peter recoils, falls at Jesus's knees, begs him to get away, calls him "Lord," and confesses his own sinfulness. Peter does not yet know Jesus's full identity—that revelation will come only after the resurrection. But at this point, Peter grasps that Jesus has come from God, and he is aware of his own sinfulness in response to this understanding.

4. Simon Peter has an appropriate response to the revelation he has received. Write a prayer of your own response to the power of Christ.

---

5. What does Jesus tell Simon Peter about his emotions (v. 10)? How does this compare with the response of the angels to the shepherds (2:8–10)?

---

6. Who are Simon Peter's business partners and what is their occupation? What is their response to Jesus's miracle of the fish (vv. 9–10)?

____

____

"From now on you will be catching people!" (v. 10). Many who have grown up in church have learned a children's song with these lyrics: "I will make you fishers of men, fishers of men, fishers of men…" Some have taken from this the idea that Jesus is saying his disciples will do ministry focused only on males. Jesus, however, doesn't use the word for males here; he uses the word for people. The task of Christ's followers is to announce the kingdom of God to and for all.

7. How do Simon and his coworkers respond to the call (v. 11)? Compare their response with what happens in v. 27. How long do they stop to think about it? What do they take with them?

____

____

____

8. Not everyone must enter vocational ministry. But every disciple is called to radical obedience. What have you left to follow Jesus? How can you live righteously in your current vocation?

____

____

____

9. Read Luke 5:12–16. How does the grateful man with leprosy respond to Jesus, both in the title he uses and in his physical positioning, even before receiving healing (v. 12)?

____

____

"Covered with leprosy" (v. 12) – The word here (lepra) translated as "leprosy" is actually a broad term that covers many skin conditions besides what is known to us today as Hansen's disease.

"Then he ordered the man to tell no one, but commanded him, 'Go and show yourself to a priest, and bring the offering for your cleansing, as Moses commanded, as a testimony to them'" (v. 14) – Jesus is no hot-shot rabbi seeking to build his platform; he is totally on mission to preach the good news in numerous towns. If the sign-seeking, miracle-gawking crowds get out of hand, they will make his mission more difficult Also, many want Jesus to be a government deliverer, but he has come to preach a different kind of good news of the kingdom. He instructs this man to do what Jewish law says should happen in the face of such a healing (see Leviticus 14:2–32), that the priests might see the glory of God. Jesus wants the religious leaders to see evidence of his life and works.

Jesus himself frequently withdrew to the wilderness and prayed (v. 16) – Jesus is getting busier, but habitual time with his Father remains a priority.

10. Read Luke 5:17–26, imagining yourself as one of the characters in the story. Which character did you choose and what were your thoughts?

____

____

____

"Your sins are forgiven" (v. 20)—Who has power on earth to forgive sin? Jesus is doing more than physical healing here. We see this reinforced in the response of the religious leaders.

"Then the experts in the law and the Pharisees" (v. 21)—The experts in Jewish law are "scribes"; and the Pharisees take seriously the Scriptures and traditions surrounding them. These would normally be good qualities. Yet sometimes knowledge hinders these religious leaders as they focus so much on externals that they miss the point. In this case, they totally miss Jesus's identity.

11. When speaking with the offended scribes and Pharisees, what title does Jesus use for himself and what does he claim he has authority to do (v. 24)?

12. Read vv. 27–32. Compare the scribes' and Pharisees' response to Jesus's healing of the paralytic with their response to Jesus's eating and drinking with tax collectors and sinners.

"Levi" (v. 27) – In the same way that Simon has a second name—Peter, here we see Levi has a second name—Matthew (compare with Matthew 5:46–47; 9:9).

13. What does Jesus say is the reason for his coming (vv. 31–32)? Do you place yourself in the category of those for whom he came? Why or why not?

"John's disciples frequently fast and pray . . . but yours continue to eat and drink with tax collectors and sinners" (v. 33). The hint here is that some think John's way is superior. Luke emphasizes sinners' attraction to Jesus, later adding to this story three other challenges to Jesus that arise when he dines with sinners (7:36–50; 15:1–32; 19:1–10). Luke even adds a parable in which Jesus compares a tax collector with a Pharisee and deems the former more "righteous" (18:11–14). Jesus hates all sin, not only cheating and sexual immorality. He hates self-righteousness and hypocrisy, too. But he loves repentance and humility.

14. Who does Jesus imply he is by his answer to the Pharisees (vv. 34–37)? And what does he assume his disciples will do after he is gone (v. 35)?

"Patch...new wineskins" (vv. 36–39)—Jesus illustrates his point with two analogies—that of fabric and of wine. New fabric shrinks when washed, so a new patch pulling on old fabric at best will make the old one pucker, and at worst will tear the garment altogether. Additionally, new wine ferments and thus stretches its wineskins. Since old wineskins are already stretched, new wine in old skins will destroy its container. One can't mix the old with the new. The Pharisees are rejecting the new, with its arrival of the kingdom and its covenant. They like the old ways. The traditions. The way things have been. The law isn't bad, it's just that the groom is here! And the new is better.

Tuesday: The Upside-Down Kingdom

1. Pray for the Spirit to grant insight and read Luke 6. As you read, notice the marks of a disciple.

> 6:1 Jesus was going through the grain fields on a Sabbath, and his disciples picked some heads of wheat, rubbed them in their hands, and ate them. 2 But some of the Pharisees said, "Why are you doing what is against the law on the Sabbath?" 3 Jesus answered them, "Haven't you read what David did when he and his companions were hungry– 4 how he entered the house of God, took and ate the sacred bread, which is not lawful for any to eat but the priests alone, and gave it to his companions?" 5 Then he said to them, "The Son of Man is lord of the Sabbath."
>
> 6 On another Sabbath, Jesus entered the synagogue and was teaching. Now a man was there whose right hand was withered. 7 The experts in the law and the Pharisees watched Jesus closely to see if he would heal on the Sabbath, so that they could find a reason to accuse him. 8 But he knew their thoughts, and said to the man who had the withered hand, "Get up and stand here." So he rose and stood there. 9 Then Jesus said to them, "I ask you, is it lawful to do good on the Sabbath or to do evil, to save a life or to destroy it?" 10 After looking around at them all, he said to the man, "Stretch out your hand." The man did so, and his hand was restored. 11 But they were filled with mindless rage and began debating with one another what they would do to Jesus.
>
> 12 Now it was during this time that Jesus went out to the mountain to pray, and he spent all night in prayer to God. 13 When morning came, he called his disciples and chose twelve of them,

whom he also named apostles: 14 Simon (whom he named Peter), and his brother Andrew; and James, John, Philip, Bartholomew, 15 Matthew, Thomas, James the son of Alphaeus, Simon who was called the Zealot, 16 Judas the son of James, and Judas Iscariot, who became a traitor.

17 Then he came down with them and stood on a level place. And a large number of his disciples had gathered along with a vast multitude from all over Judea, from Jerusalem, and from the sea-coast of Tyre and Sidon. They came to hear him and to be healed of their diseases, 18 and those who suffered from unclean spirits were cured. 19 The whole crowd was trying to touch him because power was coming out from him and healing them all.

20 Then he looked up at his disciples and said:

"Blessed are you who are poor, for the kingdom of God belongs to you.

21 Blessed are you who hunger now, for you will be satisfied.

Blessed are you who weep now, for you will laugh.

22 Blessed are you when people hate you, and when they exclude you and insult you and reject you as evil on account of the Son of Man! 23 Rejoice in that day, and jump for joy because your reward is great in heaven. For their ancestors did the same things to the prophets.

24 But woe to you who are rich, for you have received your comfort already.

25 Woe to you who are well satisfied with food now, for you will be hungry.

Woe to you who laugh now, for you will mourn and weep.

26 Woe to you when all people speak well of you, for their ancestors did the same things to the false prophets.

27 "But I say to you who are listening: Love your enemies, do good to those who hate you, 28 bless those who curse you, pray for those who mistreat you. 29 To the person who strikes you on the cheek, offer the other as well, and from the person who takes away your coat, do not withhold your tunic either. 30 Give to everyone who asks you, and do not ask for your possessions back from the person who takes them away. 31 Treat others in the same way that you would want them to treat you.

32 "If you love those who love you, what credit is that to you? For even sinners love those who love them. 33 And if you do good to those who do good to you, what credit is that to you? Even sinners do the same. 34 And if you lend to those from whom you hope to be repaid, what credit is that to you? Even sinners lend to sinners, so that they may be repaid in full. 35 But love your enemies, and

do good, and lend, expecting nothing back. Then your reward will be great, and you will be sons of the Most High, because he is kind to ungrateful and evil people. 36 Be merciful, just as your Father is merciful.

37 "Do not judge, and you will not be judged; do not condemn, and you will not be condemned; forgive, and you will be forgiven. 38 Give, and it will be given to you: A good measure, pressed down, shaken together, running over, will be poured into your lap. For the measure you use will be the measure you receive."

39 He also told them a parable: "Someone who is blind cannot lead another who is blind, can he? Won't they both fall into a pit? 40 A disciple is not greater than his teacher, but everyone when fully trained will be like his teacher. 41 Why do you see the speck in your brother's eye, but fail to see the beam of wood in your own? 42 How can you say to your brother, 'Brother, let me remove the speck from your eye,' while you yourself don't see the beam in your own? You hypocrite! First remove the beam from your own eye, and then you can see clearly to remove the speck from your brother's eye.

43 "For no good tree bears bad fruit, nor again does a bad tree bear good fruit, 44 for each tree is known by its own fruit. For figs are not gathered from thorns, nor are grapes picked from brambles. 45 The good person out of the good treasury of his heart produces good, and the evil person out of his evil treasury produces evil, for his mouth speaks from what fills his heart.

46 "Why do you call me 'Lord, Lord,' and don't do what I tell you?

47 "Everyone who comes to me and listens to my words and puts them into practice—I will show you what he is like: 48 He is like a man building a house, who dug down deep and laid the foundation on bedrock. When a flood came, the river burst against that house but could not shake it because it had been well built. 49 But the person who hears and does not put my words into practice is like a man who built a house on the ground without a foundation. When the river burst against that house, it collapsed immediately and was utterly destroyed!"

The Sabbath was a day set apart. Like a vacation day. Its purpose was not to take away fun or make life more difficult for the sick or hungry or injured. God mandated a break for his people after they had lived in slavery for hundreds of years without a day off. The God of vacations wanted his people to take a break from their labor. But traditions turned the Sabbath into a day when even showing mercy got called into question. In several ways, Jesus reveals that he has authority on earth to bring Sabbath. How does he do that (6:1–5)?

"Picked some heads of wheat, rubbed them in their hands, and ate them" (6:1). Jewish law disallows Sabbath use of an instrument to harvest, such as a sickle (see Deut. 23:24–25). The disciples are simply rubbing the wheat to remove the chaff so they can eat it. But the Pharisees object. Jesus answers their objection with a story from the Scriptures:

"David... entered the house of God, took and ate the sacred bread, which is not lawful for any to eat but the priests alone, and gave it to his companions" (vv. 3–5). Jesus knew his Bible. The instructions for the holy bread appear in Leviticus 24:5–9:

> "You shall take fine flour and bake twelve loaves from it; two tenths of an ephah shall be in each loaf. And you shall set them in two piles, six in a pile, on the table of pure gold before the Lord. And you shall put pure frankincense on each pile, that it may go with the bread as a memorial portion as a food offering to the Lord. Every Sabbath day Aaron shall arrange it before the Lord regularly; it is from the people of Israel as a covenant forever. And it shall be for Aaron and his sons, and they shall eat it in a holy place, since it is for him a most holy portion out of the Lord's food offerings, a perpetual due."

The bread is replaced weekly on the Sabbath, and it is to be eaten by the priests.

Knowing this, we are better prepared to understand the story about what David and his men did with this bread (1 Samuel 21:1–6). At this point in David's story, he has just confirmed that King Saul wants him dead, so he and his men have fled. Meanwhile, it's the Sabbath, and the new bread has just replaced the week-old loaves, which are available for the priests to eat. Here's what happened:

David went to Ahimelech the priest in Nob. Ahimelech was shaking with fear when he met David, and said to him, "Why are you by yourself with no one accom*panying you?"

David replied to Ahimelech the priest, "The king instructed me to do something, but he said to me, 'Don't let anyone know the reason I am sending you or the instructions I have given you.' I have told my soldiers to wait at a certain place. Now what do you have at your disposal? Give me five loaves of bread, or whatever can be found."

The priest replied to David, "I don't have any ordinary bread at my disposal. Only holy bread is available, and then only if your soldiers have abstained from relations with women."

David said to the priest, "Certainly women have been kept away from us, just as on previous occasions when I have set out. The soldiers' equipment is holy, even on an ordinary journey. How much more so will they be holy today, along with their equipment!"

So the priest gave him holy bread, for there was no bread there other than the Bread of the Presence. It had been removed from before the Lord in order to replace it with hot bread on the day it had been taken away.

David acted with the priest's permission to show mercy to his hungry men, meeting a human need.

Jesus's logic is this: If not-yet-king David gave his men bread on the Sabbath in cooperation with the priest as an act of mercy, how much more could The Son of Man, who is lord of the Sabbath, allow his disciples to eat the wheat growing in the field?

2. What do you think is Jesus's main point?

____

____

3. What is the general attitude of the scribes and Pharisees (vv. 7, 11)?

____

____

4. What does Jesus's knowledge of their thoughts reveal about him (v. 8)?

____

____

"Jesus said to them, 'I ask you, is it lawful to do good on the Sabbath or to do evil, to save a life or to destroy it?'" (vv. 9–10). The point of the Sabbath as God designed it for the Jewish people was rest and joy and restoration. The religious leaders turned it into a burden. Jesus does nothing here that can be construed as work, anyway. He simply speaks healing and it happens, and they get upset that this wonderful miracle has restored a suffering man.

5. What does Jesus do all night before calling his apostles (vv. 12–15)? What does this suggest about what his followers should do to imitate him?

____

____

6. Why does it say the people came from all over (vv. 17, 19)?

____

____

7. Whom does Jesus single out for healing (v. 18)?

____

8. Jesus's kingdom is backward from what everyone expects. We tend to think rich is good, as is being full of good food, laughing, and being loved. How does Jesus's upside-down kingdom work (vv. 20–26)?

____

____

9. We tend to hate our enemies, do good to people we like, and strike back when injured. How does Jesus's kingdom differ (vv. 27–31)?

____

____

____

10. What is Jesus's rationale for going beyond usual expectations (vv. 32–34)?

11. What two reasons does he give for being so different (v. 35)? How do you measure up here?

12. What is God like (vv. 35–36)?

13. What is the standard by which we'll be judged (vv. 37–38)?

14. Summarize Jesus's thoughts on hypocrisy (vv. 39–42).

15. Read vv. 43–45. Circle uses of "good" and "evil." What evidence reveals that a person is right on the inside?

Jesus asks, **"Why do you call me 'Lord, Lord,' and don't do what I tell you?"** (v. 46). He puts a high premium both on listening to and doing his words (vv. 47–49). You have just read a lot of his words. What do you need to put into practice? Pray for a heart to hear and obey with the Spirit's help.

Wednesday: Jesus, Lord of Life

1. Ask the Holy Spirit to illuminate your reading of Scripture and read Luke 7. Pay close attention to Jesus's ministry, and how it lifts up the powerless and "outsiders." Circle the word "worthy."

> 7:1 After Jesus had finished teaching all this to the people, he entered Capernaum. 2 A centurion there had a slave who was highly regarded, but who was sick and at the point of death. 3 When the centurion heard about Jesus, he sent some Jewish elders to him, asking him to come and heal his slave.
>
> 4 When they came to Jesus, they urged him earnestly, "He is worthy to have you do this for him 5 because he loves our nation and even built our synagogue."
>
> 6 So Jesus went with them. When he was not far from the house, the centurion sent friends to say to him, "Lord, do not trouble yourself, for I am not worthy to have you come under my roof! 7 That is why I did not presume to come to you. Instead, say the word, and my servant must be healed. 8 For I too am a man set under authority, with soldiers under me. I say to this one, 'Go!' and he goes, and to another, 'Come!' and he comes, and to my slave, 'Do this!' and he does it."
>
> 9 When Jesus heard this, he was amazed at him. He turned and said to the crowd that followed him, "I tell you, not even in Israel have I found such faith!" 10 So when those who had been sent returned to the house, they found the slave well.
>
> 11 Soon afterward Jesus went to a town called Nain, and his disciples and a large crowd went with him. 12 As he approached the town gate, a man who had died was being carried out, the only son of his mother (who was a widow), and a large crowd from the town was with her. 13 When the Lord saw her, he had compassion for her and said to her, "Do not weep." 14 Then he came up and touched the bier, and those who carried it stood still. He said, "Young man, I say to you, get up!"
>
> 15 So the dead man sat up and began to speak, and Jesus gave him back to his mother.

16 Fear seized them all, and they began to glorify God, saying, "A great prophet has appeared among us!" and "God has come to help his people!" 17 This report about Jesus circulated throughout Judea and all the surrounding country.

18 John's disciples informed him about all these things. So John called two of his disciples 19 and sent them to Jesus to ask, "Are you the one who is to come, or should we look for another?" 20 When the men came to Jesus, they said, "John the Baptist has sent us to you to ask, 'Are you the one who is to come, or should we look for another?'" 21 At that very time Jesus cured many people of diseases, sicknesses, and evil spirits, and granted sight to many who were blind. 22 So he answered them, "Go tell John what you have seen and heard: The blind see, the lame walk, lepers are cleansed, the deaf hear, the dead are raised, the poor have good news proclaimed to them. 23 Blessed is anyone who takes no offense at me."

24 When John's messengers had gone, Jesus began to speak to the crowds about John: "What did you go out into the wilderness to see? A reed shaken by the wind? 25 What did you go out to see? A man dressed in soft clothing? Look, those who wear soft clothing and live in luxury are in the royal palaces! 26 What did you go out to see? A prophet? Yes, I tell you, and more than a prophet. 27 This is the one about whom it is written, 'Look, I am sending my messenger ahead of you, who will prepare your way before you.' 28 I tell you, among those born of women no one is greater than John. Yet the one who is least in the kingdom of God is greater than he is." 29 (Now all the people who heard this, even the tax collectors, acknowledged God's justice because they had been baptized with John's baptism. 30 However, the Pharisees and the experts in religious law rejected God's purpose for themselves because they had not been baptized by John.)

31 "To what then should I compare the people of this generation, and what are they like? 32 They are like children sitting in the marketplace and calling out to one another,

"'We played the flute for you, yet you did not dance;
we wailed in mourning, yet you did not weep.'

33 For John the Baptist has come eating no bread and drinking no wine, and you say, 'He has a demon!' 34 The Son of Man has come eating and drinking, and you say, 'Look at him, a glutton and a drunk, a friend of tax collectors and sinners!' 35 But wisdom is vindicated by all her children."

36 Now one of the Pharisees asked Jesus to have dinner with him, so he went into the Pharisee's house and took his place at the table. 37 Then when a woman of that town, who was a sinner, learned that Jesus was dining at the Pharisee's house, she brought

an alabaster jar of perfumed oil. 38 As she stood behind him at his feet, weeping, she began to wet his feet with her tears. She wiped them with her hair, kissed them, and anointed them with the perfumed oil. 39 Now when the Pharisee who had invited him saw this, he said to himself, "If this man were a prophet, he would know who and what kind of woman this is who is touching him, that she is a sinner."

40 So Jesus answered him, "Simon, I have something to say to you."

He replied, "Say it, Teacher."

41 "A certain creditor had two debtors; one owed him 500 silver coins, and the other 50. 42 When they could not pay, he canceled the debts of both. Now which of them will love him more?"

43 Simon answered, "I suppose the one who had the bigger debt canceled."

Jesus said to him, "You have judged rightly." 44 Then, turning toward the woman, he said to Simon, "Do you see this woman? I entered your house. You gave me no water for my feet, but she has wet my feet with her tears and wiped them with her hair. 45 You gave me no kiss of greeting, but from the time I entered she has not stopped kissing my feet. 46 You did not anoint my head with oil, but she has anointed my feet with perfumed oil. 47 Therefore I tell you, her sins, which were many, are forgiven, thus she loved much; but the one who is forgiven little loves little."

48 Then Jesus said to her, "Your sins are forgiven." 49 But those who were at the table with him began to say among themselves, "Who is this, who even forgives sins?" 50 He said to the woman, "Your faith has saved you; go in peace."

"A centurion had a slave" (v. 1). Once again, Luke chooses to highlight the faith of the least likely person. Centurions are Gentiles, Roman officers in charge of one hundred soldiers. They're occupiers. And this centurion is a slaveowner. In the mind of Luke's readers, this guy would be the least likely person to exhibit faith.

2. The Jewish officials who know the centurion describe him as "worthy." How does this man differ from most in his position (v. 5)? How does he describe himself (v. 6)? What title does he use to describe Jesus (v. 6)?

"Say the word, and my servant must be healed" (v. 7). The centurion has helped to build the very synagogue where Jesus healed a demon-possessed man (Luke 4:33, 7:5). This military officer, one in a chain of command, believes Jesus has the authority to speak healing without even having to be present or to touch the ill person.

3. What is Jesus's response to this Gentile's declaration, and to what does he compare it (v. 9)?

___

___

"A man ... the only son of his mother (who was a widow)" (v. 12). In a world in which women depend on men for their livelihood, this woman is doubly helpless. She has already lost her husband. And now she has lost her only son. In addition to the loss of a beloved child, she is placed in a desperate economic situation. Note once again how Luke, in crafting his Gospel, focuses on the outsider, the powerless, the one with nothing to offer in his readers' minds.

"The bier" (v. 14). Corpses were transported on movable frames to the grave, typically outside of a town or city. Once at the tomb, Jewish practice was for mourners to place the corpse on a ledge inside the tomb to complete the decaying process (think of the ledge where Jesus lay). Myrrh and spices only slightly slowed the process of decomposition. After about a year, when remains were reduced to bones, the person was literally "gathered to his people" (Gen. 25:39). That is, the bones were collected and placed in an ossuary, a box where one's ancestors' bones were already stored. The ossuary was slightly longer than the male femur, the body's longest bone.

"So the dead man sat up and began to speak" (v. 15). This man's speaking is evidence that he has been restored from death to life. Luke will record Jesus raising the dead twice—this widow's son and the daughter of Jairus (8:55). John adds another: Lazarus, brother of Mary and Martha (John 11:43).

4. What does it say about Jesus that he raises the dead?

___

___

"And Jesus gave him back to his mother" (v. 15). The words in the text here are the exact ones found in the Septuagint (70 BC Hebrew-to-Greek translation) version of the story about Elijah raising the widow's son (1 Kings 17:23)—a story Jesus cited earlier when he asserted that a prophet is without honor in his own country and that outsiders often have more faith than "insiders" (Luke 4:26). Elijah's raising a widow's son and Jesus's raising this widow's son have many parallels.

"The blind see, the lame walk, lepers are cleansed, the deaf hear, the dead are raised, the poor have good news proclaimed to them" (v. 22). John sends some of his disciples to make sure Jesus is the Promised One. Jesus replies not with a "yes" or "no," but a list of what the Scriptures said will serve as evidence. Thus far in the Gospel of Luke, we have seen each of these happening, except for the deaf hearing. The miracles harken back to the prophecies describing Messiah's arrival that Jesus read in the synagogue from the scroll and said he was fulfilling (see Luke 3:18–21). Recall, also, that John is sitting in a dark prison cell (4:18), probably wondering why this promised king is not delivering him. In Jesus's reply, he leaves out the line in Isaiah's prophecy about captives being released. Luke will later record how Jesus "releases" a "captive." Jesus seems focused on releasing people from a different sort of prison than one with literal bars. John is doubtless confused about what to expect from this king and his kingdom.

"Blessed is the one who is not offended by me" (v. 23). The word here translated as "offended" has its root in the same word from which we get the word "scandalized." It means to be tripped up, entrapped, or enticed to sin. Jesus acknowledges that he is saying a hard thing, both for John and the crowd.

5. John was later beheaded for standing up to an immoral ruler. He never did get released from prison. Have you ever felt like God did not keep his word in a way you expected? If so, how? Jesus heals many people, but most don't receive healing. Jesus feeds many of the hungry, but people still go hungry. Why do you think he heals some but not all?

____

____

"Jesus began to speak to the crowds about John" (v. 24). Jesus does not rebuke John or his people for asking hard questions. And lest the crowd think less of John for his doubts, Jesus affirms him publicly. The Lord asks the crowd why they went to the wilderness to follow John. He reminds them it wasn't to see reeds in the wind (reeds still exist in great quantities at Bethany Beyond the Jordan today). And it sure wasn't because John wore fancy clothes. No, the people went to John because he was a prophet.

"Yes, I tell you, and more than a prophet...my messenger... who will prepare" (v. 26). Jesus affirms that John fulfills Malachi's prophecy about the forerunner (Mal. 2:17—3:1). So not only was John a prophet—he was the promised prophet who came with a special task. Of all humans, Jesus says, John is the greatest. Such affirmation!

"Yet the one who is least in the kingdom of God is greater than he is" (v. 28). John was part of the Old Covenant system. The Holy Spirit had not yet descended. Jesus is announcing new wine, good news: In the kingdom of God, Jesus's followers can be greater than John!

6. How did the sinners respond to Jesus's words vs. the religious people (vv. 29–30)? With which group do you most identify—the outwardly righteous or those who acknowledge their need?

---

7. Recall that some said John's people fasted and prayed while Jesus's followers ate and drank (Luke 5:33). A similar contrast reappears in vv. 31–34. Jesus associates John's people with wailing and mourning and his own followers as inviting dancing. But no matter which approach they take, the people criticize. What is the crowd's conclusion about the two approaches (vv. 33–34)?

"But wisdom is vindicated by all her children" (v. 35). In Proverbs 1 and 31, chapters that serve as bookends in a collection of proverbs in Old Testament wisdom literature, wisdom is personified as a woman. The Hebrew word for "wisdom" linguistically has a feminine form. "Wisdom" in the Greek is *sophia*, a word that also has a feminine gender form. In Proverbs 31, we read a catalogue of what wisdom looks like embodied as a woman in an upper-class agrarian culture. She is filled with faithful teachings, caring for the needy, buying and selling real estate, making clothing for her family, working hard, directing servants. At the end of all her amazing works, the writer concludes, "her children rise up and call her blessed" (v. 28). Her works speak for her, and her children and husband justify her with their testimony. Why mention Lady Wisdom here? John's and Jesus's works reveal that they are neither demons nor gluttons. Their works reveal their wisdom, and their followers can testify to their goodness, just like Lady Wisdom's children testified to her goodness.

8. Re-read vv. 36–50. Notice the contrasts between the person who is educated in the truth (Pharisee) and the outsider (the woman). Circle all forms of the word "sinner."

____

____

"An alabaster jar of perfumed oil" (v. 37). Alabaster is a light, soft stone often used at this time to hold ointment and perfume.

"Stood behind him at his feet...wet his feet" (v. 38). Often people picture New Testament dinner scenes with everyone sitting around a table, as in Da Vinci's "The Last Supper." But we should actually imagine everyone leaning on one elbow stretched out around a low surface with their feet behind them. We know from later in the story that Jesus's dirty feet, which this woman anoints and kisses, have not been cleaned by his host (v. 43).

"[Simon] said to himself, 'If this man were a prophet, he would know...'" (v. 39). Simon the Pharisee doubts Jesus's ability to "know things." One thing Simon knows is that this woman is a sinner.

9. How does Jesus show that he does indeed know thoughts (vv. 40–48)?

____

____

Note: Jesus had mercy on the widow who lost her only son. He has personified wisdom as a female, and now he has vindicated a woman considered "a sinner."

10. Fill in the contrasts that Jesus enumerates:

Simon did not (v. 44):
The woman did (v. 44):

Simon did not (v. 45):
The woman did (v. 45):

Simon did not (v. 46):
The woman did (v. 46):

11. What is the point of Jesus's story in this context (vv. 41–43)? The greater awareness of our sin and God's grace, the greater our love for him. What debt has Jesus cancelled for you?

____

____

12. What powers do we see Jesus exercising in this story—powers that only God has (v. 40–49)?

____

____

13. What saved this woman (v. 50)?

____

____

Thursday: Oceans 12

1. Pray for the Spirit to grant insight into the Scriptures and read Luke 8:1–25.

8:1 Sometime afterward he went on through towns and villages, preaching and proclaiming the good news of the kingdom of God. The twelve were with him, 2 and also some women who had been healed of evil spirits and disabilities: Mary (called Magdalene), from whom seven demons had gone out, 3 and Joanna the wife of Cuza (Herod's household manager), Susanna, and many others who provided for them out of their own resources.

4 While a large crowd was gathering and people were coming to Jesus from one town after another, he spoke to them in a parable: 5 "A sower went out to sow his seed. And as he sowed, some fell along the path and was trampled on, and the wild birds devoured it. 6 Other seed fell on rock, and when it came up, it withered because it had no moisture. 7 Other seed fell among the thorns, and they grew up with it and choked it. 8 But other seed fell on good soil and grew, and it produced a hundred times as much grain." As he said this, he called out, "The one who has ears to hear had better listen!"

9 Then his disciples asked him what this parable meant. 10 He said, "You have been given the opportunity to know the secrets of the kingdom of God, but for others they are in parables, so that although they see they may not see, and although they hear they may not understand.

11 "Now the parable means this: The seed is the word of God. 12 Those along the path are the ones who have heard; then the devil comes and takes away the word from their hearts, so that they may not believe and be saved. 13 Those on the rock are the ones who receive the word with joy when they hear it, but they have no root. They believe for a while, but in a time of testing fall away. 14 As for the seed that fell among thorns, these are the ones who hear, but as they go on their way they are choked by the worries and riches and pleasures of life, and their fruit does not mature. 15 But as for the seed that landed on good soil, these are the ones who, after hearing the word, cling to it with an honest and good heart, and bear fruit with steadfast endurance.

16 "No one lights a lamp and then covers it with a jar or puts it under a bed, but puts it on a lampstand so that those who come in can see the light. 17 For nothing is hidden that will not be revealed, and nothing concealed that will not be made known and brought to light. 18 So listen carefully, for whoever has will be given more, but whoever does not have, even what he thinks he has will be taken from him."

19 Now Jesus' mother and his brothers came to him, but they could not get near him because of the crowd. 20 So he was told, "Your mother and your brothers are standing outside, wanting to

see you." 21 But he replied to them, "My mother and my brothers are those who hear the word of God and do it."

22 One day Jesus got into a boat with his disciples and said to them, "Let's go across to the other side of the lake." So they set out, 23 and as they sailed he fell asleep. Now a violent windstorm came down on the lake, and the boat started filling up with water, and they were in danger. 24 They came and woke him, saying, "Master, Master, we are about to die!" So he got up and rebuked the wind and the raging waves; they died down, and it was calm. 25 Then he said to them, "Where is your faith?" But they were afraid and amazed, saying to one another, "Who then is this? He commands even the winds and the water, and they obey him!"

Women Mentioned in the Gospel of Luke

- Elizabeth (Luke 1)
- Mary, mother of Jesus (mentioned twelve times)
- Anna (Luke 2)
- Herodias (Luke 3)
- Many widows in Elijah's day (Luke 3)
- Widow of Zarephath (Luke 3)
- Simon's mother-in-law (Luke 3)
- Widow in Nain (Luke 7)
- Wisdom personified as a woman (Luke 7)
- Sinful woman who anoints Jesus and is forgiven (Luke 7)
- Women who travel with and support Jesus and his disciples: Mary Magdalene, Joanna, Susanna, others (Luke 8)
- Jairus' daughter and her parents (Luke 8)
- Hemorrhaging woman (Luke 8)
- Martha and Mary of Bethany (Luke 10)
- A woman who says, "Blessed is the womb that bore you and the breasts that nursed you!" (Luke 11)
- Queen of the South (Luke 11)
- Families divided: mother / daughter; mother-in-law / daughter-in-law (Luke 14)
- Woman who had been crippled for eighteen years (Luke 13)
- Parable of the Kingdom of God being like a woman mixing yeast and flour (Luke 13)
- Jesus likens himself to a mother hen who protects her brood (Luke 13)
- Disciples must "hate" their father, mother, wife, children, brothers, and sisters (Luke 14)
- Parable of a woman who lost and found a coin and rejoices with her friends (Luke 15)
- Mention of men divorcing their wives or marrying divorced women (Luke 16)

- Lot's wife (Luke 17)
- Two women grinding grain: one taken, one left (Luke 17)
- Parable of a widow fighting an unjust judge for her rights (Luke 18)
- "Honor your father and mother" (Luke 18)
- Disciples who have left wives...parents, children and possessions will be rewarded (Luke 18)
- Widows whose property is devoured (Luke 20)
- Sadducees question the resurrection with story of a woman who had seven husbands (Luke 20)
- Widow who offered all she had (Luke 22)
- Pregnant and nursing women fleeing in the days of Jerusalem's destruction (Luke 21)
- Servant girl who challenges Peter (Luke 22)
- Wailing women in the crowd on the way to Jesus's crucifixion (Luke 23)
- The women from Galilee who watch Jesus' crucifixion from a distance (Luke 23)
- The women who see where Jesus is buried and prepare spices and ointments for his body (Luke 23)
- Mary Magdalene, Joanna, Mary of James, and other women who find Jesus's tomb empty (Luke 24)
- Two messengers speak with women; they remember Jesus' words and tell the other disciples (Luke 24)
- Two disciples ("Cleopas" and possibly his wife in 24:18) on the road to Emmaus (Luke 24)
- Two disciples tell Jesus how some women of their group had gone to the tomb and saw a vision of angels (Luke 24)

2. List the people who travelled with Jesus as he preached and proclaimed the good news of the kingdom of God (8:1–3). Some of these we will look at in depth later.

____

____

____

3. Christianity has a long tradition of women from all social classes financially supporting kingdom work, and humble people have received their ministry. Some give; some go; some do both. What resources can you use to further the reach of the good news?

Bailing out
Thunder rolls
The boat lists
Waves reaching high
Rock our minds
Like questions
Who is this guy?
Yet the God-man naps
Blissfully believes
Trusts his father
But
How can you sleep
In turmoil
Shut out the world
Like we don't even exist
I thought God never slept
Who are you anyway?
Wake up Jesus
How can you be everywhere
And so unaware?
Please
Save
Us
Deliver, rescue
Isn't that what you do?
Calm the storm
Still the rage
Let quiet reign
Listen to the peace
That hits
Like a sweet blast
A cool whisper-breeze
Light on my face
I almost smell the fresh salted fish
Roasting on a charcoal fire.

—Misty Hedrick

4. Sometimes people say receiving income from a woman violates a male's manhood. How do the details in Luke 8:1–3 answer such an idea?

5. Why does Jesus say he often veils his meaning by speaking in parables (v. 10)?

Jesus is the master of subtlety, and we do well to study how he communicates truth. Often he "tells it slant" rather than coming right out with assertions, answers, and proclamations.

Complete the right column of the chart to show the meaning of Jesus's parable about four kinds of soil. The seed represents the Word of God (v. 11):

Seed on path (v. 5)	Trampled on Birds devoured	v. 12
Seed on rock (v. 6)	Withered No moisture	v. 13
Seed on thorns (v. 7)	Choked	v. 14
Good soil (v. 8)	Produced 100X the grain	v. 15

6. Which of the first three above poses the greatest risk for you?

____

____

"So listen carefully" (v. 18). This is Jesus's "practical application" for his disciples, his imperative. He follows it with a reason:

"For whoever has will be given more, but whoever does not have, even what he thinks he has will be taken from him" (v. 18). Think of all the examples Luke has given of people with plenty of "light" who have missed who Jesus is and what he is doing. Contrast that with the examples of those Luke has introduced to readers who have little "light," yet they show great faith. For those of us exposed to spiritual resources, the words come as a warning. We must listen carefully and respond to the light we have been granted.

"My mother and my brothers are those who hear the word of God and do it" (v. 21). Spiritual reproduction trumps physical reproduction. People assume here that being a member of Jesus's biological family will bring insider benefits. Yet Jesus emphasizes that his true family is people who hear and do God's word. "Spirit is thicker than blood."

7. Re-read vv. 22–25. What do you make of the detail that Jesus slept through a violent storm on a boat?

---

8. What does this miracle further reveal about the scope of Jesus's power?

In 1792, a German woman named Katharina A. von Schlegel wrote a hymn translated into English in 1855 by another woman, Jane L. Borthwick. The hymn is known to us as "Be Still My Soul." And von Schlegel included in her work a line that references the above story:

> Be still, my soul: the waves and wind still know
> His voice who ruled them while He dwelt below

For what do you need a reminder that if Jesus has the power to calm the winds and waves, he can certainly handle our needs?

The great Dutch painter Rembrandt van Rijn painted "Storm on the Sea of Galilee" in 1633. It was stolen in 1990 (and not recovered) in what is considered the biggest art heist in history. Find a picture of it online, meditate on it (notice how Rembrandt painted himself holding the rope and looking at the viewer) and imagine yourself waking Jesus in your storm.

FRIDAY: JESUS, LORD OVER DEMONS AND DEATH

1. Ask the Holy Spirit to help you understand the Scriptures; read Luke 8:26–56. As you do, notice Jesus's power over the unseen world. Underline the words "daughter," "twelve," and forms of the word "beg." Also circle each time one tells another to leave or sends away.

26 So they sailed over to the region of the Gerasenes, which is opposite Galilee. 27 As Jesus stepped ashore, a certain man from the town met him who was possessed by demons. For a long time this man had worn no clothes and had not lived in a house, but among the tombs. 28 When he saw Jesus, he cried out, fell down before him, and shouted with a loud voice, "Leave me alone, Jesus, Son of the Most High God! I beg you, do not torment me!" 29 For Jesus had started commanding the evil spirit to come out of the man. (For it had seized him many times, so he would be bound with chains and shackles and kept under guard. But he would break the restraints and be driven by the demon into deserted places.) 30 Jesus then asked him, "What is your name?" He said, "Legion," because many demons had entered him. 31 And they began to beg him not to order them to depart into the abyss. 32 Now a large herd of pigs was feeding there on the hillside, and the demonic spirits begged Jesus to let them go into them. He gave them permission. 33 So the demons came out of the man and went into the pigs, and the herd of pigs rushed down the steep slope into the lake and drowned. 34 When the herdsmen saw what had happened, they ran off and spread the news in the town and countryside. 35 So the people went out to see what had happened, and they came to Jesus. They found the man from whom the demons had gone out, sitting at Jesus' feet, clothed and in his right mind, and they were afraid. 36Those who had seen it told them how the man who had been demon-possessed had been healed. 37 Then all the people of the Gerasenes and the surrounding region asked Jesus to leave them alone, for they were seized with great fear. So he got into the boat and left. 38 The man from whom the demons had gone out begged to go with him, but Jesus sent him away, saying, 39 "Return to your home, and declare what God has done for you." So he went away, proclaiming throughout the whole town what Jesus had done for him.

40 Now when Jesus returned, the crowd welcomed him because they were all waiting for him. 41 Then a man named Jairus, who was a leader of the synagogue, came up. Falling at Jesus' feet, he pleaded with him to come to his house, 42 because he had an only daughter, about twelve years old, and she was dying.

As Jesus was on his way, the crowds pressed around him. 43 Now a woman was there who had been suffering from a hemorrhage for twelve years but could not be healed by anyone. 44 She came up behind Jesus and touched the edge of his cloak, and at once the bleeding stopped. 45 Then Jesus asked, "Who was it who touched me?" When they all denied it, Peter said, "Master, the crowds are surrounding you and pressing against you!"

46 But Jesus said, "Someone touched me, for I know that power has gone out from me." 47 When the woman saw that she could not escape notice, she came trembling and fell down before him. In the presence of all the people, she explained why she had touched him and how she had been immediately healed. 48 Then he said to her, "Daughter, your faith has made you well. Go in peace."

49 While he was still speaking, someone from the synagogue leader's house came and said, "Your daughter is dead; do not trouble the teacher any longer." 50 But when Jesus heard this, he told him, "Do not be afraid; just believe, and she will be healed." 51 Now when he came to the house, Jesus did not let anyone go in with him except Peter, John, and James, and the child's father and mother. 52 Now they were all wailing and mourning for her, but he said, "Stop your weeping; she is not dead but asleep!" 53 And they began making fun of him because they knew that she was dead. 54 But Jesus gently took her by the hand and said, "Child, get up." 55 Her spirit returned, and she got up immediately. Then he told them to give her something to eat. 56 Her parents were astonished, but he ordered them to tell no one what had happened.

2. What did you notice about "daughter," "twelve," and themes of sending away?

---

3. List all the ways in which demon possession has manifested itself in the tortured man's life (vv. 27–30). Include the location where he stayed.

"Leave me alone, Jesus, Son of the Most High God! (v. 28). Notice that the demons know exactly who Jesus is: He is the Son. The Most High God is his father. "Son of the Most High" is the same name the angel told Mary her son would be called (Luke 1:32). The demons' statement fulfills prophecy.

"I beg you, do not torment me!" (v. 28). Notice that the evil spirits submit to Jesus. In fact, twice they beg him to do something—not to torment them and to let them inhabit pigs (vv. 28, 32), the latter request of which he grants. They are no match for Jesus. Even the demons must obey the Lord. Nothing happens beyond his control.

"Legion" (v. 30)—Jesus speaks to the demon and asks its name. "Legion" is the reply. A Roman legion was comprised of between four thousand and six thousand soldiers. So, it's possible this man has thousands of demons within him. But "legion" can also be hyperbole for "many." Compare the man's situation with the description of Mary Magdalene earlier in this chapter (v. 2). She was said to have been healed of seven demons. This man's situation is dire.

"A large herd of pigs" (v. 32)—Jesus and his group have sailed to the country of the Gerasenes (v. 26), which is said to be opposite Galilee, so Jesus has traveled into Gentile territory. The presence of a herd of pigs, prohibited in Jewish law, further suggests spiritual darkness, from the perspective of Luke's readers. Once again, Jesus has healed a person in the most pitiable of circumstances. The fact that when the demons move from this man, they take out an entire herd of swine also suggests the number of demons was large.

"They [the people] were afraid" (v. 35). Luke uses the words fear or afraid often to show human responses to angels' appearances and to Jesus's demonstrations of power. Translators sometimes substitute the word "respect" when the underlying text actually says "fear," because they want to avoid giving the impression that the Scriptures teach one's relationship with God should be terror-filled. Indeed it shouldn't, but sometimes we go too far in the other direction, downplaying appropriate responses to the power of God. Pulitzer-winning author Annie Dillard in *Teaching a Stone to Talk* writes this,

> On the whole, I do not find Christians, outside of the catacombs, sufficiently sensible of conditions. Does anyone have the foggiest idea what sort of power we so blithely invoke? Or, as I suspect, does no one believe a word of it? The churches are children playing on the floor with their chemistry sets, mixing up a batch of TNT to kill a Sunday morning. It is madness to wear ladies' straw hats and velvet hats to church; we should all be wearing crash helmets. Ushers should issue life preservers and signal flares; they should lash us to our pews.

4. What are the reactions of the groups who see this miracle (vv. 34–37)?

____

____

5. After Jesus heals him, how has the demon-possessed man visibly changed (v. 35)? Where will he now make his residence (v. 38)?

6. The man released from spiritual bondage begs to leave everything behind and be allowed to travel with Jesus, like the women from Galilee (8:1–3). But Jesus has a different mission for him. What does Jesus tell him to do, and what is the man's response (v. 39)?

7. We see that some are called to leave all and travel with Jesus, but this follower is called to return home. What implications do you see for those seeking to follow Jesus today?

"When Jesus returned" (v. 40)—The way Luke tells this story, it looks like Jesus has crossed into Gentile territory only for this one man. He goes, the man meets him, the demoniac is delivered, Jesus tells him to go home, and Jesus returns to Galilee.

8. Compare and contrast the social power (or lack of it) for Jairus and for the bleeding woman (vv. 41, 43).

9. What hints does the text give of Jairus's desperation (vv. 41–42)? Of the bleeding woman's desperation (v. 43)?

“From a hemorrhage for twelve years” (v. 43)—Usually a “hemorrhage” brings to mind profuse bleeding from a ruptured blood vessel. That is not what’s happening here. The literal wording is “a flow of blood”;and the word here is the same as the one used in the Septuagint (Greek translation of the Hebrew Bible) to refer to a woman’s menstrual flow. Such being the case, she has been ritually unclean for more than a decade. According to Levitical law, certain emissions were ritually unclean and thus required separation from the community. The “unclean” status was not the same as sinful nor was the requirement of separation intended as a punishment. Nevertheless, everywhere this woman sat would have become unclean. Everything she touched became unclean. And she couldn’t participate in the faith community in her unclean state.. Again, not all sicknesses or illnesses are connected with sin or demon possession, including this one. This is an issue of ritual impurity.

10. What were you doing twelve years ago? That’s how long this woman has been bleeding, and twelve is also the age of Jairus’s daughter.

Looking left
Glancing right
I smell jasmine
But I taste the salty blood
Of my bitten lip
12 years I groaned alone
My money gone
But nothing helped
No one could heal
Me
Unclean
Can I hide it–
My soul’s torment
Long enough to get
Close enough to rip
Pull the thread of power
People press in
Touch me
Untouchable
Unreachable
As I bleed out
I stretch

Plunge for his hem
And I know
Instantly
I've touched the garment
Of God
I weep
Could it be that easy?
12 years
12 years in a bloody hell
But he stops
Turns around
Oh Jesus, no
Don't single me out
But he did
What he does
He heals
Whom he loves

—Misty Hedrick

"At once the bleeding stopped" (v. 44).This woman could have been anemic, or in the advanced stages of ovarian cancer. Such bleeding has numerous possible medical causes. But whatever the reason, she has probably been weak and in pain. She touches Jesus's robe, and immediately she is healed.

"I know that power has gone out from me" (v. 46). Jesus was not drained of power. Rather, he felt power proceed from himself.

"When the woman saw that she could not escape notice..." (v. 47)—Jesus expects her to publicly testify to what God has done for her—even if it requires revealing something personal in public.

11. How has God delivered you? Sustained you through illness that may not end this side of heaven? Delivered you from porn? Abortion? Depression? Broken relationships? Slander? A broken body? Endless longing? From selfishness? Pride? A critical spirit? Granting the ability to trust even if there's never a happy ending? In what circumstance(s) can you testify to God's goodness?

"Daughter..." (v. 48)—This is the only story in the entire New Testament in which we read about Jesus calling anyone "daughter." Lest anyone doubt how precious a daughter is, Luke's listener has just heard about Jairus's cherished daughter who is twelve years old—she's been alive for as long as this woman has been unclean.

12. What was it that made this woman well (v. 48)? Do you see a pattern of cause and effect in miraculous healings?

"Go in peace" (v. 48). This woman has already been healed, but Jesus restores her holistically, saying the equivalent of "Shalom." She can quit seeking medical care, enjoy energy again, and be restored to the community. While the physical healing is instant, the social and emotional flourishing has only begun.

13. How do you think Jairus feels about the delay this woman has caused? What has Jesus's stopping for an "interruption" done to make Jairus's situation worse? How is the glory of God seen in this timing?

---

14. Who are the initial witnesses of Jesus's raising of Jairus's daughter (v. 51)?

---

15. What does Jesus tell her parents to do after they witness this miracle (v. 56)?

---

16. In what do you need to trust God for his perfect timing?

Saturday: This Is That!

Scripture: "So the dead man sat up and began to speak, and Jesus gave him to his mother" (Luke 7:15).

Like the desert in Israel's forty years of wandering, the landscape itself played a role in the story of the town of Shunem. In fact, the setting communicated so much that it functioned almost as a character. Shunem's people took pride in its heritage: About eight hundred years before Jesus came to this town, Elisha had brought a woman's dead child back to life.

Elsewhere even before that, Elisha's mentor, Elijah, had restored to life a widow's dead son—her only son. Having done so, the biblical text records, Elijah "gave him to his mother" (1 Kings 17:23).

Some of the best prophets raise the dead.

Just on the other side of Shunem's hill, assuming we have the location right, sat another town with a history. Abraham's grandson Jacob had given the site to his son, Issachar, observing that it lay on "pleasant" land—"Na-ee-ma." The Greeks later nicknamed the village "Nain."

As Luke in his Gospel prepares to tell a new story that takes place in this locale, he is answering a question for his readers: Who is this Jesus? As we pick up the narrative in Nain, the Lord has just spoken into healing the sick-unto-death slave of a centurion. Following that event, Jesus has arrived, followers in tow, at the entrance to Nain's walled city.

But something has kept the group from entering: a funeral procession is exiting through the city gates. Consequently, in the same way that Americans pull cars over when a funeral procession goes by, everyone with Jesus stopped and watched the bier go by, listening to the mourners wailing. Then they did what any good Jew would do: they joined the procession.

In the first century, dead bodies were carried outside of town, as, right away, the corpse began decomposing. So, this funeral procession was probably headed for the family tomb.

Imagine the mother's grief. She is a widow, so she's already "buried" her husband, and that means she probably depended on her son for survival. Now he is gone too—her only son.

This woman has no movie footage, no audio recordings, no photos, maybe not even any drawings—only memories as she mourns the loss of her loved one's gait, voice, and eyes. If his face is wrapped in a cloth (as Jesus's will be after he dies), this mother is thinking she would never again look on her son's countenance.

What does Jesus do?

"He had compassion for her and said to her, 'Do not weep.'"

Imagine someone saying that to any parent bereft of a child! The immediate question would be, "Why. Ever. Not?"

Jesus knows he is about to change her weeping to joy. He comes forward and touches the bier, and its bearers stand still. Our Lord says, 'Young man, I say to you, rise!' Then, the dead man sat up and began to speak. And Jesus gave him to his mother" (see Luke 7:11–15).

Imagine standing in that crowd watching the overjoyed mother. You're thinking, "What? Again? He must be some prophet! And not a minor prophet like Amos or Zephaniah. But the kind who can raise the dead. Like Elijah! And Elisha!" Imagine you're in Luke's original audience. You're thinking, "This is like that!"

Who is this man? Who can do such a thing?

Who, indeed. And Jesus's whole conquering death part will get even better....

For memorization: "Fear seized them all, and they began to glorify God, saying, 'A great prophet has appeared among us!' and 'God has come to help his people!'" (Luke 7:16).

Prayer: *Oh, Lord, You have ultimate power over death. Thank you for new life! Help me to love you, stand in awe of you, honor you, glorify you, and spread the word.*

Week 4 of 7

Jesus: The One Sent from Heaven (Luke 9–12)

Sunday: Six Words That Changed My Life

Scripture: "Now as they went on their way, Jesus entered a certain village where a woman named Martha welcomed him as a guest. She had a sister named Mary, who sat at the Lord's feet and listened to what he said. But Martha was distracted with all the preparations she had to make, so she came up to him and said, "Lord, don't you care that my sister has left me to do all the work alone? Tell her to help me." But the Lord answered her, "Martha, Martha, you are worried and troubled about many things, but one thing is needed. Mary has chosen the best part; it will not be taken away from her" (Luke 10:38–42).

I am Sandra—daughter of Ann, of Velma, of Ella...all the way back to Eve. But the genetic line stops with me. Like the dinosaur, now extinct, I'm a Sandra-saur. I will never give birth.

Although I went to college, I had no intention of pursuing a career. I dated my high-school sweetheart, and I knew even in my freshman year that I would marry this guy. My main vocational goal was to be a mommy. It was my only aspiration.

When we married at ages 21 and 20, Gary and I wanted at least three children. It never dawned on me that we might face the prospect of no kids at all. If anything, I figured we'd have nineteen like Susannah Wesley and wonder how to handle them all.

After five years of marriage, during which Gary earned a master's degree in theology, we decided it was time to expand our little family of two. But a year went by with no success. And then another. Finally, I went to the doctor. But a third year passed.

Then it happened—the positive pregnancy test.

We partied. We celebrated. We cheered. Yet, elation turned to agony soon when I miscarried. Then miscarried again. And again. We had seven early pregnancy losses.

After that, we pursued adoption, but in three years' time, three adoptions fell through.

Spiritually, I wondered if God was punishing me. Emotionally, I felt unstable with hormones fluctuating wildly. The greatest trauma of all, though, was my crisis of womanhood. What was I supposed to do and who was I supposed be?

I had always heard that a Christian woman's highest calling is motherhood. Where did that leave me? When I went to college, I didn't go to prepare myself for a career. To be honest, I didn't really believe in women having vocations.

As I write that now, it still astonishes me, as I consider how narrow my perspective was. I left no room for the apostle Paul's statement that the unmarried state, if chosen for eternal purposes, can be a higher calling than marriage. Where would my view have left tent-making Priscilla? Or the woman in Proverbs 31 who, though a wife and mom, sold belts and real estate? Or Lydia, the seller of purple from Thyatira? Or Philip's four virgin daughters who prophesied? I didn't see then what I do now—that godly womanhood cuts its fabric from a varied pattern book, and its garments are not "one size fits all."

At that point, both my spiritual mentor and my husband encouraged me to attend seminary. They recognized a gift for teaching in me that I couldn't see myself.

To my amazement, the Lord provided the money for tuition. Reluctantly, I enrolled in classes, but I still had serious doubts. Was I intruding in a man's world? Was I really supposed to go? Did doing so suggest that I devalued motherhood?

I awoke the first day of class and felt nervous as I vacillated between wearing pants or a dress, necklace or earrings only. When it came time to leave, I still had nagging doubts about what I was setting out to do. And I knew that whatever is of doubt is sin.

As I walked through the living room on my way out the front door, I stopped. I simply couldn't go without peace. I had to know I was making the right choice. I slipped to my knees in front of the couch, and I prayed (more like begged): "Lord, if this violates what you want me to do, please stop me. I just want to do what you want."

Has God ever spoken simple words to you? He certainly answered me that day. I didn't hear an audible voice, but the words memorized years earlier that came to my mind might as well have been: *Mary has chosen what is better.*

I thought of the story behind the words. Martha was in the kitchen doing the traditional "woman" thing. She was being domestic. Meanwhile, Mary sat at Jesus' feet learning theology. When kitchen-woman complained that student-woman had messed up priorities, Jesus set her straight. "Mary has chosen what is better."

I got up knowing exactly what I was supposed to do. I knew seminary was where God wanted me. I had no idea what I would do with my education, but I knew the step I needed to take for that day. I confess that such direct leading from God has been rare throughout my life, but that day God used Jesus's own words to a female disciple to propel me forward.

Today, Gary and I are the adoptive parents of a grown daughter, and I teach at the same seminary where I took classes. If you told me twenty-five years ago that I'd have an "only child" and teach at a graduate school helping to train pastors and ministry workers, I would have laughed. Out loud. And shaken my head at you. Maybe even my finger.

Motherhood is a high and noble calling, but it is not the only calling—or even the ultimate calling. Following Jesus Christ wherever He leads is the ultimate calling.

Mary has chosen what is better.

Have you chosen to follow, no matter the cost?

For memorization: "Only one thing is needed. Mary has chosen what is better, and it will not be taken away from her." (Luke 10:42, NIV)

Prayer: *Dear Lord, Your words are the best words of all. They give life and direction and peace. Help me to follow you no matter where you lead. And help me to hold my plans in open palms, always ready to change them at your prompting. Fill me with your life-giving words that I might obey them and pass them on so they can make a difference in the* *lives of those I encounter. In the name of Christ through the power of the Spirit, Amen.*

Monday: The Christ of God (S-h-h-h)

1. Pray for the Spirit's help and read Luke 9:1–36. Circle the words "kingdom," "power," "authority," and "glory." Put a star by stories in which Jesus demonstrates his power.

> 9:1 After Jesus called the twelve together, he gave them power and authority over all demons and to cure diseases, 2 and he sent them out to proclaim the kingdom of God and to heal the sick. 3 He said to them, "Take nothing for your journey—no staff, no bag, no bread, no money, and do not take an extra tunic. 4 Whatever house you enter, stay there until you leave the area. 5 Wherever they do not receive you, as you leave that town, shake the dust off your feet as a testimony against them." 6 Then they departed and went throughout the villages, proclaiming the good news and healing people everywhere.
>
> 7 Now Herod the tetrarch heard about everything that was happening, and he was thoroughly perplexed because some people were saying that John had been raised from the dead, 8 while others were saying that Elijah had appeared, and still others that one of the prophets of long ago had risen. 9 Herod said, "I had John beheaded, but who is this about whom I hear such things?" So Herod wanted to learn about Jesus.
>
> 10 When the apostles returned, they told Jesus everything they had done. Then he took them with him and they withdrew privately to a town called Bethsaida. 11 But when the crowds found out, they followed him. He welcomed them, spoke to them about the kingdom of God, and cured those who needed healing. 12 Now the day began to draw to a close, so the twelve came and said to Jesus, "Send the crowd away, so they can go into the surrounding villages and countryside and find lodging and food because we are in an isolated place." 13 But he said to them, "You give them something to eat." They replied, "We have no more than five loaves and two fish—unless we go and buy food for all these people." 14 (Now about 5,000 men were there.) Then he said to his disciples, "Have them sit down in groups of about fifty each." 15 So they did as Jesus directed, and the people all sat down.
>
> 16 Then he took the five loaves and the two fish, and looking up to heaven he gave thanks and broke them. He gave them to the

disciples to set before the crowd. 17 They all ate and were satisfied, and what was left over was picked up—twelve baskets of broken pieces.

18 Once when Jesus was praying by himself and his disciples were nearby, he asked them, "Who do the crowds say that I am?" 19 They answered, "John the Baptist; others say Elijah; and still others that one of the prophets of long ago has risen." 20 Then he said to them, "But who do you say that I am?" Peter answered, "The Christ of God." 21 But he forcefully commanded them not to tell this to anyone, 22 saying, "The Son of Man must suffer many things and be rejected by the elders, chief priests, and experts in the law, and be killed, and on the third day be raised."

23 Then he said to them all, "If anyone wants to become my follower, he must deny himself, take up his cross daily, and follow me. 24 For whoever wants to save his life will lose it, but whoever loses his life because of me will save it. 25 For what does it benefit a person if he gains the whole world but loses or forfeits himself? 26 For whoever is ashamed of me and my words, the Son of Man will be ashamed of that person when he comes in his glory and in the glory of the Father and of the holy angels. 27 But I tell you most certainly, there are some standing here who will not experience death before they see the kingdom of God."

9:28 Now about eight days after these sayings, Jesus took with him Peter, John, and James, and went up the mountain to pray. 29 As he was praying, the appearance of his face was transformed, and his clothes became very bright, a brilliant white. 30 Then two men, Moses and Elijah, began talking with him. 31 They appeared in glorious splendor and spoke about his departure that he was about to carry out at Jerusalem. 32 Now Peter and those with him were quite sleepy, but as they became fully awake, they saw his glory and the two men standing with him. 33 Then as the men were starting to leave, Peter said to Jesus, "Master, it is good for us to be here. Let us make three shelters, one for you and one for Moses and one for Elijah"—not knowing what he was saying. 34 As he was saying this, a cloud came and overshadowed them, and they were afraid as they entered the cloud. 35 Then a voice came from the cloud, saying, "This is my Son, my Chosen One. Listen to him!" 36 After the voice had spoken, Jesus was found alone. So they kept silent and told no one at that time anything of what they had seen.

2. What do you notice about Jesus's power in today's reading?

___

___

"Whatever house you enter, stay there until you leave the area" (v. 4). Luke will record similar instructions in 10:7–8. At this time and place in history, religious philosophers went begging from house to house. But Jesus's disciples are to differ in their approach. No begging. No snobbery. No upgrading. Stay where you're invited. Eat what's put in front of you. No seeking income. Keep the focus on the people and the message.

"Shake the dust off your feet as a testimony against them" (v. 5). Shaking off dust was symbolic for removing uncleanness—a sign of rejection. Those who reject are rejected. The disciples have good news and they are to focus their ministry on those who hear and receive.

3. Jesus commissions the twelve. What exactly does he send them to do (vv. 1, 2, 6)?

---

4. Jesus limits those to whom he gives miracle-working power, and his miracles happen for specific purposes—he does not always rescue or heal. What happens to Jesus's relative John the Baptist (v. 9)? What is Herod's question about Jesus? What spiritual questions do you think this outcome raised for John's disciples, for John's community, and/or for Jesus's disciples?

"Now about 5,000 men were there" (v. 14). The Greek word here for "men" is usually translated "males," and not the more generic "people." So, picture the ground covered with about five thousand blankets filled with households full of men, women, and children. Jesus feeds many more than five thousand.

5. Jesus's miracle of the loaves and fish answers Herod's question about who Jesus is. Who do the crowds say Jesus is (v. 19)? Adding to the testimony of angels (2:11), the Father (3:22); demons (4:41), and Jesus himself (4:18), who does Peter say Jesus is (9:20)?

6. Once again Jesus insists, this time forcefully (v. 21), that his disciples must conceal what they know about the Lord's identity; then he reveals for the first time what he will do (v. 22). Ancient prophecies about the Messiah refer to him both healing and taking the throne as a literal king. Yet he must first be the suffering servant and die in this upside-down kingdom. Not knowing this, many in Jesus's circle have nationalistic expectations about Messiah overthrowing Rome. How would such expectations make Jesus's public ministry during his first coming more difficult?

7. If you were close friends with a royal family, what benefits might you expect? Contrast that with what Jesus says his followers must do (vv. 23–27).

8. How can seeking political power on behalf of the church sometimes undermine its overall mission?

"Until they see the kingdom of God" (v. 27)—This is possibly a reference to seeing Jesus revealed in his glory, which will happen in about eight days (v. 28).

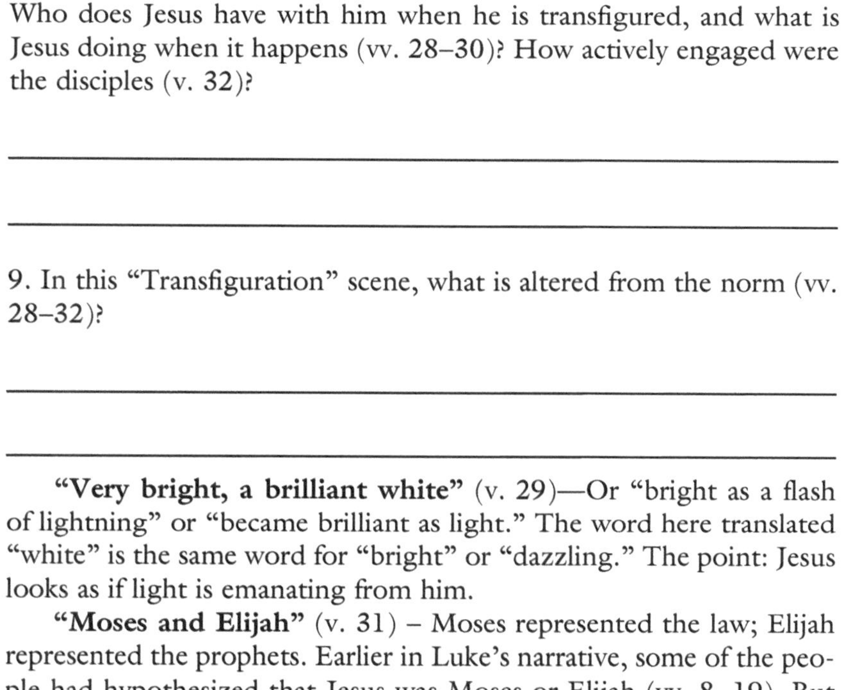

Who does Jesus have with him when he is transfigured, and what is Jesus doing when it happens (vv. 28–30)? How actively engaged were the disciples (v. 32)?

9. In this "Transfiguration" scene, what is altered from the norm (vv. 28–32)?

"Very bright, a brilliant white" (v. 29)—Or "bright as a flash of lightning" or "became brilliant as light." The word here translated "white" is the same word for "bright" or "dazzling." The point: Jesus looks as if light is emanating from him.

"Moses and Elijah" (v. 31) – Moses represented the law; Elijah represented the prophets. Earlier in Luke's narrative, some of the people had hypothesized that Jesus was Moses or Elijah (vv. 8, 19). But clearly Jesus is not one of these men, because they appear with him. In fact, later Luke will point out that Jesus fulfills both the law and the prophets (24:36–49). In the past when Moses went up a mountain to receive the law, his face shone (Exodus 34). Now Jesus has gone up a mountain to pray, and not only does his face glow, but Moses and Elijah appear with him.

10. What are Moses and Elijah talking to Jesus about (v. 31)?

"They saw his glory and the two men standing with him" (v. 32). What the disciples saw were not angels. Nor ghosts. They were men. And they were not flying or floating. They were standing.

"'Let us make three shelters, one for you and one for Moses and one for Elijah'—not knowing what he was saying" (v. 33). Peter is talking nonsense. Who can blame him? To provide some context for his words, in Jewish history, before the temple was built, God himself dwelled in a tabernacle—or a moving structure. A tent. Peter is acknowledging here that he is seeing the glory of God.

"A cloud came and overshadowed them" (v. 34). While Peter is still speaking, those who are with Jesus become engulfed in a cloud. The word "overshadowed" here is the same one the angel used when he told Mary, "The Most High will overshadow you" (1:35).

11. Compare what the voice says to Jesus's companions here (9:35) with what the voice said to Jesus at his baptism (3:22). How are the two events similar? What do all these details indicate about who Jesus really is?

___

___

___

12. What did the disciples do with their newfound information at this point (v. 36)? (They will wait until after Pentecost to talk about the Transfiguration publicly.)

___

___

Tuesday: Self-Congratulations vs. Discipleship

1. Ask the Holy Spirit to help you understand and read Luke 9:37–62.

> 37 Now on the next day, when they had come down from the mountain, a large crowd met him. 38 Then a man from the crowd cried out, "Teacher, I beg you to look at my son—he is my only child! 39 A spirit seizes him, and he suddenly screams; it throws him into convulsions and causes him to foam at the mouth. It hardly ever leaves him alone, torturing him severely. 40 I begged your disciples to cast it out, but they could not do so." 41 Jesus answered, "You unbelieving and perverse generation! How much longer must I be with you and endure you? Bring your son here." 42 As the boy was approaching, the demon threw him to the ground and shook him

with convulsions. But Jesus rebuked the unclean spirit, healed the boy, and gave him back to his father. 43 Then they were all astonished at the mighty power of God.

But while the entire crowd was amazed at everything Jesus was doing, he said to his disciples, 44 "Take these words to heart, for the Son of Man is going to be betrayed into the hands of men." 45 But they did not understand this statement; its meaning had been concealed from them, so that they could not grasp it. Yet they were afraid to ask him about this statement.

46 Now an argument started among the disciples as to which of them might be the greatest. 47 But when Jesus discerned their innermost thoughts, he took a child, had him stand by his side, 48 and said to them, "Whoever welcomes this child in my name welcomes me, and whoever welcomes me welcomes the one who sent me, for the one who is least among you all is the one who is great."

49 John answered, "Master, we saw someone casting out demons in your name, and we tried to stop him because he is not a disciple along with us." 50 But Jesus said to him, "Do not stop him, for whoever is not against you is for you."

51 Now when the days drew near for him to be taken up, Jesus set out resolutely to go to Jerusalem. 52 He sent messengers on ahead of him. As they went along, they entered a Samaritan village to make things ready in advance for him, 53 but the villagers refused to welcome him because he was determined to go to Jerusalem. 54 Now when his disciples James and John saw this, they said, "Lord, do you want us to call fire to come down from heaven and consume them?" 55 But Jesus turned and rebuked them, 56 and they went on to another village.

57 As they were walking along the road, someone said to him, "I will follow you wherever you go." 58 Jesus said to him, "Foxes have dens and the birds in the sky have nests, but the Son of Man has no place to lay his head." 59 Jesus said to another, "Follow me." But he replied, "Lord, first let me go and bury my father." 60 But Jesus said to him, "Let the dead bury their own dead, but as for you, go and proclaim the kingdom of God." 61 Yet another said, "I will follow you, Lord, but first let me say goodbye to my family." 62 Jesus said to him, "No one who puts his hand to the plow and looks back is fit for the kingdom of God."

2. Jesus has given the apostles all authority over demons and diseases (9:1). Yet what happens when they encounter a boy with a demon (v. 40)? And what is Jesus's response to their seeming inability (v. 41)?

3. What does Jesus's miracle suggest about his identity (v. 43)?

4. While everyone is amazed and marveling, Jesus is not reading the "press reports." He knows the road ahead is filled with suffering rather than applause. So, he has something serious on his mind. What is it (v. 44)?

5. While Jesus is thinking about what his kingdom will require of him in Jerusalem, the disciples have status and self-promotion on their minds. What are they arguing about (v. 46)?

6. In this instance, Jesus answers—not by telling the disciples to become like a child, but to be like him. What is Jesus doing in his example that they need to emulate (v. 48)? And how does this differ from what his followers are doing?

7. In reaction to what other ministers are doing, John has the mentality of "we're better" and "we're exclusive" (v. 49). What is Jesus's response to that and why (v. 50)?

"Days drew near for him to be taken up" (v. 51). The verb translated here as "taken up" appears four times in the New Testament in reference to the ascension of Jesus, which will happen in Jerusalem.

"Jesus set out resolutely to go to Jerusalem" (v. 51). Jesus knows the horrors of betrayal, crucifixion, and death that await him. Yet he is beyond willing—he's resolute—to do the will of God. Mt. Hermon, where the Transfiguration happened, lies in Syria, one hundred miles north of Jerusalem. So, Jesus starts out on the long walk south through Samaria to get to Jerusalem in time for Passover.

8. Jesus sends an advance team into a Samaritan village to arrange lodging (v. 52), but Jesus is unwelcome there (v. 53). Why?

____

9. James and John are incensed by the Samaritans' behavior. Their master has been insulted—perhaps because Jews insist on Jerusalem as the place of sacrifice, while Samaritans point to the mountain where their ancestors worshiped (see Judges 9:7; John 4). At any rate, members of Jesus's inner circle propose a solution (v. 54). What is Jesus's response to their suggestion (vv. 55–56)? Why do you think he responds the way he does?

____

____

____

____

10. Summarize in a few words each of Luke's three short vignettes about following Jesus. What do the three together communicate (vv. 57–62)?

____

____

____

"The Son of Man has no place to lay his head" (v. 58). Notice how Jesus identifies himself. One would expect the Son of Man to have the greatest privileges on earth, yet he does not even have a pillow to call his own.

"I will follow you wherever you go" (v. 51). On the surface, this is a great statement of commitment, yet Luke includes it in a section on the cost of discipleship. Such a statement can come from a humble, willing heart. But the same words can come from a heart of over-confidence that's self-congratulatory.

"First let me go and bury my father" (v. 59). Some think this interaction means the man's father is still alive, with death not even imminent. If that's what he means, the man expects to delay for years before following Jesus.

Who Were the Samaritans?

Mount Gerizim overlooks the city of Nablus in Israel's West Bank. And for centuries the site has served as the holiest places for Samaritan people. As they tell it, Gerizim is the mountain their ancestor Abraham ascended with Isaac to sacrifice him. The place is also, they believe, where Joshua took the wandering children of Israel to offer their first sacrifices after they entered the Promised Land. Yet according to the Jewish version, both of these events happened on Mount Moriah, the future site of Jerusalem's Temple Mount.

Rather than building a temple in Jerusalem, as the Jewish people did, the Samaritans built their temple on Mount Gerizim. The earliest evidence of worship on the latter dates to 2,500 years ago.

The conflict between Jews and Samaritans grew more heated at the time of Alexander the Great and his conquests in the fourth century B.C. Rejecting Greek culture, the people living on Mount Gerizim became more isolated, and by the second century B.C., they insisted Mount Gerizim, not Jerusalem, was the primary holy place. Meanwhile, some second-century Jewish writings accused the Samaritans of being pagans and foreigners. By the time of Jesus, the schism had become so deep that Jews typically walked the long way around Samaria to avoid going through unfriendly territory.

Source: *Archeology Magazine*, Sept/Oct 2021

I'm more inclined to think the man is cleverly giving a religious 'honor your father" excuse for his delay in following Jesus, suggesting he needs up to a year for his father's body to decompose.

Jewish burial at the time of Christ was typically a two-part process. Shortly after death, the corpse was laid on a shelf cut out of the wall of a rock-hewn tomb. This was the primary burial. The second burial happened about a year later, after the flesh had fully decomposed. At that time, family members reentered the tomb and carefully moved the bones into an ossuary. "Gathering" these bones following the primary burial was considered an important duty of a son.[1] The man in this story seems to be suggesting that only after he has fulfilled this duty to "bury his father" would he have freedom to follow Jesus.

Whatever the meaning, the man is giving an excuse for why he cannot follow Jesus. And Jesus tolerates no excuses. He is not suggesting that it's good to dishonor parents, a clear violation of the Law. Nor is Jesus suggesting the man could not attend his father's funeral. Rather, the Lord is addressing priorities and the cost of following Him. Jesus and his kingdom come before all obligations.

"Let the dead bury their own dead, but as for you, go and proclaim the kingdom of God" (v. 60) – In a play on words, Jesus says the spiritually dead can bury the physically dead, while those who are spiritually alive must go and tell of God's kingdom.

"I will follow you, Lord, but first..." (v. 61). Spiritual obligations trump social ones. When Elijah laid the prophet's mantle on Elisha, signaling the latter's call to ministry, Elisha asked first to bid his parents goodbye. Elijah allowed him to do so (1 Kings 19:19–20), but the one greater than Elijah summons with a call that must take precedence over all.

"No one who puts his hand to the plow and looks back is fit for the kingdom of God" (v. 62). A person who plows must always keep eyes on the end of the row, or the row turns out crooked. Someone who plows while looking back is unfit to plow.

11. What has following Christ cost you? Are there costs you're refusing to pay or resisting against? If so, what? Talk to God about them.

---

1. Source: Richard Neitzel Holzapfel, Jeffrey R. Chadwick, Frank F. Judd Jr., and Thomas A. Wayment, "Jesus and the Ossuaries: First-Century Jewish Burial Practices and the Lost Tomb of Jesus," in *Behold the Lamb of God: An Easter Celebration*, ed. Richard Neitzel Holzapfel, Frank F. Judd Jr., and Thomas A. Wayment (Provo, UT: Religious Studies Center, Brigham Young University, 2008), 201.

Wednesday: God First, Then Neighbor

1. Pray for the Spirit's wisdom and read Luke 10. Underline instances where Jesus does, says, and affirms the opposite of what his readers might expect. Circle references to Father, Son, and Holy Spirit.

> 10:1 After this the Lord appointed seventy-two others and sent them on ahead of him two by two into every town and place where he himself was about to go. 2 He said to them, "The harvest is plentiful, but the workers are few. Therefore ask the Lord of the harvest to send out workers into his harvest. 3 Go! I am sending you out like lambs surrounded by wolves. 4 Do not carry a money bag, a traveler's bag, or sandals, and greet no one on the road. 5 Whenever you enter a house, first say, 'May peace be on this house!' 6 And if a peace-loving person is there, your peace will remain on him, but if not, it will return to you. 7 Stay in that same house, eating and drinking what they give you, for the worker deserves his pay. Do not move around from house to house. 8 Whenever you enter a town and the people welcome you, eat what is set before you. 9 Heal the sick in that town and say to them, 'The kingdom of God has come upon you!' 10 But whenever you enter a town and the people do not welcome you, go into its streets and say, 11 'Even the dust of your town that clings to our feet we wipe off against you. Nevertheless know this: The kingdom of God has come.' 12 I tell you, it will be more bearable on that day for Sodom than for that town!
>
> 13 "Woe to you, Chorazin! Woe to you, Bethsaida! For if the miracles done in you had been done in Tyre and Sidon, they would have repented long ago, sitting in sackcloth and ashes. 14 But it will be more bearable for Tyre and Sidon in the judgment than for you! 15 And you, Capernaum, will you be exalted to heaven? No, you will be thrown down to Hades!
>
> 16 "The one who listens to you listens to me, and the one who rejects you rejects me, and the one who rejects me rejects the one who sent me."
>
> 17 Then the seventy-two returned with joy, saying, "Lord, even the demons submit to us in your name!" 18 So he said to them, "I

saw Satan fall like lightning from heaven. 19 Look, I have given you authority to tread on snakes and scorpions and on the full force of the enemy, and nothing will hurt you. 20 Nevertheless, do not rejoice that the spirits submit to you, but rejoice that your names stand written in heaven."

21 On that same occasion Jesus rejoiced in the Holy Spirit and said, "I praise you, Father, Lord of heaven and earth, because you have hidden these things from the wise and intelligent and revealed them to little children. Yes, Father, for this was your gracious will. 22 All things have been given to me by my Father. No one knows who the Son is except the Father, or who the Father is except the Son and anyone to whom the Son decides to reveal him."

23 Then Jesus turned to his disciples and said privately, "Blessed are the eyes that see what you see! 24 For I tell you that many prophets and kings longed to see what you see but did not see it, and to hear what you hear but did not hear it."

25 Now an expert in religious law stood up to test Jesus, saying, "Teacher, what must I do to inherit eternal life?" 26 He said to him, "What is written in the law? How do you understand it?" 27 The expert answered, "Love the Lord your God with all your heart, with all your soul, with all your strength, and with all your mind, and love your neighbor as yourself." 28 Jesus said to him, "You have answered correctly; do this, and you will live."

29 But the expert, wanting to justify himself, said to Jesus, "And who is my neighbor?" 30 Jesus replied, "A man was going down from Jerusalem to Jericho, and fell into the hands of robbers, who stripped him, beat him up, and went off, leaving him half dead. 31 Now by chance a priest was going down that road, but when he saw the injured man, he passed by on the other side. 32 So too a Levite, when he came up to the place and saw him, passed by on the other side. 33 But a Samaritan who was traveling came to where the injured man was, and when he saw him, he felt compassion for him. 34 He went up to him and bandaged his wounds, pouring olive oil and wine on them. Then he put him on his own animal, brought him to an inn, and took care of him. 35 The next day he took out two silver coins and gave them to the innkeeper, saying, 'Take care of him, and whatever else you spend, I will repay you when I come back this way.' 36 Which of these three do you think became a neighbor to the man who fell into the hands of the robbers?" 37 The expert in religious law said, "The one who showed mercy to him." So Jesus said to him, "Go and do the same."

38 Now as they went on their way, Jesus entered a certain village where a woman named Martha welcomed him as a guest.

> 39 She had a sister named Mary, who sat at the Lord's feet and listened to what he said. 40 But Martha was distracted with all the preparations she had to make, so she came up to him and said, "Lord, don't you care that my sister has left me to do all the work alone? Tell her to help me." 41 But the Lord answered her, "Martha, Martha, you are worried and troubled about many things, 42 but one thing is needed. Mary has chosen the best part; it will not be taken away from her."

2. What does Jesus do that's unexpected?

____

____

3. What did you notice about the members of the Trinity (Father, Son, and Holy Spirit)?

____

____

"The Lord appointed seventy-two others" (v. 1). Up to this point, Jesus has sent only his twelve apostles. Manuscripts of Luke's Gospel have been copied differently in a few places through the centuries, such that today some say "seventy" here, while others say "seventy-two." Twelve times six is seventy-two, so it's possible Jesus is multiplying the group to six times that of the original twelve apostles. But there's another option: Genesis 9 lists what is sometimes called "the table of nations," which consists of seventy nations descended from Noah. Luke could be noting that Jesus is prefiguring a sending to the nations. Either way, no major areas of doctrine are affected by this question. Many think the women who traveled with Jesus are part of this number.

"I am sending you" (v. 3). The word for "sending" here is the same root for the word "apostle." In fact, to be an apostle is to be a "sent one." The New Testament refers to "the twelve," to "the apostles," to "apostles," and to "disciples." Sometimes "the apostles" also refers to the twelve. But in other New Testament references, the word "apostle" refers to a church planter who is separate from the original twelve (James, brother of Jesus; Paul; Barnabas; Epaphroditus). Junia is one such person (Rom. 16:7). Elsewhere, Tabitha is called a disciple (Acts 9:36).

4. What does Jesus say about the harvest of souls his "sent ones" will encounter? What are they to do about the shortage, and what is Jesus doing (vv. 2–3)?

____

____

"Do not carry ... sandals, and greet no one on the road" (v. 4). Jesus is not saying his disciples must travel barefooted. He wants them to travel light. He's also not prohibiting them from simply waving or saying hello. Jesus wants his disciples to keep focused on the task rather than getting delayed.

"If a peace-loving person is there, your peace will remain on him, but if not, it will return to you" (v. 6). Mission organizations today base their advice, "Look for a person of peace," on the words of Jesus found here (vv. 5–11). The Spirit is working ahead of the harvesters, so they are to look for people whom the Spirit has already prepared with receptive hearts. The harvest is ready, and few workers exist, so those ready to reap need to prioritize the people "ripe for harvest." Jesus wants his sent-ones to focus on the people, men and women alike, who welcome them and their words rather than arguing or wasting time persuading those with hard hearts.

5. Why does Jesus allow the disciples to eat and drink the food (without asking for upgrades) of receptive people (v. 7)?

____

____

"More bearable on that day for Sodom than for that town!" (v. 12)—The author of Genesis records how Lot hosted two angels lodging in Sodom, and the people of that town came and demanded to be allowed to force sex on these strangers (Gen. 19). Jesus compares flagrant immorality with a rejection of the good news, and he says the city associated with the former, Sodom, would bear less guilt.

"Chorazin...Bethsaida" (v. 13)— "Chorazin" is not otherwise mentioned in Scripture, which suggests that Jesus performed miracles we don't even know about. Bethsaida is the hometown of three of the apostles—Phillip, Andrew, and Peter. We know from Mark's Gospel that Jesus healed a blind man in Bethsaida (Mark 8:22).

"Tyre and Sidon" (v. 12)—The two port cities of Tyre and Sidon, on the shores of Phoenicia, appear several times in the Old Testament. After Israel enters the Promised Land, God's people fail to conquer Sidon (Judges 1:31), whose gods are mentioned on a couple of occasions (Judges 10:6–16; 1 Kings 11). Consequently, Sidon remained a Gentile city in northern Israel at the time of the Conquest led by Joshua in the thirteenth century BC. Later, in the time of the kings, temples in Jerusalem were built with materials from Tyre and Sidon—both the first temple (1 Chron. 22:4; 1 Kings 7:13–51) and the one Ezra rebuilt (Ezra 3:7). The Sidonian town of Zarephath (eight miles south) is where Elijah raised the widow's only son (1 Kings 17:8–24), a miracle Jesus keeps bringing up when contrasting Jewish and Gentile responses to God's truth. He seems to be saying, in short, that if the outsiders had been given as much opportunity to see miracles as were the insiders, the outsiders would have repented—unlike the insiders.

6. Jesus invested the twelve with power and authority to cast out demons. But they failed. Now the broader group of sent-ones return celebrating a different result. What are they rejoicing about (v. 17)? And what does Jesus say is a better source of joy (vv. 18–19)?

____

____

"I saw Satan fall" (v. 18). This could also be translated as "I was seeing Satan..."—not that Jesus got a glimpse of the past, but that he was actually present at the event. Centuries before the events Luke records, Isaiah wrote: "How you have fallen from heaven, morning star, son of the dawn! You have been cast down to the earth, you who once laid low the nations!" (Isa. 14:12). Many believe this refers to the fall of the accuser, and that the event happened before the fall of humanity in the Garden of Eden. Pride had lifted him, but God cast him down, though the evil one still has limited access to heaven for a time (Job 1). For Jesus to say he "saw Satan fall" speaks both of Jesus's existing before his own birth and of what little power fallen angels have in comparison with God. The demons' obedience to those sent by Christ should be expected, as Satan has always been subject to God's authority. Rejoicing over the obedience of those destined for defeat is short-sighted; eternal life sourced in the All-Powerful, pre-existent Christ who will defeat Satan with one little word—that's far better!

"Fall like lightning from heaven" (v. 18)—How does lightning fall from heaven? With a powerful, quick flash. If you blink, you miss it.

"Jesus rejoiced in the Holy Spirit" (v. 21). While on the subject of what people rejoice about, Luke includes what Jesus rejoices about in the Holy Spirit: that his Father, Lord of heaven and earth, has hidden these things from the wise and intelligent and revealed them to little children, which was his will. Notice the focus on humility. Also notice that all three persons of the Trinity are in view here.

7. Consider Luke's audience. The Gospel writer has focused on insiders/outsiders and how God's view differs from their own perspective of those who have standing before God. How does Jesus's contrast of wise/intelligent vs. little children support his argument?

8. Luke has also focused on exploring the question, "Who is Jesus?" What does v. 22 add to how readers are to answer this question?

---

9. On the subject of priorities in rejoicing, what does Jesus suggest makes the disciples extraordinarily blessed (vv. 23–24)?

---

10. What does the Law expert correctly say sums up the Law (v. 27)? Notice he does not define it as doing specific works, but rather the focus of one's love.

"Jesus said ... 'Do this, and you will live" (v. 28). "Jesus said... 'Go and do the same'" (v. 37). The Parable of the Good Samaritan begins with Jesus's exhortation to "do" what is life-giving. Then Jesus tells a story about how to be a neighbor, bookending the story with "Go and do."

11. How does this Law expert reveal that he is "wise and intelligent," yet he's missing the spirit of the Law (v. 29)?

---

12. Think about whom Jesus's listeners have identified as the insiders and whom they would have considered the outsiders in the story we know as "The Good Samaritan" (vv. 25–37)?

Priest	Insider	What does he do?	Is he a neighbor?
Levite	Insider	What does he do?	Is he a neighbor?
Samaritan	Outsider	What does he do?	Is he a neighbor?

"Priest" (v.31) – The descendants of Aaron, Moses's brother, comprise a subset of Levites. These people have responsibility for aspects of temple worship. Not all Levites are priests, but all priests are to be Levites. The priests are the first-class religious insiders.

"Levite" (v. 32) – Levites are the tribe descended from Jacob's son, Levi, but not of Aaron. They are second-class religious insiders.

"Samaritan" (v. 33) – Samaritans are the no-class outsiders to priests and Levites. In the previous chapter, Luke records a story about how Samaritans refused to show hospitality to Jesus and his disciples due to religious differences (9:52). To a Jewish person at the time of Jesus, a Samaritan was a mere half-breed with bad theology.

"Two silver coins" (v. 35)—Luke refers to specific coins: "denarii." Experts propose different values for a denarii. Some say their value equals two weeks' care; others estimate the amount to be enough to cover care for two months. A denarius equals either one or two days' earnings for the average worker—the same amount the Jews used to pay their annual temple tax. Regardless of amount, this Samaritan is very generous with a stranger.

> "By making a Samaritan, not a fellow Jew, the hero of his parable, Jesus was simultaneously critiquing his own people for not living up to God's commands and insisting that compassion must be shown across ethnic and religious boundaries."
>
> —John Dickson, *Bullies and Saints: An Honest Look at the Good and Evil of Christian History*

"The one who showed mercy to him" (v. 37) – It appears that the one speaking cannot even bring himself to say it: "the Samaritan."

13. Regardless of how much two denarii would purchase, what is extraordinary about the Samaritan's actions?

____

____

14. Notice that Jesus answers a question ("Who is my neighbor?") with a story followed by a question: "Which of these three do you think became a neighbor...?" (v. 36). What is the difference between helping someone properly defined as neighbor and becoming someone's neighbor?

____

____

"Mary, who sat at the Lord's feet and listened" (v. 39). In the Book of Acts, Luke will later write that Paul "sat at the feet of Gamaliel" (Acts 22:3). That is, Paul received his rabbinical instruction from Gamaliel. Here Mary is taking on the physical posture of a student with the first recorded rabbi in history to teach a female. She prioritized doing so over doing traditional women's work—domestic tasks. That is not to say such work is of little worth. Rather, she has priorities that go against cultural norms if adhering to such norms conflicts with gospel priorities.

15. What did Martha choose, and what did Mary choose that was better and lasting (v. 42)?

16. What priorities do you need to have, even if they challenge cultural norms?

Thursday: Getting the Point vs. Missing the Point

1. Pray for the Spirit to grant insight and read Luke 11.

> 11:1 Now Jesus was praying in a certain place. When he stopped, one of his disciples said to him, "Lord, teach us to pray, just as John taught his disciples." 2 So he said to them, "When you pray, say:
>
> 'Father, may your name be honored;
> may your kingdom come.
> 3 Give us each day our daily bread,
> 4 and forgive us our sins,
> for we also forgive everyone who sins against us.
> And do not lead us into temptation.'"
>
> 5 Then he said to them, "Suppose one of you has a friend, and you go to him at midnight and say to him, 'Friend, lend me three loaves of bread, 6 because a friend of mine has stopped here while on a journey, and I have nothing to set before him.' 7 Then he will reply from inside, 'Do not bother me. The door is already shut, and my children and I are in bed. I cannot get up and give you anything.' 8 I tell you, even though the man inside will not get up and give

him anything because he is his friend, yet because of the first man's sheer persistence he will get up and give him whatever he needs.

9 "So I tell you: Ask, and it will be given to you; seek, and you will find; knock, and the door will be opened for you. 10 For everyone who asks receives, and the one who seeks finds, and to the one who knocks, the door will be opened. 11 What father among you, if your son asks for a fish, will give him a snake instead of a fish? 12 Or if he asks for an egg, will give him a scorpion? 13 If you then, although you are evil, know how to give good gifts to your children, how much more will the heavenly Father give the Holy Spirit to those who ask him!"

14 Now he was casting out a demon that was mute. When the demon had gone out, the man who had been mute began to speak, and the crowds were amazed. 15 But some of them said, "By the power of Beelzebul, the ruler of demons, he casts out demons!" 16 Others, to test him, began asking for a sign from heaven. 17 But Jesus, realizing their thoughts, said to them, "Every kingdom divided against itself is destroyed, and a divided household falls. 18 So if Satan too is divided against himself, how will his kingdom stand? I ask you this because you claim that I cast out demons by Beelzebul. 19 Now if I cast out demons by Beelzebul, by whom do your sons cast them out? Therefore they will be your judges. 20 But if I cast out demons by the finger of God, then the kingdom of God has already overtaken you. 21 When a strong man, fully armed, guards his own palace, his possessions are safe. 22 But when a stronger man attacks and conquers him, he takes away the first man's armor on which the man relied and divides up his plunder. 23 Whoever is not with me is against me, and whoever does not gather with me scatters.

24 "When an unclean spirit goes out of a person, it passes through waterless places looking for rest but not finding any. Then it says, 'I will return to the home I left.' 25 When it returns, it finds the house swept clean and put in order. 26 Then it goes and brings seven other spirits more evil than itself, and they go in and live there, so the last state of that person is worse than the first."

27 As he said these things, a woman in the crowd spoke out to him, "Blessed is the womb that bore you and the breasts at which you nursed!" 28 But he replied, "Blessed rather are those who hear the word of God and obey it!"

29 As the crowds were increasing, Jesus began to say, "This generation is a wicked generation; it looks for a sign, but no sign will be given to it except the sign of Jonah. 30 For just as Jonah became a sign to the people of Nineveh, so the Son of Man will be

a sign to this generation. 31 The queen of the South will rise up at the judgment with the people of this generation and condemn them, because she came from the ends of the earth to hear the wisdom of Solomon—and now, something greater than Solomon is here! 32 The people of Nineveh will stand up at the judgment with this generation and condemn it, because they repented when Jonah preached to them—and now, something greater than Jonah is here!

33 "No one after lighting a lamp puts it in a hidden place or under a basket, but on a lampstand, so that those who come in can see the light. 34 Your eye is the lamp of your body. When your eye is healthy, your whole body is full of light, but when it is diseased, your body is full of darkness. 35 Therefore see to it that the light in you is not darkness. 36 If then your whole body is full of light, with no part in the dark, it will be as full of light as when the light of a lamp shines on you."

37 As he spoke, a Pharisee invited Jesus to have a meal with him, so he went in and took his place at the table. 38 The Pharisee was astonished when he saw that Jesus did not first wash his hands before the meal. 39 But the Lord said to him, "Now you Pharisees clean the outside of the cup and the plate, but inside you are full of greed and wickedness. 40 You fools! Didn't the one who made the outside make the inside as well? 41 But give from your heart to those in need, and then everything will be clean for you.

42 "But woe to you Pharisees! You give a tenth of your mint, rue, and every herb, yet you neglect justice and love for God! But you should have done these things without neglecting the others. 43 Woe to you Pharisees! You love the best seats in the synagogues and elaborate greetings in the marketplaces! 44 Woe to you! You are like unmarked graves, and people walk over them without realizing it!"

45 One of the experts in religious law answered him, "Teacher, when you say these things, you insult us too." 46 But Jesus replied, "Woe to you experts in religious law as well! You load people down with burdens difficult to bear, yet you yourselves refuse to touch the burdens with even one of your fingers! 47 Woe to you! You build the tombs of the prophets whom your ancestors killed. 48 So you testify that you approve of the deeds of your ancestors because they killed the prophets and you build their tombs! 49 For this reason also the wisdom of God said, 'I will send them prophets and apostles, some of whom they will kill and persecute,' 50 so that this generation may be held accountable for the blood of all the prophets that has been shed since the beginning of the world, 51 from the blood of Abel to the blood of Zechariah, who was killed between the

altar and the sanctuary. Yes, I tell you, it will be charged against this generation. 52 Woe to you experts in religious law! You have taken away the key to knowledge! You did not go in yourselves, and you hindered those who were going in."

53 When he went out from there, the experts in the law and the Pharisees began to oppose him bitterly and to ask him hostile questions about many things, 54 plotting against him to catch him in something he might say.

2. What are the priorities on Jesus's prayer list (vv. 2–4)?

____

____

"Do not lead us into temptation" (v. 4). We know from other places in Scripture that God does not tempt people to sin (James 1:13). The idea here, then, is asking God for help to avoid and overcome temptation—for God to lead away from sin and toward good, preventing the tempter from even having access. Remember from the Book of Job how the tempter had to get God's permission even to allow Job to be tested (Job 1:6–12)? The word translated in Luke as "tempted" could also be translated "testing" or "trials." It's not wrong for us to ask God to alleviate our trials, but our deliverance from evil itself is a desire on Jesus's lips. God is ultimately in control over all, including the evil one. The believer looks to God for help in succeeding where we, in our own strength, would fail. (For Protestants, the Lord's Prayer ends with, "for thine is the kingdom and the power and the glory forever." All this is true, but the benediction was added for public use and was not in Jesus's original prayer.)

3. Asking, seeking, and knocking seem to express the same idea using different images: God invites persistence. What do Jesus's words about prayer suggest about the Father's character (vv. 9–13)?

____

____

4. What seems to be the best gift of all to request (v. 13)?

____

"How much more will the heavenly Father give the Holy Spirit to those who ask him!" (v. 13). Since Pentecost, all who believe receive the Holy Spirit. But the Spirit's absence or presence does not actually seem to be what Jesus has in view here. In the context, the Lord is talking about persisting in prayer, persevering when we must keep waiting and asking. As we wait, we ask, "Help me be Spirit-filled," "Help me know your ways," and "Please, grant me wisdom." God delights in lavishing on us the Spirit to help us to wait well and live wisely in the circumstances in which we find ourselves.

5. For what do you need to ask the Spirit's help?

____

____

6. By what power do some think Jesus performs his miracles (vv. 15–16)? What is his argument as he counters their accusations (vv. 17–23)?

____

____

7. What is the actual source of Jesus's power and what are the ramifications (v. 20)?

____

____

8. In Jesus's example, who is the strong man and who is the stronger (vv. 21–22)?

____

____

9. How do you think Jesus felt when people accused him of exercising Satanic power? Have you ever been accused of doing evil when you were doing good?

10. In this conversation, what evidence do you find that Jesus has power over and understands how the spirit world operates (vv. 20–26)?

"A woman in the crowd spoke out to him, 'Blessed is the womb that bore you and the breasts at which you nursed!'" (v. 27) – This interaction is the third time in four chapters that Luke inserts a story that challenges traditional views of women's identity, role, and priorities. The first time, Jesus's mother and siblings have sought access to him, and he says his true mother and siblings are those who do God's will. Then, when Mary is sitting in theology class and Martha wants her to help in the kitchen, Jesus tells Martha that Mary is actually the one with the right priorities. Now, in this instance, a woman in the crowd is saying how Jesus's mother has received God's favor, as demonstrated by having such an awesome son. Jesus replies to this woman by saying that those who are actually blessed hear and obey God's word. The spiritual takes priority over the biological.

11. Do you prioritize your spiritual family? Are there members of your spiritual family who feel they don't belong? How can you help?

12. What does Jesus say his increasing crowds are looking for? And what evidence do they already have (vv. 29–32)?

"The queen of the South will rise up at the judgment ... because she came from the ends of the earth" (v. 31). We find this queen's story in 1 Kings 10:1–13 (and again in 2 Chron. 9:1–12). Her kingdom, Sheba, has been identified as being in either southern Arabia or Ethiopia in East Africa:

> 10:1 When the queen of Sheba heard about Solomon, she came to challenge him with difficult questions. 2 She arrived in Jerusalem with a great display of pomp, bringing with her camels carrying spices, a very large quantity of gold, and precious gems. She visited Solomon and discussed with him everything that was on her mind. 3 Solomon answered all her questions; there was no question too complex for the king. 4 When the queen of Sheba saw for herself Solomon's extensive wisdom, the palace he had built, 5 the food in his banquet hall, his servants and attendants, their robes, his cup-bearers, and his burnt offerings which he presented in the Lord's temple, she was amazed. 6 She said to the king, "The report I heard in my own country about your wise sayings and insight was true! 7 I did not believe these things until I came and saw them with my own eyes. Indeed, I didn't hear even half the story! Your wisdom and wealth surpass what was reported to me. 8 Your attendants, who stand before you at all times and hear your wise sayings, are truly happy! 9 May the Lord your God be praised because he favored you by placing you on the throne of Israel! Because of the Lord's eternal love for Israel, he made you king so you could make just and right decisions." 10 She gave the king 120 talents of gold, a very large quantity of spices, and precious gems. The quantity of spices the queen of Sheba gave King Solomon has never been matched. 11 (Hiram's fleet, which carried gold from Ophir, also brought from Ophir a very large quantity of fine timber and precious gems. 12 With the timber the king made supports for the Lord's temple and for the royal palace and stringed instruments for the musicians. No one has seen so much of this fine timber to this very day.) 13 King Solomon gave the queen of Sheba everything she requested, besides what he had freely offered her. Then she left and returned to her homeland with her attendants.

The queen's arrival with gold and spices (myrrh and frankincense?) looking for the wise one has been compared with magi who came bearing gold, frankincense, and myrrh to honor Wisdom in the flesh. Once again Luke cites Jesus as holding up a Gentile—and a woman, at that—to argue that those with limited "light" have welcomed God's revelation more than those who have much.

This passage had a different application in the fifteenth century when women were disallowed from testifying in the French court: Christine de Pizan argues in her book, *The City of Ladies*, that if Jesus said the Queen of the South will testify against a nation at the end of the age, surely a woman's nature cannot eliminate her from giving testimony in a local civil court.

"The people of Nineveh will stand up at the judgment with this generation and condemn it, because they repented" (v. 32). Jonah was God's prophet in Israel whom the Lord sent to Nineveh. Jonah was so unhappy about God showing mercy to Assyrians that he ran the other way, but God got the last word. And Nineveh repented. (You can find that story in the Book of Jonah.) In citing the Queen of the South pursuing wisdom and Nineveh repenting, Jesus (and Luke in telling these stories) has once again contrasted religious insiders with outsiders, and the outsiders come out looking better.

13. Luke is still answering the question, "Who is Jesus?" In this section, who is Jesus saying he is better than (vv. 29–32)?

____

____

14. In vv. 33–36, circle forms of the words for "light" and "darkness." Jesus talks about others being able to see the light. What do you think he means when he speaks of being "full of light" (v. 36)?

____

____

15. Jesus has been focusing on wisdom and love and repentance and being full of light. What offends the Pharisee about Jesus (v. 38)?

____

16. Summarize Jesus's sharp rebuke (vv. 39–44).

____

____

____

When a religious law expert tells Jesus he's insulting not only the Pharisees, but the lawyers too (v. 45), Jesus loads it on with three more "woes" for the lawyers.

17. Summarize his second round of rebukes (vv. 46–52). Notice Jesus reserves his harshest rebukes for people with full access to Scripture who are full of spiritual pride and hypocrisy.

"You build the tombs of the prophets whom your ancestors killed" (v. 46). Building a tomb is a sign of respect, as is visiting one. Yet, these religious leaders built tombs for the very people their ancestors killed and whose words they all dishonored. These leaders honored the prophets' deaths, but not their lives.

"The blood of all the prophets that has been shed since the beginning of the world, from the blood of Abel to the blood of Zechariah" (vv. 50–51). The first murder readers encounter in the Scriptures is the murder of righteous Abel by his brother, Cain (Gen. 4:1–16). Here Jesus describes Abel as one of the prophets.

The last murder recorded in the Hebrew Bible of Jesus's day (the books appeared in a different order then) was that of Zechariah the priest as he tried to preach to God's people in Judah. We find the story in 2 Chronicles 24:20–22; it took place at the time of King Joash (eighth or ninth century BC):

> 24:20 God's Spirit energized Zechariah son of Jehoiada the priest. He stood up before the people and said to them, "This is what God says: 'Why are you violating the commands of the Lord? You will not be prosperous. Because you have rejected the Lord, he has rejected you!'" 21 They plotted against him and by royal decree stoned him to death in the courtyard of the Lord's temple. 22 King Joash disregarded the loyalty Zechariah's father Jehoiada had shown him and killed Jehoiada's son. As Zechariah was dying, he said, "May the Lord take notice and seek vengeance!"

God's people have a long history of rejecting him and/or missing the point, while those with much less access to truth often do a better job of embracing it. Let that be a warning to those of us with much access to Scripture and to Bible teaching.

"You have taken away the key to knowledge! You did not go in yourselves, and you hindered those who were going in" (v. 52). Not only do Jesus's hearers, religious as they are, fail to enter the kingdom themselves, but by their rejection of the truth in how they live, they "throw away the key" that might allow others to enter through the door to knowledge. They are supposed to draw people to the light, but instead they prevent others from seeing the light. We see this phenomenon in every century—those who claim the name of God make his name odious to others by their actions.

18. Does Jesus's example change their hearts? What effect do his words have on their behavior (vv. 53–54)?

___

___

19. In what areas in your own life do you say and believe one thing, but do another?

___

___

20. Ask God to search your heart for attitudes of superiority toward others with less "light." Pray for yourself and for the church and her witness, that God's people would live lives consistent with the one we claim to follow.

Friday: Pursue Lasting Treasure

1. Pray for the Spirit to grant insight and then read Luke 12. Circle all the references to hypocrisy, to fear, and to lasting treasure.

> 12:1 Meanwhile, when many thousands of the crowd had gathered so that they were trampling on one another, Jesus began to speak first to his disciples, "Be on your guard against the yeast of the Pharisees, which is hypocrisy. 2 Nothing is hidden that will not be revealed, and nothing is secret that will not be made known. 3 So then whatever you have said in the dark will be heard in the light, and what you have whispered in private rooms will be proclaimed from the housetops.

4 "I tell you, my friends, do not be afraid of those who kill the body, and after that have nothing more they can do. 5 But I will warn you whom you should fear: Fear the one who, after the killing, has authority to throw you into hell. Yes, I tell you, fear him! 6 Aren't five sparrows sold for two pennies? Yet not one of them is forgotten before God. 7 In fact, even the hairs on your head are all numbered. Do not be afraid; you are more valuable than many sparrows.

8 "I tell you, whoever acknowledges me before men, the Son of Man will also acknowledge before God's angels. 9 But the one who denies me before men will be denied before God's angels. 10 And everyone who speaks a word against the Son of Man will be forgiven, but the person who blasphemes against the Holy Spirit will not be forgiven. 11 But when they bring you before the synagogues, the rulers, and the authorities, do not worry about how you should make your defense or what you should say, 12 for the Holy Spirit will teach you at that moment what you must say."

13 Then someone from the crowd said to him, "Teacher, tell my brother to divide the inheritance with me." 14 But Jesus said to him, "Man, who made me a judge or arbitrator between you two?" 15 Then he said to them, "Watch out and guard yourself from all types of greed because one's life does not consist in the abundance of his possessions." 16 He then told them a parable: "The land of a certain rich man produced an abundant crop, 17 so he thought to himself, 'What should I do, for I have nowhere to store my crops?' 18 Then he said, 'I will do this: I will tear down my barns and build bigger ones, and there I will store all my grain and my goods. 19 And I will say to myself, "You have plenty of goods stored up for many years; relax, eat, drink, celebrate!"' 20 But God said to him, 'You fool! This very night your life will be demanded back from you, but who will get what you have prepared for yourself?' 21 So it is with the one who stores up riches for himself, but is not rich toward God."

22 Then Jesus said to his disciples, "Therefore I tell you, do not worry about your life, what you will eat, or about your body, what you will wear. 23 For there is more to life than food, and more to the body than clothing. 24 Consider the ravens: They do not sow or reap, they have no storeroom or barn, yet God feeds them. How much more valuable are you than the birds! 25 And which of you by worrying can add an hour to his life? 26 So if you cannot do such a very little thing as this, why do you worry about the rest? 27 Consider how the flowers grow; they do not work or spin. Yet I tell you, not even Solomon in all his glory was clothed like one of

these! 28 And if this is how God clothes the wild grass, which is here today and tomorrow is tossed into the fire to heat the oven, how much more will he clothe you, you people of little faith! 29 So do not be overly concerned about what you will eat and what you will drink, and do not worry about such things. 30 For all the nations of the world pursue these things, and your Father knows that you need them. 31 Instead, pursue his kingdom, and these things will be given to you as well.

32 "Do not be afraid, little flock, for your Father is well pleased to give you the kingdom. 33 Sell your possessions and give to the poor. Provide yourselves purses that do not wear out—a treasure in heaven that never decreases, where no thief approaches and no moth destroys. 34 For where your treasure is, there your heart will be also.

35 "Get dressed for service and keep your lamps burning; 36 be like people waiting for their master to come back from the wedding celebration, so that when he comes and knocks, they can immediately open the door for him. 37 Blessed are those slaves whom their master finds alert when he returns! I tell you the truth, he will dress himself to serve, have them take their place at the table, and will come and wait on them! 38 Even if he comes in the second or third watch of the night and finds them alert, blessed are those slaves! 39 But understand this: If the owner of the house had known at what hour the thief was coming, he would not have let his house be broken into. 40 You also must be ready because the Son of Man will come at an hour when you do not expect him."

41 Then Peter said, "Lord, are you telling this parable for us or for everyone?" 42 The Lord replied, "Who then is the faithful and wise manager, whom the master puts in charge of his household servants, to give them their allowance of food at the proper time? 43 Blessed is that slave whom his master finds at work when he returns. 44 I tell you the truth, the master will put him in charge of all his possessions. 45 But if that slave should say to himself, 'My master is delayed in returning,' and he begins to beat the other slaves, both men and women, and to eat, drink, and get drunk, 46 then the master of that slave will come on a day when he does not expect him and at an hour he does not foresee, and will cut him in two, and assign him a place with the unfaithful. 47 That servant who knew his master's will but did not get ready or do what his master asked will receive a severe beating. 48 But the one who did not know his master's will and did things worthy of punishment will receive a light beating. From everyone who has been given much, much will be required, and from the one who has been entrusted with much, even more will be asked.

49 "I have come to bring fire on the earth—and how I wish it were already kindled! 50 I have a baptism to undergo, and how distressed I am until it is finished! 51 Do you think I have come to bring peace on earth? No, I tell you, but rather division! 52 For from now on there will be five in one household divided, three against two and two against three. 53 They will be divided, father against son and son against father, mother against daughter and daughter against mother, mother-in-law against her daughter-in-law and daughter-in-law against mother-in-law."

54 Jesus also said to the crowds, "When you see a cloud rising in the west, you say at once, 'A rainstorm is coming,' and it does. 55 And when you see the south wind blowing, you say, 'There will be scorching heat,' and there is. 56 You hypocrites! You know how to interpret the appearance of the earth and the sky, but how can you not know how to interpret the present time?

57 "And why don't you judge for yourselves what is right? 58 As you are going with your accuser before the magistrate, make an effort to settle with him on the way, so that he will not drag you before the judge, and the judge hand you over to the officer, and the officer throw you into prison. 59 I tell you, you will never get out of there until you have paid the very last cent!"

"Many thousands of the crowd had gathered ... Jesus began to speak first to his disciples" (v. 1). Notice Jesus's priority in training.

"Be on your guard against the yeast of the Pharisees, which is hypocrisy" (v. 1). After a scathing rebuke of the Pharisees and religious law experts, Jesus warns his disciples about what to do so they themselves will have a different end.

"So then whatever you have said in the dark will be heard in the light" (v. 3). Jesus had said something similar when he was going from town to town (see Luke 8:17). The person living a life in which his or her words, actions, and thoughts are consistent feels no fear when hearing all will be exposed. But the greatest horror for a hypocrite is exposure—and Jesus promises that one day all will be revealed. The appropriate response is repentance and confession.

2. Where do you see hypocrisy in yourself? Confess your sin to God ask him to help you stay on guard. Do you need to confess to another human?

___

3. We can fear God, or we can fear people. What does Jesus recommend and why (vv. 4–6)?

____

____

4. Jesus immediately follows his "fear God!" exhortation with reminders of God's care and the command to be unafraid. How do you reconcile being told to fear with being told to not be afraid? What reasons does Jesus give (v. 6)?

____

____

5. A righteous person lives consistently with the knowledge that God sees all, living not in the fear of humans, but in the fear of God, who has infinitely more power. How does this knowledge affect bearing witness to God in the face of human opposition (vv. 8–12)?

____

____

"When they bring you before the synagogues, the rulers, and the authorities" (v. 11) – Notice the sources of opposition—both Jew and Gentile. Persecution of the righteous has a long history of coming both from within and without.

6. Jesus is talking about God as judge of all, and a man in the crowd tries to pull Jesus into judging a legal dispute between this man and his brother. Even if the speaker has been treated unjustly (and we don't know if he has), Jesus looks beyond temporal concerns to eternal ones (vv. 13–21). He has just warned against hypocrisy. What does he warn to guard against in this situation, and what is his rationale (v. 15)?

____

____

7. Jesus, speaking to his disciples, continues his exhortation to prioritize eternal over temporal pursuits, using food and clothing as examples. What evidence does Jesus give of God's care in providing food (v. 24)? Of God's care in providing clothing (vv. 27–28)?

____

____

8. Contrast what Gentiles pursue (vv. 29–30) with what Jesus's followers are to pursue (v. 31).

____

____

"Little flock" (v. 32) – Throughout the Old Testament the prophets describe God as Israel's shepherd (e.g., Isaiah 40:11; Psalm 79:13; Ezekiel 34:11–24). The most famous is probably David's shepherd psalm, Psalm 23, which begins, "The Lord is my shepherd." In the New Testament, Jesus is the Good Shepherd who cares for his flock and seeks lost sheep (see John 10). Here, he addresses his audience affectionately as "little flock."

9. Earlier, Luke records Jesus talking about fear, including exhortations to fear God, yet not be afraid. Why does Jesus instruct God's "little flock" to be unafraid (v. 32)?

____

____

10. What two commands or imperatives does Jesus give for demonstrating that someone prioritizes kingdom investments over temporal concerns (v. 33)?

____

____

11. Jesus's kingdom is the opposite of what the world teaches. What kinds of purses are created by selling possessions? What kinds of treasures are created by giving to the poor (v. 33)?

____

____

____

12. It is often said that people will invest in what they love. But how does such thinking differ from the order Jesus lays out (v. 34)? Why do you think that is?

____

____

____

"Get dressed for service" (v. 35). More literally, "Let your loins stay girded." The picture is of a person prepared to run, with the outer garment tucked up in the belt to avoid tripping.

"Keep your lamps burning" (v. 35). In a world without electricity or matches, Jesus adds another idiom for staying ready.

"Be like people waiting for their master to come back from the wedding celebration" (v. 36). Jesus gives a third example of what it looks like to stay ready for the master's return. Wedding feasts could last for days, so the master at one such feast has stayed gone for a while. When he finally returns home after the long delay, he wants to find his staff ready for his arrival. He certainly doesn't want to stand outside pounding on the door and, upon entry, find his estate in disarray.

13. If this particular master is pleased with the vigilance of the servants, what will he do (v. 37)?

____

____

"Second or third watch of the night" (v. 38) – In the Jewish understanding, a night had three watches. The second or third watch fell between 10 PM and 6 AM. Romans had four watches, the second and third of which would fall between 9 PM and 3 AM. Regardless of which Jesus means here, the idea is clear—if the master returns in the middle of the night, at the least expected time, any slaves found dressed and waiting for him are blessed.

Jesus likens the owner's return to a thief in the night (vv. 39–40), and Peter wonders if Jesus is talking only to the disciples or to everyone (v. 41). But Jesus does not answer him directly. What does Jesus say is the fate of the slave whom the master finds working upon his return (vv. 42–44)?

14. What is the fate of the slave who "begins to beat the other slaves, both men and women, and to eat, drink, and get drunk," assuming the master will stay gone (v. 45–47)?

____

____

15. Why does the one who knew his masters will and disobeyed receive a more severe punishment than the slave who did not know the master's will and disobeyed (v. 48)?

____

____

16. Why are Jesus's words bad news for people given great spiritual privileges but who are still disobedient to what they know?

____

____

17. Following Jesus brings a great cost in this life. He says he will greatly divide households (vv. 49–53). What women does he say will be divided over him (v. 53)?

____

____

18. Jesus gives two indicators that the people know about predicting weather (vv. 54–56), yet he calls them hypocrites for failing to similarly read their present times. What signs are the people missing that announce the kingdom of God in their midst?

---

19. Jesus has been talking about the future, when God will judge the world. A focus on the future was supposed to affect how people acted in their earthly lives. What would it look like if the man who asked Jesus to serve as judge were to apply the commands Jesus gave in vv. 57–59?

Saturday: Rainmaker

Scripture: "Because of the first man's sheer persistence [his friend] will get up and give him whatever he needs" (Luke 11:9).

In the summer of 1998, our city—Dallas, Texas—had fifty-six days that registered more than 100 degrees. More than sixty days of ninety-plus temperatures passed without rain. On one of those days, while driving with my little girl, I spotted a grass fire. Alarmed, I called the fire department.

Several days later, we drove by the spot where the flames had scorched the earth. My daughter wanted to know, "Why is the ground black?" "Is it safe?" "What causes fires?"

I explained to her how the grass in our city needed a drink.

"What can we do?" she asked.

"Pray."

She insisted I do so immediately. "Pray now. Right now."

So, I focused on the highway and asked God for rain.

Seconds after I said "Amen," a drop splatted on my windshield. I looked around, thinking a passing truck was leaking fluid. Then splash! Another drop. And then another.

From her car seat, my daughter screamed, "HE SAID YES! HE SAID YES!"

I remember that story so vividly because such answers differ from the norm. My more typical reality is laboring for years to see a change in a heart, a provision, direction. In fact, years after this event happened, I recounted that story to a friend who said, envy in her voice, "I wish God would answer my prayers like that."

And honestly, I agree! I wish God would answer my prayers like that, too. All of them.

But he doesn't normally answer that quickly, and he purposefully won't. We know this, because Jesus taught his disciples to persist in asking—even to the point of annoyance, as if such a thing were possible. The one who is the exact representation of the Father told his followers to expect waiting as part of the process—and for that waiting to drive them to ask again. Then, he told a story....

Imagine a world without electricity in which an entire family sleeps in a one-room house. Everybody has to go to bed at the same time. The candles and fire must go out after everyone's all settled. The kids resist sleep. So you sing them lullabies. You tell their favorite stories. You get them the drinks they insist they must have. And finally, everyone drifts off to sleep.

But a few hours later, a noise jars you awake. You listen for it again. Someone's knocking on the window above your head. You sit up and strain to hear. Your friend whispers through the cracks in the wall. "You have to share some of your food. I have an unexpected guest, and the grocery store closed hours ago."

"Sorry. Can't help."

"Yes, you can! You have to help me!"

"I can't. Everybody's bedded down. I'll wake the kids if I crawl over them to get to the cupboard. Don't you have another friend you can ask?"

"Help me!"

"Sh-h-h! I can't."

"I'm not leaving till you help me."

"Ugh!" *She'll wake up everybody anyway if she keeps insisting,* you think, so you crawl over the family and scrounge around for leftovers.

Jesus said that's what prayer should be like. God loves his children. But even if his love were to have a limit, he would be moved to answer by our sheer persistence.

So keep knocking, seeking, asking.

For memorization: "If you then, although you are evil, know how to give good gifts to your children, how much more will the heavenly Father give the Holy Spirit to those who ask him!" (Luke 11:3).

Prayer: *Heavenly Father, teach me the patience of unanswered prayer. Help me persist in asking, seeking, and knocking. In the name of your Son, amen.*

Week 5 of 7

Jesus the Master Teacher (Luke 13–16)

Sunday: Jesus Frees the Captive

Scripture: "Thus Jesus asked, 'What is the kingdom of God like? To what should I compare it? It is like a mustard seed that a man took and sowed in his garden. It grew and became a tree, and the wild birds nested in its branches'" (Luke 13:18–19).

Jesus and his disciples are walking somewhere on a Sabbath, and they feed themselves by taking some heads of grain in a field. And what do the religious leaders do? They object, because Jesus and his team have done "work."

When this happens, Jesus reminds his listeners of a story in the Scriptures about how a priest gave David and his hungry men leftover consecrated bread on the Sabbath. Jesus concludes by declaring that the Son of Man is "lord of the Sabbath" (Luke 6:5).

Soon after that on another Sabbath, Jesus does something more public and equally unexpected: he heals a man with a withered hand (v. 10). Again, the Sabbath-police object, because their traditions have turned God's designated weekly day of rest into a time when they prohibit others from showing mercy.

In both scenarios, Jesus establishes himself as Lord of the Sabbath. He is not actually breaking Sabbath law; he is showing how their interpretation of Sabbath law has led to practices that actually contradict the intent of the day.

Now, it is yet another Saturday in the ancient Near East. Jesus is where we expect to find him—in the synagogue teaching. He sees a woman who has endured being bent over for eighteen years. (Do you remember what were you doing eighteen years ago? That's a long time.) Sometimes Luke attributes physical problems to disease, and sometimes he attributes them to spiritual bondage. In this case, he attributes the suffering to a disabling spirit (13:11).

The woman in question is not in line for healing. Instead, Jesus initiates the interaction. He spots her, he calls her over, and he says to her, "Woman, you are freed from your infirmity." Then, he places his hands on her.

Imagine her shock when she can stand straight. "Praise God!" she exclaims. For the first time in nearly two decades, she rises up vertical. Instead of seeing people's shoes she sees their faces. She stands slack-jawed. And the crowd marvels.

But the president of the synagogue scowls. Why? You guessed it—Jesus has healed, once again, on the Sabbath. So, what does the angry president do? Rather than address Jesus, the one who committed the so-called crime of working on the Sabbath, he turns to the least powerful person in the room, the woman who came expecting nothing but a worship service. And he bullies her: "There are six days on which work should be done," he insists. "So come and be healed on those days. But not on the Sabbath."

But the healer intervenes. He has no tolerance for grace-killing. Instead, he publicly answers the man with words intended for the entire group of joy-smashers: "You hypocrites! Does not each of you on the Sabbath loose his ox or his donkey from its stall and lead it to water? (Yes. Duh.) Then shouldn't this woman, a daughter of Abraham whom Satan bound for eighteen long years, be loosed from this imprisonment on the Sabbath day?"

The Anointed One indeed releases people from prison (Isa. 61:1; Luke 4:18)—just not the kind of prison in which John the Baptist was locked up. And isn't the Sabbath the best time to release a daughter of Abraham from such a prison? In suggesting as much, Jesus clarifies the true meaning of "Sabbath"—as a day for replacing bondage with freedom, a day for a shalom-fest. What better day to celebrate the rest of God and provide a reason for God's people to rejoice?

Jesus's response humiliates his adversaries, but the crowd loves what he has done. Jesus has freed a woman from prison, yet another evidence of the arrival of the kingdom.

Everyone looking forward to the kingdom has expected a king to ride into Jerusalem on a trusty steed and overtake their occupiers, the Romans. But in Jesus's first coming, he brings a different kind of deliverance, freeing captives from different kinds of prisons.

Seeing the opportunity to help his listeners understand how his kingdom differs from what they expect, Jesus borrows examples from the farm and from domestic space. First, he compares the kingdom to a mustard seed. Sure, such seeds are smaller than a pinhead, but they grow large enough to support birds' nests. The kingdom is like that. And the kingdom is also like yeast—"that a woman takes and mixes with three measures of flour until all the dough rises." Yeast infiltrates invisibly, changing everything.

That's what the kingdom is like. Jesus is the Lord of the Sabbath, the freer of captives, the defender of the bullied, the King of the Kingdom. And he changes everything.

For memorization: "Again he [Jesus] said, 'To what should I compare the kingdom of God? It is like yeast that a woman took and mixed with three measures of flour until all the dough had risen'" (Luke 13:20–21).

Prayer: *Thank you, Father, that you grant rest. That you see us when we're invisible, strengthen us when we're weak, free us from spiritual bondage. Purify us from our hypocrisy. And make us fit for your glorious upside-down kingdom. Thank you for sending your beloved Son, in whose name we pray through the power of the Spirit, Amen.*

Monday: King of the Upside-Down Kingdom

1. Pray for insight and read Luke 13–16. Circle every use of the world "repent."

> 13:1 Now there were some present on that occasion who told him about the Galileans whose blood Pilate had mixed with their sacrifices. 2 He answered them, "Do you think these Galileans were worse sinners than all the other Galileans because they suffered these things? 3 No, I tell you! But unless you repent, you will all

perish as well! 4 Or those eighteen who were killed when the tower in Siloam fell on them, do you think they were worse offenders than all the others who live in Jerusalem? 5 No, I tell you! But unless you repent you will all perish as well!"

6 Then Jesus told this parable: "A man had a fig tree planted in his vineyard, and he came looking for fruit on it and found none. 7 So he said to the worker who tended the vineyard, 'For three years now, I have come looking for fruit on this fig tree, and each time I inspect it I find none. Cut it down! Why should it continue to deplete the soil?' 8 But the worker answered him, 'Sir, leave it alone this year too, until I dig around it and put fertilizer on it. 9 Then if it bears fruit next year, very well, but if not, you can cut it down.'"

10 Now he was teaching in one of the synagogues on the Sabbath, 11 and a woman was there who had been disabled by a spirit for eighteen years. She was bent over and could not straighten herself up completely. 12 When Jesus saw her, he called her to him and said, "Woman, you are freed from your infirmity." 13 Then he placed his hands on her, and immediately she straightened up and praised God. 14 But the president of the synagogue, indignant because Jesus had healed on the Sabbath, said to the crowd, "There are six days on which work should be done! So come and be healed on those days, and not on the Sabbath day." 15 Then the Lord answered him, "You hypocrites! Does not each of you on the Sabbath untie his ox or his donkey from its stall and lead it to water? 16 Then shouldn't this woman, a daughter of Abraham whom Satan bound for eighteen long years, be released from this imprisonment on the Sabbath day?" 17 When he said this, all his adversaries were humiliated, but the entire crowd was rejoicing at all the wonderful things he was doing.

18 Thus Jesus asked, "What is the kingdom of God like? To what should I compare it? 19 It is like a mustard seed that a man took and sowed in his garden. It grew and became a tree, and the wild birds nested in its branches."

20 Again he said, "To what should I compare the kingdom of God? 21 It is like yeast that a woman took and mixed with three measures of flour until all the dough had risen."

22 Then Jesus traveled throughout towns and villages, teaching and making his way toward Jerusalem. 23 Someone asked him, "Lord, will only a few be saved?" So he said to them, 24 "Exert every effort to enter through the narrow door because many, I tell you, will try to enter and will not be able to. 25 Once the head of the house gets up and shuts the door, then you will stand outside and start to knock on the door and beg him, 'Lord, let us in!' But he will

answer you, 'I don't know where you come from.' 26 Then you will begin to say, 'We ate and drank in your presence, and you taught in our streets.' 27 But he will reply, 'I don't know where you come from! Go away from me, all you evildoers!' 28 There will be weeping and gnashing of teeth when you see Abraham, Isaac, Jacob, and all the prophets in the kingdom of God but you yourselves thrown out. 29 Then people will come from east and west, and from north and south, and take their places at the banquet table in the kingdom of God. 30 But indeed, some are last who will be first, and some are first who will be last."

31 At that time, some Pharisees came up and said to Jesus, "Get away from here because Herod wants to kill you." 32 But he said to them, "Go and tell that fox, 'Look, I am casting out demons and performing healings today and tomorrow, and on the third day I will complete my work. 33 Nevertheless I must go on my way today and tomorrow and the next day, because it is impossible that a prophet should be killed outside Jerusalem.' 34 O Jerusalem, Jerusalem, you who kill the prophets and stone those who are sent to you! How often I have longed to gather your children together as a hen gathers her chicks under her wings, but you would have none of it! 35 Look, your house is forsaken! And I tell you, you will not see me until you say, 'Blessed is the one who comes in the name of the Lord!'"

14:1 Now one Sabbath when Jesus went to dine at the house of a leader of the Pharisees, they were watching him closely. 2 There right in front of him was a man whose body was swollen with fluid. 3 So Jesus asked the experts in religious law and the Pharisees, "Is it lawful to heal on the Sabbath or not?" 4 But they remained silent. So Jesus took hold of the man, healed him, and sent him away. 5 Then he said to them, "Which of you, if you have a son or an ox that has fallen into a well on a Sabbath day, will not immediately pull him out?" 6 But they could not reply to this.

7 Then when Jesus noticed how the guests chose the places of honor, he told them a parable. He said to them, 8 "When you are invited by someone to a wedding feast, do not take the place of honor because a person more distinguished than you may have been invited by your host. 9 So the host who invited both of you will come and say to you, 'Give this man your place.' Then, ashamed, you will begin to move to the least important place. 10 But when you are invited, go and take the least important place, so that when your host approaches he will say to you, 'Friend, move up here to a better place.' Then you will be honored in the presence of all who share the meal with you. 11 For everyone who exalts himself will be humbled, but the one who humbles himself will be exalted."

12 He said also to the man who had invited him, "When you host a dinner or a banquet, don't invite your friends or your brothers or your relatives or rich neighbors so you can be invited by them in return and get repaid. 13 But when you host an elaborate meal, invite the poor, the crippled, the lame, and the blind. 14 Then you will be blessed because they cannot repay you, for you will be repaid at the resurrection of the righteous."

15 When one of those at the meal with Jesus heard this, he said to him, "Blessed is everyone who will feast in the kingdom of God!" 16 But Jesus said to him, "A man once gave a great banquet and invited many guests. 17 At the time for the banquet he sent his slave to tell those who had been invited, 'Come, because everything is now ready.' 18 But one after another they all began to make excuses. The first said to him, 'I have bought a field, and I must go out and see it. Please excuse me.' 19 Another said, 'I have bought five yoke of oxen, and I am going out to examine them. Please excuse me.' 20 Another said, 'I just got married, and I cannot come.' 21 So the slave came back and reported this to his master. Then the master of the household was furious and said to his slave, 'Go out quickly to the streets and alleys of the city, and bring in the poor, the crippled, the blind, and the lame.' 22 Then the slave said, 'Sir, what you instructed has been done, and there is still room.' 23 So the master said to his slave, 'Go out to the highways and country roads and urge people to come in, so that my house will be filled. 24 For I tell you, not one of those individuals who were invited will taste my banquet!'"

25 Now large crowds were accompanying Jesus, and turning to them he said, 26 "If anyone comes to me and does not hate his own father and mother, and wife and children, and brothers and sisters, and even his own life, he cannot be my disciple. 27 Whoever does not carry his own cross and follow me cannot be my disciple. 28 For which of you, wanting to build a tower, doesn't sit down first and compute the cost to see if he has enough money to complete it? 29 Otherwise, when he has laid a foundation and is not able to finish the tower, all who see it will begin to make fun of him. 30 They will say, 'This man began to build and was not able to finish!' 31 Or what king, going out to confront another king in battle, will not sit down first and determine whether he is able with 10,000 to oppose the one coming against him with 20,000? 32 If he cannot succeed, he will send a representative while the other is still a long way off and ask for terms of peace. 33 In the same way therefore not one of you can be my disciple if he does not renounce all his own possessions.

34 "Salt is good, but if salt loses its flavor, how can its flavor be restored? 35 It is of no value for the soil or for the manure pile; it is to be thrown out. The one who has ears to hear had better listen!"

15:1 Now all the tax collectors and sinners were coming to hear him. 2 But the Pharisees and the experts in the law were complaining, "This man welcomes sinners and eats with them."

3 So Jesus told them this parable: 4 "Which one of you, if he has a hundred sheep and loses one of them, would not leave the ninety-nine in the open pasture and go look for the one that is lost until he finds it? 5 Then when he has found it, he places it on his shoulders, rejoicing. 6 Returning home, he calls together his friends and neighbors, telling them, 'Rejoice with me because I have found my sheep that was lost.' 7 I tell you, in the same way there will be more joy in heaven over one sinner who repents than over ninety-nine righteous people who have no need to repent.

8 "Or what woman, if she has ten silver coins and loses one of them, does not light a lamp, sweep the house, and search thoroughly until she finds it? 9 Then when she has found it, she calls together her friends and neighbors, saying, 'Rejoice with me, for I have found the coin that I had lost.' 10 In the same way, I tell you, there is joy in the presence of God's angels over one sinner who repents."

11 Then Jesus said, "A man had two sons. 12 The younger of them said to his father, 'Father, give me the share of the estate that will belong to me.' So he divided his assets between them. 13 After a few days, the younger son gathered together all he had and left on a journey to a distant country, and there he squandered his wealth with a wild lifestyle. 14 Then after he had spent everything, a severe famine took place in that country, and he began to be in need. 15 So he went and worked for one of the citizens of that country, who sent him to his fields to feed pigs. 16 He was longing to eat the carob pods the pigs were eating, but no one gave him anything. 17 But when he came to his senses, he said, 'How many of my father's hired workers have food enough to spare, but here I am dying from hunger! 18 I will get up and go to my father and say to him, "Father, I have sinned against heaven and against you. 19 I am no longer worthy to be called your son; treat me like one of your hired workers."' 20 So he got up and went to his father. But while he was still a long way from home his father saw him, and his heart went out to him; he ran and hugged his son and kissed him. 21 Then his son said to him, 'Father, I have sinned against heaven and against you; I am no longer worthy to be called your son.' 22 But the father said to his slaves, 'Hurry! Bring the best

robe, and put it on him! Put a ring on his finger and sandals on his feet! 23 Bring the fattened calf and kill it! Let us eat and celebrate, 24 because this son of mine was dead, and is alive again—he was lost and is found!' So they began to celebrate.

25 "Now his older son was in the field. As he came and approached the house, he heard music and dancing. 26 So he called one of the slaves and asked what was happening. 27 The slave replied, 'Your brother has returned, and your father has killed the fattened calf because he got his son back safe and sound.' 28 But the older son became angry and refused to go in. His father came out and appealed to him, 29 but he answered his father, 'Look! These many years I have worked like a slave for you, and I never disobeyed your commands. Yet you never gave me even a goat so that I could celebrate with my friends! 30 But when this son of yours came back, who has devoured your assets with prostitutes, you killed the fattened calf for him!' 31 Then the father said to him, 'Son, you are always with me, and everything that belongs to me is yours. 32 It was appropriate to celebrate and be glad, for your brother was dead, and is alive; he was lost and is found.'"

16:1 Jesus also said to the disciples, "There was a rich man who was informed of accusations that his manager was wasting his assets. 2 So he called the manager in and said to him, 'What is this I hear about you? Turn in the account of your administration, because you can no longer be my manager.' 3 Then the manager said to himself, 'What should I do, since my master is taking my position away from me? I'm not strong enough to dig, and I'm too ashamed to beg. 4 I know what to do so that when I am put out of management, people will welcome me into their homes.' 5 So he contacted his master's debtors one by one. He asked the first, 'How much do you owe my master?' 6 The man replied, '100 measures of olive oil.' The manager said to him, 'Take your bill, sit down quickly, and write 50.' 7 Then he said to another, 'And how much do you owe?' The second man replied, '100 measures of wheat.' The manager said to him, 'Take your bill, and write 80.' 8 The master commended the dishonest manager because he acted shrewdly. For the people of this world are more shrewd in dealing with their contemporaries than the people of light. 9 And I tell you, make friends for yourselves by how you use worldly wealth, so that when it runs out, you will be welcomed into the eternal homes.

10 "The one who is faithful in a very little is also faithful in much, and the one who is dishonest in a very little is also dishonest in much. 11 If then you haven't been trustworthy in handling worldly wealth, who will entrust you with the true riches? 12 And

if you haven't been trustworthy with someone else's property, who will give you your own? 13 No servant can serve two masters, for either he will hate the one and love the other, or he will be devoted to the one and despise the other. You cannot serve God and money."

14 The Pharisees (who loved money) heard all this and ridiculed him. 15 But Jesus said to them, "You are the ones who justify yourselves in men's eyes, but God knows your hearts. For what is highly prized among men is utterly detestable in God's sight.

16 "The law and the prophets were in force until John; since then, the good news of the kingdom of God has been proclaimed, and everyone is urged to enter it. 17 But it is easier for heaven and earth to pass away than for one tiny stroke of a letter in the law to become void.

18 "Everyone who divorces his wife and marries someone else commits adultery, and the one who marries a woman divorced from her husband commits adultery.

19 "There was a rich man who dressed in purple and fine linen and who feasted sumptuously every day. 20 But at his gate lay a poor man named Lazarus whose body was covered with sores, 21 who longed to eat what fell from the rich man's table. In addition, the dogs came and licked his sores.

22 "Now the poor man died and was carried by the angels to Abraham's side. The rich man also died and was buried. 23 And in Hades, as he was in torment, he looked up and saw Abraham far off with Lazarus at his side. 24 So he called out, 'Father Abraham, have mercy on me, and send Lazarus to dip the tip of his finger in water and cool my tongue because I am in anguish in this fire.' 25 But Abraham said, 'Child, remember that in your lifetime you received your good things and Lazarus likewise bad things, but now he is comforted here and you are in anguish. 26 Besides all this, a great chasm has been fixed between us, so that those who want to cross over from here to you cannot do so, and no one can cross from there to us.' 27 So the rich man said, 'Then I beg you, father—send Lazarus to my father's house 28 (for I have five brothers) to warn them so that they don't come into this place of torment.' 29 But Abraham said, 'They have Moses and the prophets; they must respond to them.' 30 Then the rich man said, 'No, father Abraham, but if someone from the dead goes to them, they will repent.' 31 He replied to him, 'If they do not respond to Moses and the prophets, they will not be convinced even if someone rises from the dead.'"

2. What does the text suggest repentance looks like?

---

3. Spend some time in prayer repenting and asking God to help you in areas where you need to change.

Tuesday: The Ruler of the Heart

1. Pray for the Spirit to grant insight and read Luke 13. Put a star by Jesus's teaching on repentance.

> 13:1 Now there were some present on that occasion who told him about the Galileans whose blood Pilate had mixed with their sacrifices. 2 He answered them, "Do you think these Galileans were worse sinners than all the other Galileans because they suffered these things? 3 No, I tell you! But unless you repent, you will all perish as well! 4 Or those eighteen who were killed when the tower in Siloam fell on them, do you think they were worse offenders than all the others who live in Jerusalem? 5 No, I tell you! But unless you repent you will all perish as well!"
>
> 6 Then Jesus told this parable: "A man had a fig tree planted in his vineyard, and he came looking for fruit on it and found none. 7 So he said to the worker who tended the vineyard, 'For three years now, I have come looking for fruit on this fig tree, and each time I inspect it I find none. Cut it down! Why should it continue to deplete the soil?' 8 But the worker answered him, 'Sir, leave it alone this year too, until I dig around it and put fertilizer on it. 9 Then if it bears fruit next year, very well, but if not, you can cut it down.'"
>
> 10 Now he was teaching in one of the synagogues on the Sabbath, 11 and a woman was there who had been disabled by a spirit for eighteen years. She was bent over and could not straighten herself up completely. 12 When Jesus saw her, he called her to him and said, "Woman, you are freed from your infirmity." 13 Then he placed his hands on her, and immediately she straightened up and praised God. 14 But the president of the synagogue, indignant because Jesus had healed on the Sabbath, said to the

crowd, "There are six days on which work should be done! So come and be healed on those days, and not on the Sabbath day." 15 Then the Lord answered him, "You hypocrites! Does not each of you on the Sabbath untie his ox or his donkey from its stall and lead it to water? 16 Then shouldn't this woman, a daughter of Abraham whom Satan bound for eighteen long years, be released from this imprisonment on the Sabbath day?" 17 When he said this, all his adversaries were humiliated, but the entire crowd was rejoicing at all the wonderful things he was doing.

18 Thus Jesus asked, "What is the kingdom of God like? To what should I compare it? 19 It is like a mustard seed that a man took and sowed in his garden. It grew and became a tree, and the wild birds nested in its branches."

20 Again he said, "To what should I compare the kingdom of God? 21 It is like yeast that a woman took and mixed with three measures of flour until all the dough had risen."

22 Then Jesus traveled throughout towns and villages, teaching and making his way toward Jerusalem. 23 Someone asked him, "Lord, will only a few be saved?" So he said to them, 24 "Exert every effort to enter through the narrow door because many, I tell you, will try to enter and will not be able to. 25 Once the head of the house gets up and shuts the door, then you will stand outside and start to knock on the door and beg him, 'Lord, let us in!' But he will answer you, 'I don't know where you come from.' 26 Then you will begin to say, 'We ate and drank in your presence, and you taught in our streets.' 27 But he will reply, 'I don't know where you come from! Go away from me, all you evildoers!' 28 There will be weeping and gnashing of teeth when you see Abraham, Isaac, Jacob, and all the prophets in the kingdom of God but you yourselves thrown out. 29 Then people will come from east and west, and from north and south, and take their places at the banquet table in the kingdom of God. 30 But indeed, some are last who will be first, and some are first who will be last."

31 At that time, some Pharisees came up and said to Jesus, "Get away from here because Herod wants to kill you." 32 But he said to them, "Go and tell that fox, 'Look, I am casting out demons and performing healings today and tomorrow, and on the third day I will complete my work. 33 Nevertheless I must go on my way today and tomorrow and the next day, because it is impossible that a prophet should be killed outside Jerusalem.' 34 O Jerusalem, Jerusalem, you who kill the prophets and stone those who are sent to you! How often I have longed to gather your children together as a hen gathers her chicks under her wings, but you would have none of

it! 35 Look, your house is forsaken! And I tell you, you will not see me until you say, 'Blessed is the one who comes in the name of the Lord!'"

"The Galileans whose blood Pilate had mixed with their sacrifices" (v. 1) – Although the story to which Jesus refers here is not one written in the Scriptures, the Jewish historian Josephus (born AD 37 in Jerusalem) records similar incidents. In Jesus's story, apparently some Jewish people had been offering animal sacrifices to God in the Jerusalem temple. Pilate had these people killed and their blood mixed with that of the animals. An abomination! A human intentionally caused this unjust suffering. Yet those observing wondered if the victims were responsible. Or if what happened was part of God's judgment. Jesus challenges such a cause/effect relationship between sin and suffering.

"But unless you repent, you will all perish as well!" (v. 3). Rather than assuming evil of the people who are suffering or even thinking their trouble is a consequence of actions by the community around them, Jesus says the better interpretation of such misfortune is that all who see it have an opportunity to search their own hearts and repent.

"Those eighteen who were killed when the tower in Siloam fell on them" (v. 4) – Jesus uses another tragedy known to his listeners to correct their thinking. A tower in Jerusalem fell on eighteen people, crushing them to death. Jesus asks those who know about it, "Do you think [the victims] were worse offenders than all the others who live in Jerusalem?" The question assumes the answer is "no." God did not single out those who died for punishment. They did nothing wrong. In this example the tragedy is not at the hands of humans, as was the previous suffering mentioned (which Pilate caused). But the people's response to tragedy should be the same: Repent (v. 5). In Jesus's story people died without warning. How does someone prepare for such an eventuality? They (and we) repent.

When terrorists attacked the U.S. on September 11, 2001, preachers speculated that the nearly three thousand deaths came as punishment from God. On the day after Christmas in 2003 when an earthquake hit the Iranian city of Bam, some theologians said people were killed as a punishment from God. Terrorists caused one of these tragedies; an earthquake caused the other. But both incidents received their share of faulty theological interpretations. Jesus's examples suggest that the only finger pointing in response to tragedy—whether at human hands or not—should be to point to oneself, seeing in tragedy a reminder of life's brevity, and to repent.

2. Of what do you need to repent?

___

___

3. For what was the fig-planter looking in his tree (v. 6)? In the parable of the fig tree, in what way is the farmer like God?

___

___

4. In Jesus's examples (blood-filled sacrifices, falling tower), the Lord focused on the need for repentance. What need is revealed in the parable of the fig tree?

___

___

5. Consider the fruit of the Spirit: love, joy, peace, patience, kindness, goodness, gentleness, faithfulness, and self-control (Gal. 5:22–23). Ask the Spirit to show where you lack good fruit. Pray, yielding these areas of your life and asking for Spirit-led transformation.

___

___

"The head of the house" (v. 25) – The word "head" in English carries the idea of authority, but in Koine Greek—the original language of the New Testament—someone reading about the head of a house probably would have pictured a literal house with a head-on top. The "head of house" is not a New Testament term, it's an old United States tax-system term. The Greek term (it's one word) that Luke uses here is a compound word joining "house" + "ruler" (*despotes*, from which we get "despot"), the latter of which usually means "lord" or "master."

"There will be weeping and gnashing of teeth when you see Abraham, Isaac, Jacob, and all the prophets in the kingdom of God" (v. 28). The men cited are the ancestors and religious leaders through whom Jesus's listeners think they have access to God. These were Jewish people who will be in the kingdom because they believed. (And even though their names are not stated, the prophets Miriam and Huldah and Anna and others are included here.)

"People will come from east and west, and from north and south, and take their places at the banquet table in the kingdom of God" (v. 29). The "nations" are not those generally envisioned as having a place at the table in the kingdom. Yet Jesus is saying the kingdom consists of Gentiles! This revelation would have come as a shock, perhaps a distasteful one, to many in the Lord's audience.

"But indeed, some are last who will be first, and some are first who will be last" (v. 30). This sentence could be a slogan for the kingdom. And it's not what the people expect. In their minds, the "kingdom" belongs to the group that shares a pedigree that's both ethnic and religiously observant. But Jesus smashes that expectation, saying the kingdom is for the humble, the repentant, and includes non-Jewish people.

6. Some of Jesus's listeners ask how many people will be in the kingdom. The Lord here redirects the focus (vv. 25–30). He describes a time when repentance comes too late. What does he envision as an appropriate response to his warning (v. 24)?

---

7. Remember back in the Samaritan village—when the people refused hospitality because Jesus was headed to Jerusalem (9:53)? As Jesus continues to travel toward his destination, he teaches in towns and villages along the way—and he is speaking to fellow Jews (13:22). In his discussion about who will and won't be saved, who are the insiders and who are the outsiders (vv. 22–30)? How does his vision of the kingdom differ from what his listeners would have expected?

"At that time, some Pharisees came up and said to Jesus, "Get away from here because Herod wants to kill you" (v. 31). Jesus's answer, which turned upside down the people's kingdom expectations, would have burned the religious leaders. Their discomfort is probably behind why they appeal to Herod to try to get Jesus to leave their territory. The Herod to whom the Pharisees refer here is Herod Antipas, the half-Samaritan, half-Idumean tetrarch whom we met in Luke 3:1. He was the son of Herod the Great, and he had a long reign of forty-two years.

"Go and tell that fox" (v. 32) – "Fox" is the nickname Jesus gives to the ruler who ordered his righteous relative, John (the Baptist), to die by beheading just to gratify a dancer. My late colleague Harold Hoehner, who wrote the definitive work on Herod Antipas, said that a person designated a "fox" at this time was "an insignificant or base person. He lacks real power and dignity, and uses cunning deceit to achieve his aims."[2] The prophet Ezekiel identified foxes with foolishness (Ezek. 13:4). Notice how Jesus does not allow himself to let fear drive him off mission.

"I am casting out demons and performing healings today and tomorrow, and on the third day I will complete my work" (v. 32). Jesus had clarity about the work God called him to do. His listeners would have heard his third-day reference as meaning he planned to stay in their geographical area for a literal three days—today, tomorrow, and the next day. But Jesus ultimately completed the work he came to do on earth "on the third day"—that is, on the day of resurrection. Doubtless, only after he was raised would it have dawned on Jesus's followers what he meant here—a prophetic prediction and a statement of purpose. Nevertheless, Jesus will indeed leave this physical locale in three literal days and go to Jerusalem. He goes on to tell why…

"Because it is impossible that a prophet should be killed outside Jerusalem. O Jerusalem, Jerusalem, you who kill the prophets and stone those who are sent to you!" (vv. 33–34). Jesus is not saying all Jewish prophet-martyrs have been killed inside Jerusalem. Earlier, he referred to Abel as a prophet/martyr (11:51), and Jerusalem did not even exist in Abel's day. Instead, Jesus's listeners probably heard his words as sad irony. Jerusalem was the city of the prophets. It was home to the temple, the sacrifices, the high priests, the experts in Moses's law, the religious leaders. It was Ground Zero for Jewish belief and practice. Of all places, Jerusalem should

2. H. W. Hoehner, *Herod Antipas* [SNTSMS], 347.

have welcomed prophets most enthusiastically. But instead, it had a reputation for smashing those who critiqued it. When prophets came declaring to the descendants of Abraham that they needed to repent, these mouthpieces of God often suffered persecution and were even killed. Jesus identifies himself here as a prophet of God headed to the place where people kill prophets. He knows what will happen, but he will go anyway.

8. Later in the Gospel of Luke, Jesus will cry over Jerusalem (19:41). What is Jesus's emotional response to Jerusalem as recorded here (v. 34)?

---

9. Jesus likens himself to a hen gathering chicks under her wings, a common biblical simile for a mother bird's loving care (Ps. 36:7) and refuge (Ruth 2:12; Ps. 17:8). At the first sign of a predator, a mother hen covers her vulnerable offspring. In what way is Jesus a loving refuge to his followers? What sort of evil threatens God's people?

"Look, your house is forsaken!" (v. 35). Throughout this passage, Jesus demonstrates that God woos his people, but those who claim to be his followers reject him. They want the benefits of God, but not the associated costs. As a result, their house has been abandoned.

"You will not see me until you say, 'Blessed is the one who comes in the name of the Lord!'" (v. 35). Jesus's final pronouncement is that it will be a long time before any hope of restoration happens. People well-versed in the Holy Week accounts of Jesus life will recognize the words "Blessed is he who comes in the name of the Lord" and may think Jesus is saying these words will be fulfilled when Jesus makes his triumphal entry into Jerusalem. But the context here is actually the rejection of God's own people, the ultimate example of which will be Jesus's crucifixion. Looking ahead, when we get to Luke's account of Jesus's entry into Jerusalem, we will see the author borrowing this quote again (Luke 19:38). In fact, three times in his Gospel, Luke references Psalm 118, from which Jesus quotes. Pilgrims chanted this psalm as they ascended into Jerusalem for festivals:

Please, Lord, deliver!
Please, Lord, grant us success!
May the one who comes in the name of the Lord be blessed.
We will pronounce blessings on you in the Lord's temple. (Ps. 118:25–26)

For now, make a mental note that Jesus makes this statement in the context of grief over his own people's rejection of him. He is looking much further into the future to a day when Israel will acknowledge him for who he really is and receive his blessing.

10. Although Jesus knew he would be crucified in Jerusalem, he refused to let fear drive him off mission. In what ways do you need to push through your own fears to follow Christ?

____

____

Wednesday: The Cost of Disipleship

1. Pray for the Holy Spirit's help in understanding, and then read Luke 14. Put a star by evidences of pride.

14:1 Now one Sabbath when Jesus went to dine at the house of a leader of the Pharisees, they were watching him closely. 2 There right in front of him was a man whose body was swollen with fluid. 3 So Jesus asked the experts in religious law and the Pharisees, "Is it lawful to heal on the Sabbath or not?" 4 But they remained silent. So Jesus took hold of the man, healed him, and sent him away. 5 Then he said to them, "Which of you, if you have a son or an ox that has fallen into a well on a Sabbath day, will not immediately pull him out?" 6 But they could not reply to this.

7 Then when Jesus noticed how the guests chose the places of honor, he told them a parable. He said to them, 8 "When you are invited by someone to a wedding feast, do not take the place of honor because a person more distinguished than you may have been invited by your host. 9 So the host who invited both of you will come and say to you, 'Give this man your place.' Then, ashamed, you will begin to move to the least important place. 10 But when you are invited, go and take the least important place, so that when

your host approaches he will say to you, 'Friend, move up here to a better place.' Then you will be honored in the presence of all who share the meal with you. 11 For everyone who exalts himself will be humbled, but the one who humbles himself will be exalted."

12 He said also to the man who had invited him, "When you host a dinner or a banquet, don't invite your friends or your brothers or your relatives or rich neighbors so you can be invited by them in return and get repaid. 13 But when you host an elaborate meal, invite the poor, the crippled, the lame, and the blind. 14 Then you will be blessed because they cannot repay you, for you will be repaid at the resurrection of the righteous."

15 When one of those at the meal with Jesus heard this, he said to him, "Blessed is everyone who will feast in the kingdom of God!" 16 But Jesus said to him, "A man once gave a great banquet and invited many guests. 17 At the time for the banquet he sent his slave to tell those who had been invited, 'Come, because everything is now ready.' 18 But one after another they all began to make excuses. The first said to him, 'I have bought a field, and I must go out and see it. Please excuse me.' 19 Another said, 'I have bought five yoke of oxen, and I am going out to examine them. Please excuse me.' 20 Another said, 'I just got married, and I cannot come.' 21 So the slave came back and reported this to his master. Then the master of the household was furious and said to his slave, 'Go out quickly to the streets and alleys of the city, and bring in the poor, the crippled, the blind, and the lame.' 22 Then the slave said, 'Sir, what you instructed has been done, and there is still room.' 23 So the master said to his slave, 'Go out to the highways and country roads and urge people to come in, so that my house will be filled. 24 For I tell you, not one of those individuals who were invited will taste my banquet!'"

25 Now large crowds were accompanying Jesus, and turning to them he said, 26 "If anyone comes to me and does not hate his own father and mother, and wife and children, and brothers and sisters, and even his own life, he cannot be my disciple. 27 Whoever does not carry his own cross and follow me cannot be my disciple. 28 For which of you, wanting to build a tower, doesn't sit down first and compute the cost to see if he has enough money to complete it? 29 Otherwise, when he has laid a foundation and is not able to finish the tower, all who see it will begin to make fun of him. 30 They will say, 'This man began to build and was not able to finish!' 31 Or what king, going out to confront another king in battle, will not sit down first and determine whether he is able with 10,000 to oppose the one coming against him with 20,000? 32 If he cannot

> succeed, he will send a representative while the other is still a long way off and ask for terms of peace. 33 In the same way therefore not one of you can be my disciple if he does not renounce all his own possessions.
>
> 34 "Salt is good, but if salt loses its flavor, how can its flavor be restored? 35 It is of no value for the soil or for the manure pile; it is to be thrown out. The one who has ears to hear had better listen!"

Once again, Luke focuses on a Sabbath-day conflict between religious leaders and Jesus (vv. 1–6). With the bent-over woman, the president of the synagogue had brought up the so-called Sabbath violation after Jesus healed her. Now, in the home of a leader of the Pharisees, the religious leaders are watching Jesus closely. In this context, a man with dropsy, or swollen with fluid, is sitting right in front of Jesus. I wonder if the Pharisees placed him there on purpose?

"But they remained silent" (v. 4). On this Sabbath, Jesus asks first—before healing—if it's lawful to heal on the Sabbath. If such a healing were truly against Sabbath law, this is the religious leaders' chance to quote the regulation. But no such regulation exists.

"But they could not reply to this" (v. 6). After Jesus heals and sends the man away, he refuses to let the issue drop. Instead, he asks, "Which of you, if you have a son or an ox that has fallen into a well on a Sabbath day, will not immediately pull him out?" If they answer saying they would show mercy, they then acknowledge having more concern for an animal than for a human in need. But they can't really say they'd leave their son in a well, either.

"Jesus noticed how the guests chose the places of honor" (v. 7). The people at this dinner party have been perfectly content to let a man suffer. They're more focused on their own honor, and their focus reveals their character. Jesus addresses their pride with a story about honor and humiliation (vv. 7–11). He summarizes his point in verse 11: "Everyone who exalts himself will be humbled, but the one who humbles himself will be exalted."

2. What are some ways we honor ourselves or seek position rather than taking the humblest place?

---

3. What does Jesus suggest is a wrong motive for hospitality (vv. 12–14)?

____

____

4. Trusting that God will reward unseen deeds at the resurrection of the righteous requires faith (v. 14). We must believe both that God sees and that he rewards. To whom can you secretly minister, invite, or give without expectation of return, knowing that God sees and will reward you in heaven?

____

"Blessed is everyone who will feast in the kingdom of God!" (v. 15). Hearing Jesus's mention of blessing in the kingdom, someone changes the subject from care for the poor to exclaiming what a blessing that feast will be. The implication is that all present are looking forward to that event because they will participate. But Jesus responds with a parable picturing how God, the ultimate host, extended an invitation, but his people declined, so the invitation is now being re-issued to "outsiders" (vv. 16– 24). Jesus ends by saying that not one initially invited will attend (v. 24)!

5. What is the master of the household's emotional response to the invitees' rejection (v. 21)?

____

____

6. Who will actually attend the feast (vv. 21, 23)?

____

7. What are some wrong priorities that keep people from accepting God's invitation (vv. 18–19)?

____

____

"If anyone comes to me and does not hate his own father and mother, and wife and children, and brothers and sisters, and even his own life, he cannot be my disciple" (v. 26).

Jesus talks in couplets about people the disciple must hate: Father and mother; wife and children; brothers and sisters. The final thing on the list is singular: one's own life. Jesus loves hyperbole. His message has been love, love, love. Yet here he says a person must hate his or her own family to be his disciple. "Hating" is a Semitic expression meaning to "love less." Notice he is talking to "large crowds" (v. 25) and not the disciples—who have already left their families to follow him. The first condition of discipleship is prioritizing human relationships behind one's relationship with Christ. Crowds often follow Jesus looking for a good meal or a nice miracle. He is not interested in his popularity. He wants hard-core commitment.

8. What relationships do you need to surrender to Christ and his lordship?

"Whoever does not carry his own cross and follow me cannot be my disciple" (v. 27) . The second condition of true discipleship is willingness to die. Often today we hear "it's a cross I must bear," by which the speaker means, "I have to put up with this job" or "I have to endure this relationship." But Jesus's hearers would have understood "carry his own cross" to mean death—and that by the most excruciating and humiliating means possible. The ancient writers, Plautus and Plutarch, describe criminals carrying the horizontal bar of the cross—the idea being that the vertical part, or the pole, remained embedded in the ground, but each person condemned to die carried his own crossbar to the place of crucifixion. Seeing someone do so would have been a fairly common occurrence in the world of Jesus. What a recruiting slogan! "Come and die."

9. In what situations do you place your personal safety and comfort over following Christ? Surrender your very life to him, offering your all, even if it means death. Jesus is worth dying for.

"Not one of you can be my disciple if he does not renounce all his own possessions" (v. 33). The third cost of following Jesus is surrendering all finances/possessions.

10. Counting a financial cost is simply good practice in other areas of life. Jesus gives two examples. Fill in the blanks.

Goal	What one calculates (vv. 28–32)
Build a tower	
King going to battle	

11. What of your possessions do you need to relinquish to be a faithful disciple?

___

___

"Salt is good, but if salt loses its flavor, how can its flavor be restored?" (v. 34). The context here is the cost of discipleship. In actuality salt cannot lose its flavor. It's impossible. And in the same way, it can't be restored.

"The one who has ears to hear had better listen!" (v. 35). Jesus ends his sobering speech with an exhortation: Listen! Can you imagine the effect of such words at a dinner party in which everyone was feeling good about their status as a spiritual insider? Complacency is the enemy of listening.

Thursday: What Makes God Rejoice

1. Pray for the Spirit to grant insight and read or listen to Luke 15. Notice the three examples Jesus gives to illustrate God's love for lost souls.

15:1 Now all the tax collectors and sinners were coming to hear him. 2 But the Pharisees and the experts in the law were complaining, "This man welcomes sinners and eats with them."

3 So Jesus told them this parable: 4 "Which one of you, if he has a hundred sheep and loses one of them, would not leave the ninety-nine in the open pasture and go look for the one that is lost until he finds it? 5 Then when he has found it, he places it on his shoulders, rejoicing. 6 Returning home, he calls together his friends and neighbors, telling them, 'Rejoice with me because I have found my sheep that was lost.' 7 I tell you, in the same way there will be more joy in heaven over one sinner who repents than over ninety-nine righteous people who have no need to repent.

8 "Or what woman, if she has ten silver coins and loses one of them, does not light a lamp, sweep the house, and search thoroughly until she finds it? 9 Then when she has found it, she calls together her friends and neighbors, saying, 'Rejoice with me, for I have found the coin that I had lost.' 10 In the same way, I tell you, there is joy in the presence of God's angels over one sinner who repents."

11 Then Jesus said, "A man had two sons. 12 The younger of them said to his father, 'Father, give me the share of the estate that will belong to me.' So he divided his assets between them. 13 After a few days, the younger son gathered together all he had and left on a journey to a distant country, and there he squandered his wealth with a wild lifestyle. 14 Then after he had spent everything, a severe famine took place in that country, and he began to be in need. 15 So he went and worked for one of the citizens of that country, who sent him to his fields to feed pigs. 16 He was longing to eat the carob pods the pigs were eating, but no one gave him anything. 17 But when he came to his senses, he said, 'How many of my father's hired workers have food enough to spare, but here I am dying from hunger! 18 I will get up and go to my father and say to him, "Father, I have sinned against heaven and against you. 19 I am no longer worthy to be called your son; treat me like one of your hired workers."' 20 So he got up and went to his father. But while he was still a long way from home his father saw him, and his heart went out to him; he ran and hugged his son and kissed him. 21 Then his son said to him, 'Father, I have sinned against heaven and against you; I am no longer worthy to be called your son.' 22 But the father said to his slaves, 'Hurry! Bring the best robe, and put it on him! Put a ring on his finger and sandals on his feet! 23 Bring the fattened calf and kill it! Let us eat and celebrate, 24 because this son of mine was dead, and is alive again—he was lost and is found!' So they began to celebrate.

25 "Now his older son was in the field. As he came and approached the house, he heard music and dancing. 26 So he called one of the slaves and asked what was happening. 27 The slave replied, 'Your brother has returned, and your father has killed the fattened calf because he got his son back safe and sound.' 28 But the older son became angry and refused to go in. His father came out and appealed to him, 29 but he answered his father, 'Look! These many years I have worked like a slave for you, and I never disobeyed your commands. Yet you never gave me even a goat so that I could celebrate with my friends! 30 But when this son of yours came back, who has devoured your assets with prostitutes, you killed the fattened calf for him!' 31 Then the father said to him, 'Son, you are always with me, and everything that belongs to me is yours. 32 It was appropriate to celebrate and be glad, for your brother was dead, and is alive; he was lost and is found.'"

2. What religious outsiders were coming to hear Jesus (v. 1)?

____

____

3. Jesus told three stories in response to a complaint by the Pharisees. What complaint do the three stories address (v. 2)?

____

____

4. The stories have something in common: in each case something precious is lost. Identify the three lost things (vv. 3–7; 8–10; 11–24).

____

____

____

5. In each case when the lost thing is found, rejoicing follows. Jesus uses the reference to rejoicing as a parallel for something that will happen in heaven. What triggers rejoicing in heaven (v. 7, v. 9, and by implication, v. 32)?

6. Why do you think Jesus seems to prefer the company of sinners and tax collectors to the religious people?

7. In the story of the lost son, what evidence do you see of true repentance (vv. 18–20)? How do the son's actions suggest a real change of heart?

8. The older son is like the religious people who criticize Jesus for hanging out with sinners. What is the older son's emotional reaction to his brother's return (vv. 28–30)? Notice that both sons are lost in their own way in this story.

"Sent him to his fields to feed pigs. He was longing to eat the carob pods the pigs were eating" (vv. 15–16). Imagine the effect of details like "pigs" and "food pigs are eating" on Jewish readers' ears. They don't touch pork—it's unclean. And this son has so debased himself that he is unworthy even to eat pig's food.

"But while he was still a long way from home his father saw him, and his heart went out to him" (v. 20). The detail of the father's seeing his lost son while he is "still a long way from home" suggests the father stands scanning the horizon with hope. Notice the father does not go into the far country to find his son and drag him back. The father lets his lost son go. But he also stands ready to welcome him back. He longs for this son who has said virtually, "I wish you were dead so I can get my inheritance already."

"He ran and hugged his son and kissed him" (v. 20). A running older man was considered undignified, especially for a wealthy landowner. But this father cares nothing for his reputation when it comes to welcoming his sinning son home and covering him in a public display of affection

9. What four expressions of celebration does the father issue to honor his returned son (v. 23)? And why does the father say he is doing so (v. 24)?

___

___

"His father came out and appealed to him" (v. 28). Notice the father's initiative is not limited to the son who is returning. He also goes out to the son who has refused to come inside. The father initiates with both.

"This son of yours came back" (v. 30). The older son cannot even bring himself to say "my brother." He describes his brother in relationship to his father, not to himself.

"Your brother was dead, and is alive" (v. 32). The father does describe the son who returned as "your brother." And that younger brother did indeed squander. He spent his inheritance on prostitutes. And the father took nothing away from the older brother to honor to the returned son. This father describes the returned sinner as formerly dead. When the father divided the assets at the time the younger son departed, the older son got his fair share. The father does not minimize what the younger son has done, but the older son fails to see the resurrection that has happened in his brother's soul. God is like this father. The Lord does not give sin a pass or minimize it, but he rejoices when a sinner repents and is restored to life.

When people read this story, often labeled "The Parable of the Prodigal Son," we frequently identify with the lost son, as we consider how we have received grace. And we have. But Jesus actually expected his readers to identify with the older son and thus to purge their (and our) lives of his attitudes. The word "prodigal" means "extravagant" and "lavish," so perhaps a more appropriate title to this story would be "The Prodigal Father." As we mature in faith, God expects us to grow into the kind of people who search for, long for, and rejoice over every sinner whom the Father loves. A mature person becomes like the father in this story. Take a moment to search your heart and repent.

10. Read the following poem by Christine Prater and imagine yourself in the story.

Then Jesus told them yet another story: "Once a man had two sons..." —Luke 15:11–31

Unnamed in the Story
The kitchen window framed the scene—
the proud posturing, the wild gesturing.
And I, with linen towel twisting
between fretting fingers, watched
as a broken boy extended his hand,
demanding honor from kindness.

For six years, I coursed my days
and minded my worries at the window,
eyes straining down an empty road,
prayer pouring from mourning lips.

In the evenings, I despaired as I watched
rough lips mouth unanswered prayers,
and low shoulders—burdened
beneath sorrow—undress in tallow light.
And I lie beside him in silent lament—
unnamed in the story but hand-in-hand
with his hurt, sitting shiva with kindness.

Each morning, I rose with the dawn,
picked limp dreams from the counter,
and kept watch at the window.
Washing, praying.
Drying, praying.

When at last our earnest prayers were answered
and our lost son's shape rose on the road,
I abandoned my post at the window.
Eyes straining to meet his.
Joy pouring from praising lips.
I clutched my miracle on the stoop
and then busied myself with preparations.

But as the celebration swelled, the sun sank
and a new agony dawned in another son.

The kitchen window framed the scene—
the proud posturing, the wild gesturing.
And I, with linen towel twisting
between fretting fingers, watched
as a broken boy pointed his finger,
resenting kindness from honor.

Christine Prater

Friday: Money Matters

1. Pray for the Holy Spirit's help and read Luke 16. Circle all references to money, poverty, and riches.

16:1 Jesus also said to the disciples, "There was a rich man who was informed of accusations that his manager was wasting his assets. 2 So he called the manager in and said to him, 'What is this I hear about you? Turn in the account of your administration, because you can no longer be my manager.' 3 Then the manager said to himself, 'What should I do, since my master is taking my position away from me? I'm not strong enough to dig, and I'm too ashamed to beg. 4 I know what to do so that when I am put out of management, people will welcome me into their homes.' 5 So he contacted his master's debtors one by one. He asked the first, 'How much do you owe my master?' 6 The man replied, '100 measures of olive oil.' The manager said to him, 'Take your bill, sit down quickly, and write 50.' 7 Then he said to another, 'And how much do you owe?' The second man replied, '100 measures of wheat.' The manager said to him, 'Take your bill, and write 80.' 8 The master commended the dishonest manager because he acted shrewdly. For the people of this world are more shrewd in dealing with their contemporaries than the people of light. 9 And I tell you, make friends for yourselves by how you use worldly wealth, so that when it runs out, you will be welcomed into the eternal homes.

10 "The one who is faithful in a very little is also faithful in much, and the one who is dishonest in a very little is also dishonest in much. 11 If then you haven't been trustworthy in handling worldly wealth, who will entrust you with the true riches? 12 And if you haven't been trustworthy with someone else's property, who

will give you your own? 13 No servant can serve two masters, for either he will hate the one and love the other, or he will be devoted to the one and despise the other. You cannot serve God and money."

14 The Pharisees (who loved money) heard all this and ridiculed him. 15 But Jesus said to them, "You are the ones who justify yourselves in men's eyes, but God knows your hearts. For what is highly prized among men is utterly detestable in God's sight.

16 "The law and the prophets were in force until John; since then, the good news of the kingdom of God has been proclaimed, and everyone is urged to enter it. 17 But it is easier for heaven and earth to pass away than for one tiny stroke of a letter in the law to become void.

18 "Everyone who divorces his wife and marries someone else commits adultery, and the one who marries a woman divorced from her husband commits adultery.

19 "There was a rich man who dressed in purple and fine linen and who feasted sumptuously every day. 20 But at his gate lay a poor man named Lazarus whose body was covered with sores, 21 who longed to eat what fell from the rich man's table. In addition, the dogs came and licked his sores.

22 "Now the poor man died and was carried by the angels to Abraham's side. The rich man also died and was buried. 23 And in Hades, as he was in torment, he looked up and saw Abraham far off with Lazarus at his side. 24 So he called out, 'Father Abraham, have mercy on me, and send Lazarus to dip the tip of his finger in water and cool my tongue because I am in anguish in this fire.' 25 But Abraham said, 'Child, remember that in your lifetime you received your good things and Lazarus likewise bad things, but now he is comforted here and you are in anguish. 26 Besides all this, a great chasm has been fixed between us, so that those who want to cross over from here to you cannot do so, and no one can cross from there to us.' 27 So the rich man said, 'Then I beg you, father—send Lazarus to my father's house 28 (for I have five brothers) to warn them so that they don't come into this place of torment.' 29 But Abraham said, 'They have Moses and the prophets; they must respond to them.' 30 Then the rich man said, 'No, father Abraham, but if someone from the dead goes to them, they will repent.' 31 He replied to him, 'If they do not respond to Moses and the prophets, they will not be convinced even if someone rises from the dead.'"

2. Jesus previously laid out the terms of discipleship, one of which was renouncing all possessions (Luke 14:33). Now he talks to his disciples (not the crowd) about what renunciation might look like. He tells

a story about an unrighteous person who has learned he will soon be fired. Knowing his authority will end before long, this man uses his access to his boss's clients and capital to plan for his own future (16:1–9). What is his end goal (v. 4)?

____

____

3. By what percentages does this man discount what his master's clients owe (vv. 6–7)?

____

____

4. How would reducing these debtors' outstanding balances endear this crooked administrator to those receiving discounts?

____

____

5. For what does the master commend this unfaithful employee (v. 8)?

____

____

6. According to Jesus, in what way are people of this world more clever or more shrewd than people of the light (v. 8)?

____

____

7. What imperative (command) does Jesus issue to his disciples as an application of this story (v. 9)? What is his reasoning behind this instruction?

8. How are you investing resources in the ultimate future? What resources can you manage more shrewdly for the sake of the kingdom?

Jesus said, "The one who is faithful in a very little is also faithful in much, and the one who is dishonest in a very little is also dishonest in much" (v. 10). Write out this verse, and as you write it, consider "little" areas of unfaithfulness or dishonesty in your life and repent. Ask God to help you be faithful with every little thing entrusted to you.

9. God wants to entrust his children with true riches. What is a test of readiness to handle true riches (vv. 11–12)?

10. Jesus describes two masters—money and God. He says no one can serve both, placing the options in love/hate contrasts. Do you love God or love money? Do you hate money or hate God? (As a reminder, Jesus uses the Semitic word for "hate" as part of an idiom meaning "love less.") What do your financial decisions reveal about your view of eternity?

11. What do the Pharisees love (v. 14)?

"The Pharisees ... ridiculed him" (v. 14). The Greek word translated here as "ridiculed" is to "turn up one's nose at" or to sneer. These people did more than disagree. The Pharisees showed open contempt for Jesus's words.

"For what is highly prized among men is utterly detestable in God's sight" (v. 15). The word translated "men" here is the broader word for "humans" (*anthrōpōn*), from which we get "anthropology." What humans highly prize, God hates.

12. In terms of material possessions, what are some things the world prizes? What does God prize?

13. Jesus divides time into two eras—(1) the Law and the prophets; and (2) the good news of the kingdom. What (or who) divided the two (v. 16)?

14. What invitation comes with the kingdom and to whom is it offered (v. 16)?

"Everyone who divorces his wife and marries someone else commits adultery, and the one who marries a woman divorced from her husband commits adultery" (v. 18). Even though the kingdom replaces the Law and the prophets, it does not render the Scriptures void. In fact, the Law and the prophets—built on "love God" and "love your neighbor"—are realized in Jesus. The king aligns with the revelation that has preceded him, so Jesus's appearing does not render previous commitments void. Marriage vows are still intact, for example. Jesus is not giving a full-length treatise about divorce here, with every possible qualification or exception. Rather, he is affirming that God's original intent from the beginning was for marriage to last until the death of one or both partners. The kingdom Jesus preaches aligns with the Law and the prophets, but it goes beyond these to bring good news. The ideal set forth in Genesis is not being contradicted but upheld.

15. In what relationships do you need to show integrity and devotion as an outworking of your relationship with the king?

____

____

Saturday: Invest in Your Own Future

Scripture: "He replied to him, 'If they do not respond to Moses and the prophets, they will not be convinced even if someone rises from the dead.'" (Luke 16:31)

Jesus has had a lot to say about money and kingdom riches. To illustrate the world's values and those of God, he tells a story in which he contrasts love of money with love of the kingdom:

> 19 "There was a rich man who dressed in purple and fine linen and who feasted sumptuously every day. 20 But at his gate lay a poor man named Lazarus whose body was covered with sores, 21 who longed to eat what fell from the rich man's table. In addition, the dogs came and licked his sores.
>
> 22 "Now the poor man died and was carried by the angels to Abraham's side. The rich man also died and was buried. 23 And in Hades, as he was in torment, he looked up and saw Abraham far off with Lazarus at his side. 24 So he called out, 'Father Abraham, have mercy on me, and send Lazarus to dip the tip of his finger in water and cool my tongue because I am in anguish in this fire.' 25 But Abraham said, 'Child, remember that in your lifetime you

> received your good things and Lazarus likewise bad things, but now he is comforted here and you are in anguish. 26 Besides all this, a great chasm has been fixed between us, so that those who want to cross over from here to you cannot do so, and no one can cross from there to us.' 27 So the rich man said, 'Then I beg you, father—send Lazarus to my father's house 28 (for I have five brothers) to warn them so that they don't come into this place of torment.' 29 But Abraham said, 'They have Moses and the prophets; they must respond to them.' 30 Then the rich man said, 'No, father Abraham, but if someone from the dead goes to them, they will repent.' 31 He replied to him, 'If they do not respond to Moses and the prophets, they will not be convinced even if someone rises from the dead.'"

The first man is rich, and Jesus gives four details that reveal what this man values. First, he dresses in purple. Purple dye at this time is often derived from snails and is expensive. Next, the man's linen—possibly a reference to his undergarments— is "fine," so he spends a lot on clothing, perhaps even apparel hidden to others. Third, this man feasts, and he does so daily—and "sumptuously." His regular fare is the Middle Eastern equivalent of white truffle and gold pizza, Beluga's Almas caviar, million-dollar lobster frittata, and chocolate opulence sundaes. Finally, his home has a gate, which suggests he has more than a house; he has an estate.

In contrast is a poor man named Lazarus. It appears he's lying at the rich man's gate, homeless, and likely even unable to walk. He certainly cannot work. His festering sores attract dogs who lick them. Gross! Further, Lazarus is so hungry that he longs to eat crumbs from the rich man's table. Notice Jesus does not say Lazarus gets to eat such crumbs. He just longs for some fragments of pizza crust and a few fish eggs.

Notice that Jesus has withheld the rich man's name, but he names Lazarus. Having one's name remembered was especially important in a world that lacked photographs, video, or audio recordings (see Isaiah 56:5). This name detail also provides a hint about whom listeners are supposed to cheer for in the story.

In addition to their food and clothing, Jesus has more contrasts for his audience—the afterlife experience of the two men. The rich man goes to torment in "Hades," but the poor man goes to "Abraham's side," or more literally his "bosom." Jesus uses figurative language here. Abraham does not have a literal "bosom" large enough for all those welcomed into a beautiful forever. The contrast is a good end and a bad end, torment vs. rest. Jesus's listeners would have understood an afterlife in the presence of Abraham as the good end of the righteous. To sum things up, the rich man got a short life of riches followed by eternal torment; the poor man got a short life of suffering followed by eternal rest.

Yet even in their differing places, the rich man has the gall to tell Abraham to send Lazarus on errands—first to touch water to his tongue and then to send Lazarus to warn his relatives. Does the rich man still think of Lazarus as below him socially (vv. 24, 27)?

Abraham denies both of the rich man's requests. Jesus denies the request for a taste of water because, even if it were possible for Lazarus to bridge the chasm between the two afterlives (which it's not), in the rich man's lifetime he already received the good things, while Lazarus received the bad things. Now the suffering or comfort has been flipped. It's as if Abraham is saying "Suffering comes in life or the hereafter—you took your pick." Instead of reducing his own comfort to alleviate the distress of another, the rich man had spent all his capital on himself. As a result, he gets exactly what he gave to Lazarus during his lifetime—no relief.

Seeing his request rejected, the rich man makes a second request. He wants Lazarus to be sent by his ancestor, or "father," Abraham to warn the family so they won't make the same choices this man has made. But Abraham denies this request because the man's brothers already have ample warning—they have Moses and the prophets "and must respond to them" (v. 29). To this the rich man argues that Lazarus's appearance would add the credibility of a miracle, a resurrection, to his message.

As Jesus tells this story, he doubtless thinks of all the miracles he has worked. How many of his own people in synagogues on multiple Saturdays have seen him heal? There was the demon-possessed man. The woman bent over. And the man with dropsy. But miracles didn't lead to belief for those with hard hearts. In fact, they seemed only to have added to the hardness. As Jesus tells the story, he puts these words in the mouth of Abraham: "If they do not respond to Moses and the prophets, they will not be convinced even if someone rises from the dead" (v. 31).

Think of Luke writing this account some years after Jesus's ascension. Although Luke does not mention that event in his Gospel, he knew Jesus had raised a literal Lazarus from the dead (John 11:1–44).

And yet that miracle motivated some people to kill Jesus (v. 53). And as if the miracle of raising Lazarus were not enough, Jesus himself rose from the dead! Yet the leaders of his people still rejected the ultimate expression of the Law and the prophets: the king and his kingdom.

How a person stewards resources reveals what he or she loves and hates. How are you spending your life? Are you spending your cash only on your own comfort, or does the suffering of the poor, the lame, the homeless, the ill and the helpless compel you to show God's love in tangible ways? Does your spending reveal that you believe the good news? What are you doing with your capital? Are you sending it ahead to provide a later reward?

For memorization: "And I tell you, make friends for yourselves by how you use worldly wealth, so that when it runs out, you will be welcomed into the eternal homes" (Luke 16:9).

Prayer: *Heavenly Father, thank you for your mercy to sinners like me. And thank you for the resources you have entrusted to me. I offer them all to you. Take and use them as you will. Please grant me the wisdom of good stewardship. Help me demonstrate my love for you by how I treat the poor, the sick, the lame, the suffering, the vulnerable. Even if I have what I consider little, help me be faithful with every bit. Grant me eyes to see how you want me to invest my worldly goods so that when they run out, I will be welcomed into eternal homes. And thank you that I serve a risen Savior. In the name of your Son through the power of the Spirit, Amen.*

Week 6 of 7

Jesus: The King Who Reigns (Luke 17–20)

Sunday: Repentance Is More Than Prayer

Scripture: "But Zacchaeus stopped and said to the Lord, 'Look, Lord, half of my possessions I now give to the poor, and if I have cheated anyone of anything, I am paying back four times as much!'" (Luke 19:8).

Come back in time with me to first-century Jericho. Jesus has just entered the town, and there's this short guy named Zach trying to see him through the crowd. Zach is a tax collector—and not just any tax collector. He's the mafia boss of taxes, so he's rich. And he got his wealth through corruption.

Now imagine you're one of the people this mob leader has ripped off. And the biggest rip-off happened twenty years ago. Let's assume it went like this: you once owned property inherited from your parents that they got from their parents. Every good childhood memory you have rests on that precious plot of soil. But one day Zach sent a couple of his thugs in suits to inform you—on behalf of the "family"—that the fee on your prime real estate was going up five hundred percent. Of course, you couldn't pay it, though you sold just about everything you owned to try to raise the money. So, Zach and his guys took your property as payment for money owed.

For the past twenty years, you and your family have had no field for planting a harvest. You've had no vineyard in which to grow grapes. You've had no cistern from which to draw water. You have suffered for the choices Zach made and forgot about. Every time you and your family have thought about your hardship, which is daily, you've had to let go of bitterness for the suffering Zach and his cronies caused you. Every time you've walked past that little piece of once-paradise, which is often, you have wrestled with forgiveness.

Then one day some of your friends tell you a rabbi named Yeshua, who may be the Promised One, is coming to town. You rush to see him, elbowing your way through the crowds. When you get to the Main Street, you think you see Zach from the back up in one of the trees. Sure enough, he's up there trying to get a good view. He's short, but you're tall, so you can see it all.

Yeshua is walking down Main when he spots Zach.

"Finally!" you think. "Justice will happen."

Then, you hear Yeshua talk to Zach. "Hurry and come down, because today I'm lodging at your house."

You think, "*Your house? That house isn't Zach's!*"

Zach shimmies down the tree to receive him gladly.

You and everybody around you—all of whom have been similarly ripped off—grumble among yourselves. It bothers all of you that the guy lucky enough to host Jesus (and being host is a big deal) is none other than the local mob boss.

For the next five years, you have to tolerate Zach talking about how what he did in the past does not matter because God has forgiven him. You think this God of his must not be so great.

Okay, that's a totally unsatisfying ending, right? And it's not the way the story actually ended. We know the version I told is wrong because being right with God (vertically) means making reparations with other humans (horizontally), correct?

Then, how about this ending?

Zach: "Lord, I'll give half of my possessions to the poor, and if I have defrauded anyone of anything, I will give back four times as much."

Awesome!

So, you go to Zach after the Master has left town. You feel thrilled out of your mind that Zach has new life. And you tell him you cannot wait to get back your old house—the house of your ancestors—not to mention the quadrupled size of the real estate!

Zach looks stunned. "You actually expect me to give up my house?"

Now it's your turn to blink. Twice. "But you stole it twenty years ago..."

Zach scoffs. "Twenty years! Buddy, you need to lose that 'victim identity.' That was a long time ago. I'm a different person now. Besides, if I had really taken your house and land, why would you wait this long to bring it up? Why would you want to ruin my life?"

His callousness only adds to your pain. You wonder if his God is real. His friends who claim to know God say you must be lying or at fault if you waited this long to say anything. You wonder if their God is real, too. Their religious friends say anyone who waits a long time to reveal an injustice must be lying or have ulterior motives. You promise yourself never to go to their house of worship because theirs is not the kind of God who is worthy of your worship.

As we see from this story, time alone does not fix an injustice. Being forgiven by God does not restore justice; forgiveness is merely the beginning of repentance. No statute of limitations exists in God's book either on confessing or on righting an injustice. Victims have many reasons for waiting to come forward, mostly because of legitimate fear and concern that doing so will only add to their wounds.

The way Jesus told the story, Zaccheus truly repented. And he understood immediately that following Christ was going to cost him in every way.

What is discipleship costing you?

For memorization: "For the Son of Man came to seek and to save the lost" (Luke 19:10).

Prayer: *Father, Thank you for hope. For repentance. That you raise the dead to life. That you long for human flourishing. That you are the kind of God who runs to the prodigal and also leaves the party to appeal to the older brother. Thank you for your heart for sinners, for the poor, and for justice. Move in my heart in such a way that I might see my need for grace and give away grace to those who need it most. Make me an instrument of your piece. In the name of your Son and through the power of the Spirit, Amen.*

Monday: The Son of Man

1. Pray for insight and read Luke 17–20. Circle all the references to "the Son of Man."

17:1 Jesus said to his disciples, "Stumbling blocks are sure to come, but woe to the one through whom they come! 2 It would be better for him to have a millstone tied around his neck and be thrown into the sea than for him to cause one of these little ones to sin. 3 Watch yourselves! If your brother sins, rebuke him. If he repents, forgive him. 4 Even if he sins against you seven times in a day, and seven times returns to you saying, 'I repent,' you must forgive him."

5 The apostles said to the Lord, "Increase our faith!" 6 So the Lord replied, "If you had faith the size of a mustard seed, you could say to this black mulberry tree, 'Be pulled out by the roots and planted in the sea,' and it would obey you.

7 "Would any one of you say to your slave who comes in from the field after plowing or shepherding sheep, 'Come at once and sit down for a meal'? 8 Won't the master instead say to him, 'Get my dinner ready, and make yourself ready to serve me while I eat and drink. Then you may eat and drink'? 9 He won't thank the slave because he did what he was told, will he? 10 So you too, when you have done everything you were commanded to do, should say, 'We are slaves undeserving of special praise; we have only done what was our duty.'"

11 Now on the way to Jerusalem, Jesus was passing along between Samaria and Galilee. 12 As he was entering a village, ten men with leprosy met him. They stood at a distance, 13 raised their voices and said, "Jesus, Master, have mercy on us." 14 When he saw them he said, "Go and show yourselves to the priests." And as they went along, they were cleansed. 15 Then one of them, when he saw he was healed, turned back, praising God with a loud voice. 16 He fell with his face to the ground at Jesus' feet and thanked him. (Now he was a Samaritan.) 17 Then Jesus said, "Were not ten cleansed? Where are the other nine? 18 Was no one found to turn back and give praise to God except this foreigner?" 19 Then he said to the man, "Get up and go your way. Your faith has made you well."

20 Now at one point the Pharisees asked Jesus when the kingdom of God was coming, so he answered, "The kingdom of God is not coming with signs to be observed, 21 nor will they say, 'Look, here it is!' or 'There!' For indeed, the kingdom of God is in your midst."

22 Then he said to the disciples, "The days are coming when you will desire to see one of the days of the Son of Man, and you will not see it. 23 Then people will say to you, 'Look, there he is!' or 'Look, here he is!' Do not go out or chase after them. 24 For just like the lightning flashes and lights up the sky from one side to the other, so will the Son of Man be in his day. 25 But first he must suffer many things and be rejected by this generation. 26 Just as it was in the days of Noah, so too it will be in the days of the Son of Man. 27 People were eating, they were drinking, they were marrying, they were being given in marriage—right up to the day Noah entered the ark. Then the flood came and destroyed them all. 28 Likewise, just as it was in the days of Lot, people were eating, drinking, buying, selling, planting, building; 29 but on the day Lot went out from Sodom, fire and sulfur rained down from heaven and destroyed them all. 30 It will be the same on the day the Son of Man is revealed. 31 On that day, anyone who is on the roof, with his goods in the house, must not come down to take them away, and likewise the person in the field must not turn back. 32 Remember Lot's wife! 33 Whoever tries to keep his life will lose it, but whoever loses his life will preserve it. 34 I tell you, in that night there will be two people in one bed; one will be taken and the other left. 35 There will be two women grinding grain together; one will be taken and the other left."

37 Then the disciples said to him, "Where, Lord?" He replied to them, "Where the dead body is, there the vultures will gather."

18:1 Then Jesus told them a parable to show them they should always pray and not lose heart. 2 He said, "In a certain city there was a judge who neither feared God nor respected people. 3 There was also a widow in that city who kept coming to him and saying, 'Give me justice against my adversary.' 4 For a while he refused, but later on he said to himself, 'Though I neither fear God nor have regard for people, 5 yet because this widow keeps on bothering me, I will give her justice, or in the end she will wear me out by her unending pleas.'" 6 And the Lord said, "Listen to what the unrighteous judge says! 7 Won't God give justice to his chosen ones, who cry out to him day and night? Will he delay long to help them? 8 I tell you, he will give them justice speedily. Nevertheless, when the Son of Man comes, will he find faith on earth?"

9 Jesus also told this parable to some who were confident that they were righteous and looked down on everyone else. 10 "Two men went up to the temple to pray, one a Pharisee and the other a tax collector. 11 The Pharisee stood and prayed about himself like this: 'God, I thank you that I am not like other people: extortion-

ists, unrighteous people, adulterers—or even like this tax collector. 12 I fast twice a week; I give a tenth of everything I get.' 13 The tax collector, however, stood far off and would not even look up to heaven, but beat his breast and said, 'God, be merciful to me, sinner that I am!' 14 I tell you that this man went down to his home justified rather than the Pharisee. For everyone who exalts himself will be humbled, but he who humbles himself will be exalted."

15 Now people were even bringing their babies to him for him to touch. But when the disciples saw it, they began to scold those who brought them. 16 But Jesus called for the children, saying, "Let the little children come to me and do not try to stop them, for the kingdom of God belongs to such as these. 17 I tell you the truth, whoever does not receive the kingdom of God like a child will never enter it."

18 Now a certain leader asked him, "Good teacher, what must I do to inherit eternal life?" 19 Jesus said to him, "Why do you call me good? No one is good except God alone. 20 You know the commandments: 'Do not commit adultery, do not murder, do not steal, do not give false testimony, honor your father and mother.'" 21 The man replied, "I have wholeheartedly obeyed all these laws since my youth." 22 When Jesus heard this, he said to him, "One thing you still lack. Sell all that you have and give the money to the poor, and you will have treasure in heaven. Then come, follow me." 23 But when the man heard this, he became very sad, for he was extremely wealthy. 24 When Jesus noticed this, he said, "How hard it is for the rich to enter the kingdom of God! 25 In fact, it is easier for a camel to go through the eye of a needle than for a rich person to enter the kingdom of God." 26 Those who heard this said, "Then who can be saved?" 27 He replied, "What is impossible for mere humans is possible for God." 28 And Peter said, "Look, we have left everything we own to follow you! 29 Then Jesus said to them, "I tell you the truth, there is no one who has left home or wife or brothers or parents or children for the sake of God's kingdom 30 who will not receive many times more in this age—and in the age to come, eternal life."

31 Then Jesus took the twelve aside and said to them, "Look, we are going up to Jerusalem, and everything that is written about the Son of Man by the prophets will be accomplished. 32 For he will be handed over to the Gentiles; he will be mocked, mistreated, and spat on. 33 They will flog him severely and kill him. Yet on the third day he will rise again." 34 But the twelve understood none of these things. This saying was hidden from them, and they did not grasp what Jesus meant.

35 As Jesus approached Jericho, a blind man was sitting by the road begging. 36 When he heard a crowd going by, he asked what

was going on. 37 They told him, "Jesus the Nazarene is passing by." 38 So he called out, "Jesus, Son of David, have mercy on me!" 39 And those who were in front scolded him to get him to be quiet, but he shouted even more, "Son of David, have mercy on me!" 40 So Jesus stopped and ordered the beggar to be brought to him. When the man came near, Jesus asked him, 41 "What do you want me to do for you?" He replied, "Lord, let me see again." 42 Jesus said to him, "Receive your sight; your faith has healed you." 43 And immediately he regained his sight and followed Jesus, praising God. When all the people saw it, they too gave praise to God.

19:1 Jesus entered Jericho and was passing through it. 2 Now a man named Zacchaeus was there; he was a chief tax collector and was rich. 3 He was trying to get a look at Jesus, but being a short man he could not see over the crowd. 4 So he ran on ahead and climbed up into a sycamore tree to see him because Jesus was going to pass that way. 5 And when Jesus came to that place, he looked up and said to him, "Zacchaeus, come down quickly because I must stay at your house today." 6 So he came down quickly and welcomed Jesus joyfully. 7 And when the people saw it, they all complained, "He has gone in to be the guest of a man who is a sinner." 8 But Zacchaeus stopped and said to the Lord, "Look, Lord, half of my possessions I now give to the poor, and if I have cheated anyone of anything, I am paying back four times as much!" 9 Then Jesus said to him, "Today salvation has come to this household because he too is a son of Abraham! 10 For the Son of Man came to seek and to save the lost."

11 While the people were listening to these things, Jesus proceeded to tell a parable because he was near to Jerusalem, and because they thought that the kingdom of God was going to appear immediately. 12 Therefore he said, "A nobleman went to a distant country to receive for himself a kingdom and then return. 13 And he summoned ten of his slaves, gave them ten minas, and said to them, 'Do business with these until I come back.' 14 But his citizens hated him and sent a delegation after him, saying, 'We do not want this man to be king over us!' 15 When he returned after receiving the kingdom, he summoned these slaves to whom he had given the money. He wanted to know how much they had earned by trading. 16 So the first one came before him and said, 'Sir, your mina has made ten minas more.' 17 And the king said to him, 'Well done, good slave! Because you have been faithful in a very small matter, you will have authority over ten cities.' 18 Then the second one came and said, 'Sir, your mina has made five minas.' 19 So the king said to him, 'And you are to be over five cities.' 20 Then another

slave came and said, 'Sir, here is your mina that I put away for safe-keeping in a piece of cloth. 21 For I was afraid of you because you are a severe man. You withdraw what you did not deposit and reap what you did not sow.' 22 The king said to him, 'I will judge you by your own words, you wicked slave! So you knew, did you, that I was a severe man, withdrawing what I didn't deposit and reaping what I didn't sow? 23 Why then didn't you put my money in the bank, so that when I returned I could have collected it with interest?' 24 And he said to his attendants, 'Take the mina from him, and give it to the one who has ten.' 25 But they said to him, 'Sir, he has ten minas already!' 26 'I tell you that everyone who has will be given more, but from the one who does not have, even what he has will be taken away. 27 But as for these enemies of mine who did not want me to be their king, bring them here and slaughter them in front of me!'"

28 After Jesus had said this, he continued on ahead, going up to Jerusalem. 29 Now when he approached Bethphage and Bethany, at the place called the Mount of Olives, he sent two of the disciples, 30 telling them, "Go to the village ahead of you. When you enter it, you will find a colt tied there that has never been ridden. Untie it and bring it here. 31 If anyone asks you, 'Why are you untying it?' just say, 'The Lord needs it.'" 32 So those who were sent ahead found it exactly as he had told them. 33 As they were untying the colt, its owners asked them, "Why are you untying that colt?" 34 They replied, "The Lord needs it." 35 Then they brought it to Jesus, threw their cloaks on the colt, and had Jesus get on it. 36 As he rode along, they spread their cloaks on the road. 37 As he approached the road leading down from the Mount of Olives, the whole crowd of his disciples began to rejoice and praise God with a loud voice for all the mighty works they had seen: 38 "Blessed is the king who comes in the name of the Lord! Peace in heaven and glory in the highest!" 39 But some of the Pharisees in the crowd said to him, "Teacher, rebuke your disciples." 40 He answered, "I tell you, if they keep silent, the very stones will cry out!"

41 Now when Jesus approached and saw the city, he wept over it, 42 saying, "If you had only known on this day, even you, the things that make for peace! But now they are hidden from your eyes. 43 For the days will come upon you when your enemies will build an embankment against you and surround you and close in on you from every side. 44 They will demolish you—you and your children within your walls—and they will not leave within you one stone on top of another because you did not recognize the time of your visitation from God."

45 Then Jesus entered the temple courts and began to drive out those who were selling things there, 46 saying to them, "It is written, 'My house will be a house of prayer,' but you have turned it into a den of robbers!"

47 Jesus was teaching daily in the temple courts. The chief priests and the experts in the law and the prominent leaders among the people were seeking to assassinate him, 48 but they could not find a way to do it, for all the people hung on his words.

2. As you read, did you see any recurring themes or repeated ideas?

____

____

3. How many references did you find to Jesus as "Son of Man"?

____

4. Repentance is more than a prayer and a feeling. In what areas do you need to repent, resulting in life change, to become more like Christ?

____

____

Tuesday: Hard-Core Discipleship

1. Pray for the Holy Spirit to grant insight and read Luke 17. Circle all references to disciples/apostles, paying attention to whom Jesus is addressing throughout this chapter.

17:1 Jesus said to his disciples, "Stumbling blocks are sure to come, but woe to the one through whom they come! 2 It would be better for him to have a millstone tied around his neck and be thrown into the sea than for him to cause one of these little ones to sin. 3 Watch yourselves! If your brother sins, rebuke him. If he repents, forgive him. 4 Even if he sins against you seven times in a day, and seven times returns to you saying, 'I repent,' you must forgive him."

5 The apostles said to the Lord, "Increase our faith!" 6 So the Lord replied, "If you had faith the size of a mustard seed, you could say to this black mulberry tree, 'Be pulled out by the roots and planted in the sea,' and it would obey you.

7 "Would any one of you say to your slave who comes in from the field after plowing or shepherding sheep, 'Come at once and sit down for a meal'? 8 Won't the master instead say to him, 'Get my dinner ready, and make yourself ready to serve me while I eat and drink. Then you may eat and drink'? 9 He won't thank the slave because he did what he was told, will he? 10 So you too, when you have done everything you were commanded to do, should say, 'We are slaves undeserving of special praise; we have only done what was our duty.'"

11 Now on the way to Jerusalem, Jesus was passing along between Samaria and Galilee. 12 As he was entering a village, ten men with leprosy met him. They stood at a distance, 13 raised their voices and said, "Jesus, Master, have mercy on us." 14 When he saw them he said, "Go and show yourselves to the priests." And as they went along, they were cleansed. 15 Then one of them, when he saw he was healed, turned back, praising God with a loud voice. 16 He fell with his face to the ground at Jesus' feet and thanked him. (Now he was a Samaritan.) 17 Then Jesus said, "Were not ten cleansed? Where are the other nine? 18 Was no one found to turn back and give praise to God except this foreigner?" 19 Then he said to the man, "Get up and go your way. Your faith has made you well."

20 Now at one point the Pharisees asked Jesus when the kingdom of God was coming, so he answered, "The kingdom of God is not coming with signs to be observed, 21 nor will they say, 'Look, here it is!' or 'There!' For indeed, the kingdom of God is in your midst."

22 Then he said to the disciples, "The days are coming when you will desire to see one of the days of the Son of Man, and you will not see it. 23 Then people will say to you, 'Look, there he is!' or 'Look, here he is!' Do not go out or chase after them. 24 For just like the lightning flashes and lights up the sky from one side to the other, so will the Son of Man be in his day. 25 But first he must suffer many things and be rejected by this generation. 26 Just as it was in the days of Noah, so too it will be in the days of the Son of Man. 27 People were eating, they were drinking, they were marrying, they were being given in marriage—right up to the day Noah entered the ark. Then the flood came and destroyed them all. 28 Likewise, just as it was in the days of Lot, people were eating, drinking, buying, selling, planting, building; 29 but on the day Lot

went out from Sodom, fire and sulfur rained down from heaven and destroyed them all. 30 It will be the same on the day the Son of Man is revealed. 31 On that day, anyone who is on the roof, with his goods in the house, must not come down to take them away, and likewise the person in the field must not turn back. 32 Remember Lot's wife! 33 Whoever tries to keep his life will lose it, but whoever loses his life will preserve it. 34 I tell you, in that night there will be two people in one bed; one will be taken and the other left. 35 There will be two women grinding grain together; one will be taken and the other left."

37 Then the disciples said to him, "Where, Lord?" He replied to them, "Where the dead body is, there the vultures will gather."

2. Jesus begins with an essential quality of a disciple: Life and teaching that align with the truth (vv. 1–3). What are some scandals in the church that have turned people from the faith or created obstacles to their interest in Christianity?

____

____

____

"Stumbling blocks are sure to come, but woe to the one through whom they come!" (v. 1). The Lord uses the metaphor of a block that makes someone fall to illustrate the cause and effect of a serious offense. In describing this "stumbling block," Luke uses the word "*skandalon*," associated with the word "trap" as a snare or enticement. In the disciples' case, a stumbling block would have included teaching and/or behavior that drove people from the truth and led to loss of faith.

"It would be better for him to have a millstone tied around his neck and be thrown into the sea" (v. 2). The "him/his" in this verse is not gender-specific in Greek—so read these as "that person." Women and men are equally capable of causing offense. The image here evokes the mafia-hit phrase, "swimming with the fishes." The consequence for a person putting a "rock of offense" in the way of another's faith is another kind of stone: a millstone. Millstones were and are typically shaped into circles that weigh more than a ton and are used as the upper stone in grinding grain.

"Cause one of these little ones to sin" (v. 2). "These little ones" is probably a term of affection for all would-be disciples, who are vulnerable. The word rendered as "sin" here is *skandalis* a form of the word translated in verse 1 as "stumbling block." Jesus is making a play on words about stumbling stones, millstones, and causing stumbles.

3. Bibles had no verse numberings until the sixteenth century, so our numbered divisions are not "inspired." The way verse 3 is divided can look like Jesus's command here goes with what follows. But it likely goes with what preceded it. Jesus has painted a sobering picture. What application does he urge (v. 3)?

---

4. On the one hand, we are not responsible for others' choices. On the other hand, we bear responsibility for how we have used our influence. Take stock of your life. Can you identify areas, patterns, and/or teachings that could cause others to lose interest in faith? If so, repent. Is there anything you'd change about your life if you knew all the secrets about how you currently live would become public knowledge?

"If your brother sins, rebuke him. If he repents, forgive him" (v. 3). The word in Greek translated here as brother is "*adelphos*" or "sibling." The city of Philadelphia is the "city of brotherly love." In Luke's use here, the word translated "brothers" can include females. That's why the NIV has translated the phrase "if your brother or sister sins...." Note Jesus doesn't say "asks for forgiveness" but "repents."

5. Do you see someone living in a pattern of habitual sin? If so, are you in the kind of relationship with this person in which you can lovingly confront (v. 3)?

---

6. It's one thing to forgive someone who is "generally sinning." But when the repeated offense affects us personally, forgiveness is much more difficult. How much forgiveness is enough, according to Jesus (v. 4)? Sometimes people have assumed from Jesus's teaching here that we must trust a person who habitually wrongs us and never changes. But forgiveness and trust are not the same thing. That said, we humans tend to rationalize reasons for refusing to forgive. Jesus lays out an astonishingly high standard. Meeting it requires faith. How can you exercise that kind of faith?

---

7. For what do the apostles ask the Lord (v. 5)?

"Faith the size of a mustard seed" (v. 6) – Previously Jesus used the tiny size of a mustard seed to illustrate that the kingdom has enormous volume rooted in a tiny seed (Luke 13:18–19). Here Jesus uses the seed's size again to teach his disciples through hyperbole that the volume of faith is not what's needed—but rather the presence of faith.

"You could say to this black mulberry tree 'Be pulled out by the roots and planted in the sea,' and it would obey you" (v. 6). The kind of tree (Gr. *sykaminos*) Jesus mentions here is in the same family as a fig tree. (We'll see it again later this week in the story about Zacchaeus.) These trees could grow for hundreds of years, giving them massive root systems. Uprooting one? And planting it in deep salt water? No way! Jesus uses foliage the disciples see daily to illustrate that a little faith can do the impossible.

8. For what do you lack faith? Ask God to help you by the power of the Spirit to trust him to do anything impossible that aligns with his will.

Jesus gives another mark of the disciple: Humility expressed in thankless acts of service viewed as just doing one's duty (vv. 7–10). While it's true that God gives rewards, he does not always do so in this life. In contrast with those who serve God for the crowds, the praise, the glory, and the benefits, Jesus's disciples are to serve their Lord without expecting rewards or praise. In fact, they see serving him as doing what's required.

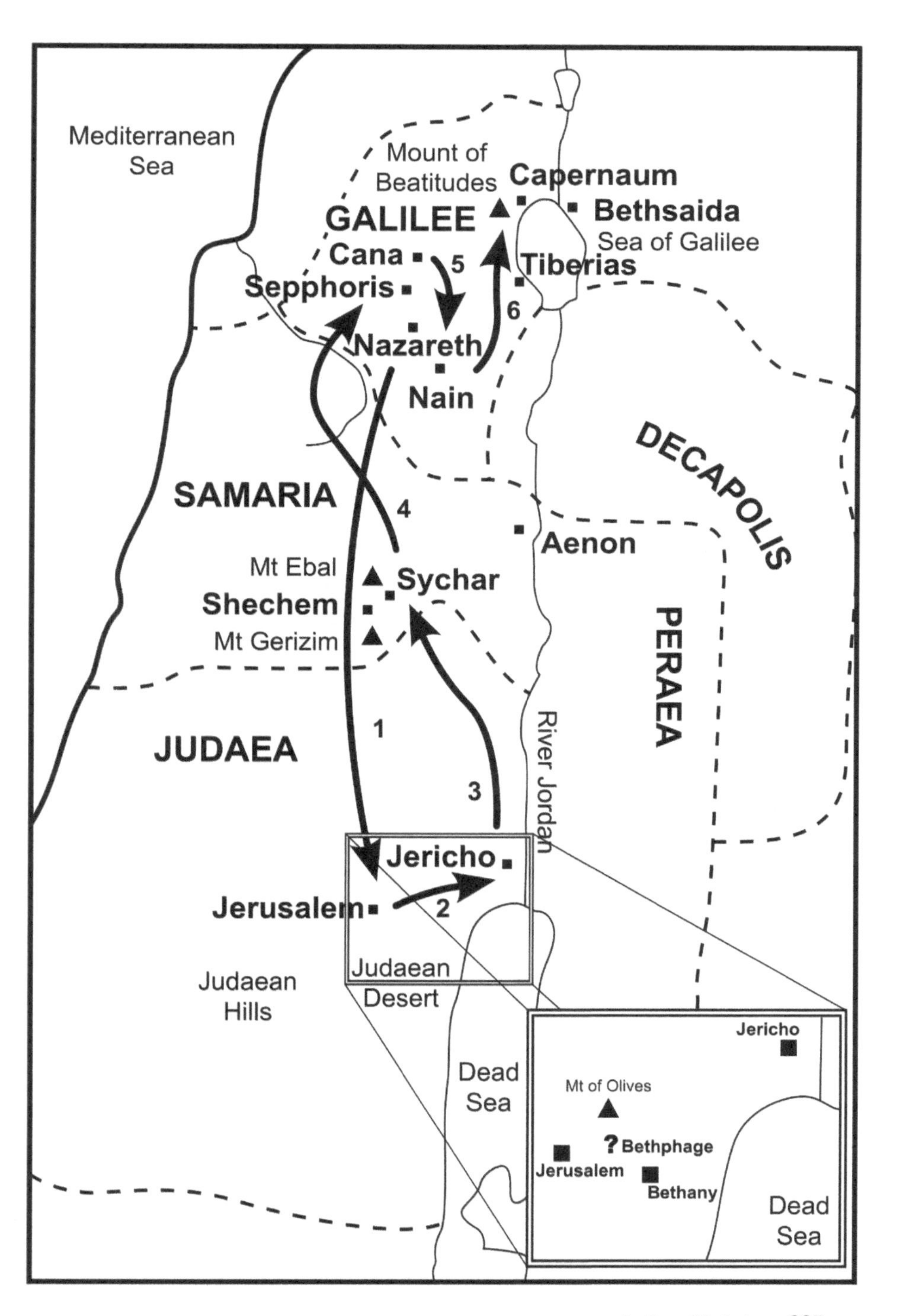
Mediterranean Sea
Mount of Beatitudes
Capernaum
Bethsaida
GALILEE
Sea of Galilee
Cana
Tiberias
Sepphoris
Nazareth
Nain
DECAPOLIS
SAMARIA
Aenon
Mt Ebal
Sychar
Shechem
Mt Gerizim
PERAEA
JUDAEA
River Jordan
1
2
3
4
5
6
Jericho
Jerusalem
Judaean Desert
Judaean Hills
Dead Sea
Jericho
Mt of Olives
? Bethphage
Jerusalem
Bethany
Dead Sea

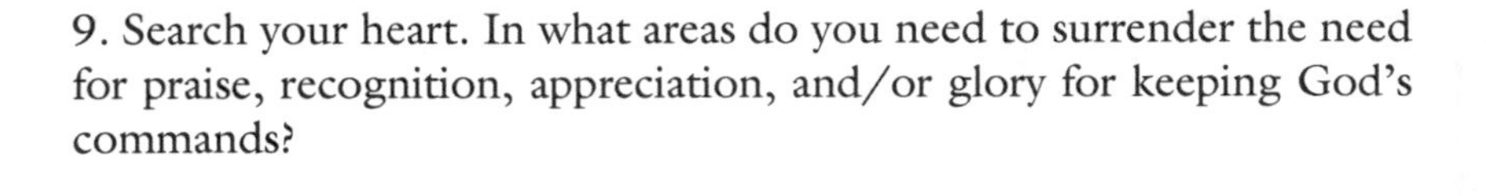

9. Search your heart. In what areas do you need to surrender the need for praise, recognition, appreciation, and/or glory for keeping God's commands?

10. In addition to humility, gratitude is another mark of a disciple. List ten things for which you're grateful.

"Now on the way to Jerusalem, Jesus was passing along between Samaria and Galilee" (v. 11). See the map on page 237. Jesus is moving south on his way to Jerusalem for Passover. He's been on this journey for a while—it's eighty miles from Galilee through Samaria to Jerusalem. He is taking a less-than-direct route, stopping in towns and villages along the way to preach the good news of the kingdom.

"Ten men with leprosy met him...stood at a distance" (v. 12). The word in the New Testament often translated as "leprosy" refers to skin conditions that affect mainly the skin, the eyes, the nose, and peripheral nerves. As mentioned in the note on Luke 5:12, the condition is broader than what is known today as Hansen's disease. There was no medical cure in Jesus's day. Because Jewish people with leprosy were considered ritually unclean, they typically stood at a distance and called out to others the word "unclean." In this narrative, they stand at a distance from Jesus and call out for mercy to the "Master."

"When [Jesus] saw them he said, "Go and show yourselves to the priests" (v. 14) – By implication, Jesus is showing mercy. Jewish law required that a person with a skin condition show it to the priest, who declares it clean or unclean (Lev. 13:1–8). Jesus is sending these ten men to go give testimony to Jewish leaders, who will probably be seeing their first cases ever of leprosy healed—and not for only one person, but for ten! In fact, Jesus sends the lepers to the priests even before he has healed them. Only "as they went along" were they cleansed (v. 14). Their obedience required literal steps of faith.

11. For Jesus to heal ten people at once is amazing, yet healing is not the focus of Luke's story here. Only one of the people healed returned to thank their healer. What was different about this one in addition to his gratitude (vv. 16–18)? Why do you think Luke chose to include these details?

"Your faith has made you well" (v. 19). The man had already been physically healed—that's why he returned to give Jesus his thanks. Note that Luke uses two different words to describe what has happened to these people—"cleansed" (v. 14) and "well" (v. 19). The source of the grateful man's full return to flourishing is his faith in Jesus, evidenced by his gratitude for the mercy he has received.

We live in an era and a part of the world where we have access to lots of biblical teaching and music with scriptural themes on podcasts, online video, and streaming. It's easy to become "immune" to so much blessing, though. Write out ten things for which you have not thanked God but for which you are grateful. Consider these prompts as starters. Think of recent examples:

- answered prayer
- safety
- deliverance from life's difficulties, sin, oppression, persecution, etc.
- for other believers
- for the privilege of serving God
- for access to Scripture and teaching
- mercy
- spiritual gifts
- God's attributes, including love, faithfulness, and justice

12. Jesus's people have waited centuries for the coming of the kingdom, so it's no surprise when a Pharisee asks him how they will know when the kingdom of God is coming (v. 20). Jesus often refers to the kingdom as coming in the future, but here his answer varies from the norm. How does Jesus's answer, which implies repentance, differ from what his listeners might expect (vv. 20–21)?

"Then he said to the disciples, 'The days are coming'" (v. 22). As is often the case, after someone asks Jesus a question and he answers publicly, he gives the disciples an expanded explanation in private. Here Jesus refers to the kingdom in the future.

"When you will desire to see one of the days of the Son of Man, and you will not see it" (v. 22). The disciples would have been familiar with the prophesy of Daniel, who portrayed "one like a son of man coming to the Ancient of days" given dominion and glory and a kingdom. When Luke calls Jesus "the Son of Man," he is building on the reference to the coming King described in Daniel. The King's dominion is said to be long lasting and not to be destroyed (Dan. 7:13–14). Jesus's kingdom is repentance and wholeness and loosing from bondage in addition to a coming earthly kingdom. Jesus tells his disciples they will desire the latter but not see it. He's warning: Things will get worse before they get better.

"First he must suffer many things and be rejected by this generation" (v. 25). Everyone has expected the Son of Man to come in glory and dominion to set up his kingdom. But some other events must happen first.

13. What unpleasant things must happen before the king sets up his physical kingdom (vv. 26–37)?

14. What do the days of Noah have in common with the days of Lot (vv. 26–30)?

"Remember Lot's wife!" (v. 32). We'll explore this story further in the weekend devotional. But suffice it to say that while Lot's wife's city was being destroyed for its sin, she looked back at her old life with longing. And she was destroyed along with the city. Her longing destroyed her.

15. What does Jesus say is the moral of the story (v. 33)?

____

____

"Two people in one bed; one will be taken and the other left... two women grinding grain together; one will be taken and the other left" (vv. 34–35). There are two kinds of people—those suddenly taken and those left on earth. The former are like people at the time of the Flood and at the destruction of Sodom. The message for the righteous in Noah's day was "Come in, fast!" The message at the destruction of Sodom was "Get out, fast!" Either way, the righteous were warned, because destruction came suddenly.

16. The disciples were looking for the kingdom to be established on earth, but Jesus clarifies that sudden judgment—like that at the time of Noah and of Lot—happens first. In response to a statement about vanishing bodies, the disciples ask "where?" What questions do Jesus's words raise for *you*?

____

____

____

Wednesday: The Heart-Changer

1. Pray for the Holy Spirit's help in understanding and read Luke 18.

> 18:1 Then Jesus told them a parable to show them they should always pray and not lose heart. 2 He said, "In a certain city there was a judge who neither feared God nor respected people. 3 There

was also a widow in that city who kept coming to him and saying, 'Give me justice against my adversary.' 4 For a while he refused, but later on he said to himself, 'Though I neither fear God nor have regard for people, 5 yet because this widow keeps on bothering me, I will give her justice, or in the end she will wear me out by her unending pleas.'" 6 And the Lord said, "Listen to what the unrighteous judge says! 7 Won't God give justice to his chosen ones, who cry out to him day and night? Will he delay long to help them? 8 I tell you, he will give them justice speedily. Nevertheless, when the Son of Man comes, will he find faith on earth?"

9 Jesus also told this parable to some who were confident that they were righteous and looked down on everyone else. 10 "Two men went up to the temple to pray, one a Pharisee and the other a tax collector. 11 The Pharisee stood and prayed about himself like this: 'God, I thank you that I am not like other people: extortionists, unrighteous people, adulterers—or even like this tax collector. 12 I fast twice a week; I give a tenth of everything I get.' 13 The tax collector, however, stood far off and would not even look up to heaven, but beat his breast and said, 'God, be merciful to me, sinner that I am!' 14 I tell you that this man went down to his home justified rather than the Pharisee. For everyone who exalts himself will be humbled, but he who humbles himself will be exalted."

15 Now people were even bringing their babies to him for him to touch. But when the disciples saw it, they began to scold those who brought them. 16 But Jesus called for the children, saying, "Let the little children come to me and do not try to stop them, for the kingdom of God belongs to such as these. 17 I tell you the truth, whoever does not receive the kingdom of God like a child will never enter it."

18 Now a certain leader asked him, "Good teacher, what must I do to inherit eternal life?" 19 Jesus said to him, "Why do you call me good? No one is good except God alone. 20 You know the commandments: 'Do not commit adultery, do not murder, do not steal, do not give false testimony, honor your father and mother.'" 21 The man replied, "I have wholeheartedly obeyed all these laws since my youth." 22 When Jesus heard this, he said to him, "One thing you still lack. Sell all that you have and give the money to the poor, and you will have treasure in heaven. Then come, follow me." 23 But when the man heard this, he became very sad, for he was extremely wealthy. 24 When Jesus noticed this, he said, "How hard it is for the rich to enter the kingdom of God! 25 In fact, it is easier for a camel to go through the eye of a needle than for a rich person to enter the kingdom of God." 26 Those who heard this said, "Then who can be

saved?" 27 He replied, "What is impossible for mere humans is possible for God." 28 And Peter said, "Look, we have left everything we own to follow you! 29 Then Jesus said to them, "I tell you the truth, there is no one who has left home or wife or brothers or parents or children for the sake of God's kingdom 30 who will not receive many times more in this age—and in the age to come, eternal life."

31 Then Jesus took the twelve aside and said to them, "Look, we are going up to Jerusalem, and everything that is written about the Son of Man by the prophets will be accomplished. 32 For he will be handed over to the Gentiles; he will be mocked, mistreated, and spat on. 33 They will flog him severely and kill him. Yet on the third day he will rise again." 34 But the twelve understood none of these things. This saying was hidden from them, and they did not grasp what Jesus meant.

35 As Jesus approached Jericho, a blind man was sitting by the road begging. 36 When he heard a crowd going by, he asked what was going on. 37 They told him, "Jesus the Nazarene is passing by." 38 So he called out, "Jesus, Son of David, have mercy on me!" 39 And those who were in front scolded him to get him to be quiet, but he shouted even more, "Son of David, have mercy on me!" 40 So Jesus stopped and ordered the beggar to be brought to him. When the man came near, Jesus asked him, 41 "What do you want me to do for you?" He replied, "Lord, let me see again." 42 Jesus said to him, "Receive your sight; your faith has healed you." 43 And immediately he regained his sight and followed Jesus, praising God. When all the people saw it, they too gave praise to God.

2. In what ways is the judge in the first story like God, the ultimate judge (vv. 1–8)? In what ways is the judge in the story different from God?

____

____

____

"There was also a widow in that city" (v. 3). The average age of widowhood in North America is about 59 years, but we should probably picture a younger woman in Jesus's world. Women married in their mid-teens, and the number-one cause of death for men was war, so many widows were in their mid-thirties. But the detail about her marital status is less about her age than her vulnerability. She is financially and socially at risk for suffering injustice, so she continually pleads for the judge to "give me justice against my adversary." Jesus uses her drive and persistence as an example for his disciples to follow.

"Nevertheless, when the Son of Man comes, will he find faith on earth?" (v. 8). Luke said that Jesus's point was this: people should always pray and not lose heart. Here Jesus once again self-identifies as the Son of Man who will establish his kingdom, and he connects faith with prayer. Jesus is physically present with them at this moment, but he is speaking of a future day when he will return to earth. At that time, he will look for faith as seen in tenacious prayer.

3. If Jesus were to return today, would he find you making prayer a priority? What evidence do you have to support your answer? If you have difficulty focusing when you pray, consider writing out your words.

Prayer in the Gospel of Luke

Luke has been called the Prayer Gospel. More than any of the other three Gospel writers, Luke emphasizes prayer. Notice how often Jesus prays before and during significant events.

People pray outside while Zechariah is in the temple (Luke 1:10)
Gabriel says Zechariah's prayer has been heard (1:13)
Anna fasts and prays day and night (2:37)
Jesus prays when heavens open at his baptism (3:21)
Jesus said to frequently retreat to wilderness to pray (5:16)
John's disciples said to frequently fast and pray (5:33)
Jesus spends all night in prayer before choosing disciples (6:12)
Disciples told to pray for those who mistreat them (6:27)
Jesus prays alone and asks disciples who the crowds say he is (9:16)
Jesus takes disciples up mountain to pray (9:28)
Jesus transfigured while praying (9:29)
Jesus teaches disciples how to pray (11:2)
Jesus teaches parable of persistent widow about prayer (18:1ff)
Jesus contrasts Pharisee's prayer with that of sinner justified (18:10–11)
Jesus cleanses temple saying it should be a house of prayer (19:46)
Jesus criticizes law experts showing off with long prayers (20:47)
Jesus exhorts followers to stay alert and pray at all times (22:36)

Jesus tells Simon he prayed for him that his faith won't fail (22:32)
Jesus tells disciples to pray they won't fall (22:39)
Jesus kneels and prays on the Mount of Olives (22:41)
Jesus, in anguish, prays even more earnestly (22:44)
Getting up from prayer, Jesus finds disciples sleeping and exhorts them to pray they won't fall into temptation (22:46)
Jesus prays, "Father, into your hands I commit my spirit" (24:46)

---

4. Luke says the intended audience for Jesus's next parable is some who were confident that they were righteous, so they looked down on everyone else (v. 9). Complete the chart contrasting the two men Jesus describes.

Kind of person	Pharisee	Tax collector
Bodily stance	(v. 11)	(v. 13)
What he prayed about	(v. 11)	(v. 13)
Evidence of character	(vv. 11, 12)	(v. 13)
How God viewed him	(v. 14)	(v. 14)
View of self	(v. 14)	(v. 14)
His future	(v. 14)	(v. 14)

5. What are some subtle and not-so-subtle ways we humans exalt ourselves?

____

____

6. Jesus values humility. In many agrarian cultures, even today, the pecking order is men, animals, women, and children. How does Jesus's treatment of children reflect both his valuing them and flipping the pecking order (vv. 15–17)?

____

____

7. What evidence do you see that the rich young ruler is using flattery to endear himself to Jesus? (v. 18–21)?

____

____

"Jesus said to him, 'Why do you call me good? No one is good except God alone'" (v. 19). In his *IVP New Testament Commentary*, Luke, Bible scholar Darrell Bock writes, "Jesus is not replying to deprecate himself... Jesus' refusal to accept the man's flattery also warns the man that Jesus will shoot straight with him."

8. The rich young leader, or ruler, demonstrates the kind of attitude seen in the Pharisee described above, unlike that of the tax collector. What evidence do you see that this rich man thinks highly of his own righteousness (v. 21)?

____

____

"When Jesus heard this, he said to him, 'One thing you still lack. Sell all that you have and give the money to the poor, and you will have treasure in heaven. Then come, follow me'" (v. 22). Make no mistake. The message here is not that everybody gets into the kingdom by becoming poor. This man has learned and memorized the law since childhood, yet he has altogether missed the point—to love God and love his neighbor. So, Jesus cuts to the heart of his idolatry. Think of the opportunity this man has—to follow Jesus himself! Yet instead he is sad. And not just sad, but very sad. Why? He is extremely rich. So, he has made his choice.

Using hyperbole, Jesus says it's easier for a camel to go through the eye of a needle than for a rich person to enter the kingdom of God (v. 25), something the disciples view as impossible. (Just like salt can't regain its flavor. Or a tree can't be planted in the sea.)

9. Why do you think Jesus says, in effect, it's impossible for a rich person to enter the kingdom? Why is wealth such an obstacle?

____

____

____

"[Jesus] replied, 'What is impossible for mere humans is possible for God'" (v. 27). People cannot save ourselves. But God saves! And his doing so requires a new heart.

10. Have you asked God to do what is humanly impossible—to save you? Why or why not?

____

____

____

11. At the opposite end is Peter, who says to Jesus, "Look, we have left everything we own to follow you! (v. 28). What does Jesus say is the reward for leaving all for the sake of the kingdom (v. 29–30)?

____

____

12. People have used Jesus's words about leaving one's spouse, siblings, parents, and children (v. 29) to justify neglect of families. How do you reconcile Jesus's teaching here with the call to love one's neighbor?

13. What are some ways people (including yourself) are tempted to prioritize biological family relationships over kingdom priorities?

14. What are some rewards people experience "in this age" for having kingdom priorities?

15. Jesus tells the Twelve what will happen in Jerusalem. Make a list of all he predicts will happen (vv. 31–33). How does this list differ from typical kingdom expectations?

16. What is the disciples' response and why (v. 34)?

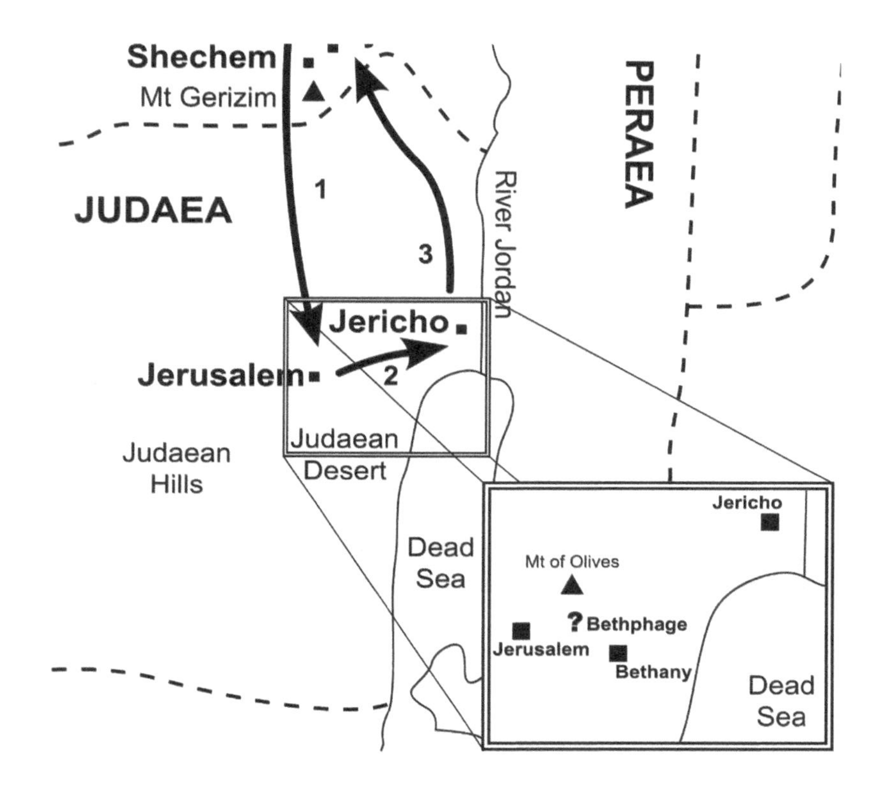

17. Locate Jericho on the above map and notice how close Jesus is getting to Jerusalem. By what titles does the beggar, who is blind, address Jesus, suggesting that this man really "sees" (vv. 38, 39, 41)?

____

____

18. Notice Jesus refrains from healing the blind man until he answers, **"What do you want me to do for you?"** (v. 41). What does the man's answer suggest about what he believes?

____

____

19. Jesus says to the blind beggar, **"Receive your sight; your faith has healed you"** (v. 42). The word translated here as "healed" is

"saved"; that is, "your faith has saved you." Do you think Jesus's reference to "faith" here means the man's faith that he would be healed or his faith in who Jesus is? Or both? Explain your answer.

---

20. How does this man's faith affect the lives of the people (v. 43)?

Thursday: Things That Make for Peace

1. Pray for the Spirit to grant insight and read or listen to Luke 19. Underline evidences of repentance.

> 19:1 Jesus entered Jericho and was passing through it. 2 Now a man named Zacchaeus was there; he was a chief tax collector and was rich. 3 He was trying to get a look at Jesus, but being a short man he could not see over the crowd. 4 So he ran on ahead and climbed up into a sycamore tree to see him because Jesus was going to pass that way. 5 And when Jesus came to that place, he looked up and said to him, "Zacchaeus, come down quickly because I must stay at your house today." 6 So he came down quickly and welcomed Jesus joyfully. 7 And when the people saw it, they all complained, "He has gone in to be the guest of a man who is a sinner." 8 But Zacchaeus stopped and said to the Lord, "Look, Lord, half of my possessions I now give to the poor, and if I have cheated anyone of anything, I am paying back four times as much!" 9 Then Jesus said to him, "Today salvation has come to this household because he too is a son of Abraham! 10 For the Son of Man came to seek and to save the lost."
>
> 11 While the people were listening to these things, Jesus proceeded to tell a parable because he was near to Jerusalem, and because they thought that the kingdom of God was going to appear immediately. 12 Therefore he said, "A nobleman went to a distant country to receive for himself a kingdom and then return. 13 And he summoned ten of his slaves, gave them ten minas, and

said to them, 'Do business with these until I come back.' 14 But his citizens hated him and sent a delegation after him, saying, 'We do not want this man to be king over us!' 15 When he returned after receiving the kingdom, he summoned these slaves to whom he had given the money. He wanted to know how much they had earned by trading. 16 So the first one came before him and said, 'Sir, your mina has made ten minas more.' 17 And the king said to him, 'Well done, good slave! Because you have been faithful in a very small matter, you will have authority over ten cities.' 18 Then the second one came and said, 'Sir, your mina has made five minas.' 19 So the king said to him, 'And you are to be over five cities.' 20 Then another slave came and said, 'Sir, here is your mina that I put away for safe-keeping in a piece of cloth. 21 For I was afraid of you because you are a severe man. You withdraw what you did not deposit and reap what you did not sow.' 22 The king said to him, 'I will judge you by your own words, you wicked slave! So you knew, did you, that I was a severe man, withdrawing what I didn't deposit and reaping what I didn't sow? 23 Why then didn't you put my money in the bank, so that when I returned I could have collected it with interest?' 24 And he said to his attendants, 'Take the mina from him, and give it to the one who has ten.' 25 But they said to him, 'Sir, he has ten minas already!' 26 'I tell you that everyone who has will be given more, but from the one who does not have, even what he has will be taken away. 27 But as for these enemies of mine who did not want me to be their king, bring them here and slaughter them in front of me!'"

28 After Jesus had said this, he continued on ahead, going up to Jerusalem. 29 Now when he approached Bethphage and Bethany, at the place called the Mount of Olives, he sent two of the disciples, 30 telling them, "Go to the village ahead of you. When you enter it, you will find a colt tied there that has never been ridden. Untie it and bring it here. 31 If anyone asks you, 'Why are you untying it?' just say, 'The Lord needs it.'" 32 So those who were sent ahead found it exactly as he had told them. 33 As they were untying the colt, its owners asked them, "Why are you untying that colt?" 34 They replied, "The Lord needs it." 35 Then they brought it to Jesus, threw their cloaks on the colt, and had Jesus get on it. 36 As he rode along, they spread their cloaks on the road. 37 As he approached the road leading down from the Mount of Olives, the whole crowd of his disciples began to rejoice and praise God with a loud voice for all the mighty works they had seen: 38 "Blessed is the king who comes in the name of the Lord! Peace in heaven and glory in the highest!" 39 But some of the Pharisees in the crowd said to him, "Teacher, rebuke your disciples." 40 He answered, "I tell you, if they keep silent, the very stones will cry out!"

41 Now when Jesus approached and saw the city, he wept over it, 42 saying, "If you had only known on this day, even you, the things that make for peace! But now they are hidden from your eyes. 43 For the days will come upon you when your enemies will build an embankment against you and surround you and close in on you from every side. 44 They will demolish you–you and your children within your walls–and they will not leave within you one stone on top of another because you did not recognize the time of your visitation from God."

45 Then Jesus entered the temple courts and began to drive out those who were selling things there, 46 saying to them, "It is written, 'My house will be a house of prayer,' but you have turned it into a den of robbers!"

47 Jesus was teaching daily in the temple courts. The chief priests and the experts in the law and the prominent leaders among the people were seeking to assassinate him, 48 but they could not find a way to do it, for all the people hung on his words.

2. In the last chapter, we saw Jesus approaching Jericho (18:35). Now he has arrived, so he enters and passes through (19:1). Inside Jesus finds Zacchaeus, about whom we read in Sunday's devotional. What fruits of repentance does Zacchaeus show (vv. 2–9)?

____

____

____

"Today salvation has come to this household because he too is a son of Abraham!" (v. 9). Since the days when Joshua and the Israelites made Jericho's "walls fall down," the city has been in Israelite territory. But there are two kinds of "children of Abraham" in Jericho—children by blood and children by faith. Jesus identifies Zacchaeus, the formerly moral outsider, as the best kind of insider now, because he has believed and repented. Later in the New Testament, Peter will tell women that they have become children of Sarah if they "do what is right without being frightened by any fear" (1 Pet. 3:6). The reason salvation has come to Zacchaeus's household "today" is not because he's just become Jewish, but because he is now *a true son of Abraham*. Zacchaeus is able to become a true son, because "The Son of Man came to seek and to save the lost" (v. 10).

3. What does this tax collector's story reveal about the heart and mission of Jesus?

____

____

4. While Jesus has an audience, he tells a parable to correct the erroneous idea that says the kingdom—in which Messiah will take his ancestor David's throne in nearby Jerusalem—will appear immediately (v. 11). Instead, Jesus focuses on what a good disciple does in the meantime (vv. 12–27). Why does the nobleman in his story go far away (v. 12)?

____

____

"Gave them ten minas" (v. 13). A *mina* was worth three to four months' wages doing a six-day-a-week job—thousands of dollars in today's U.S. currency. The soon-to-be-king in the story leaves this money with his various servants so they can run his business in his absence.

5. How do the citizens express their animosity for their future ruler (v. 14)?

____

____

6. What is the principle behind why the now-king, upon his return, gives the first slave authority over ten cities (v. 17)?

____

____

7. What reason does the third slave give for a lack of earning at least some interest on the king's investment (vv. 21, 23)?

____

____

8. How do you think the wicked servant's reason made the king feel? By what standard does the now-king judge the wicked slave and why (vv. 22–26)?

____

____

9. What is the end of those who did not want the king to rule over them (v. 27)? What have their actions revealed about their failure to plan for the future?

____

____

10. What are you doing in the interim as you await the king's return? How are you using the resources (of every kind) entrusted to you to plan for a long-term future?

____

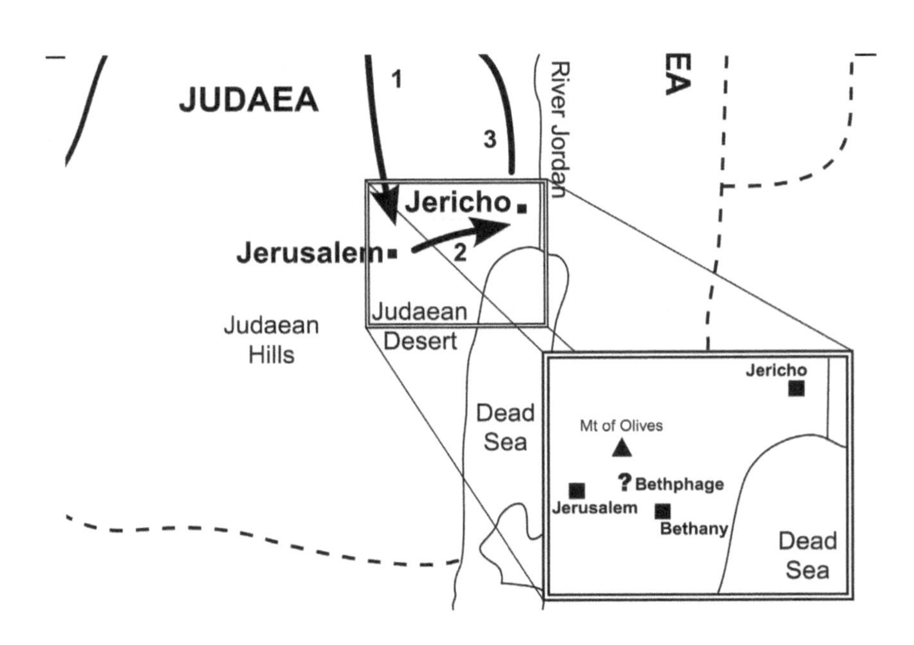

Jesus has almost reached Jerusalem, so he makes preparation to enter the city. Locate "Bethphage and Bethany," at the place called the "Mount of Olives" (v. 29) on the map on the previous page.

11. Jesus plans to enter Jerusalem in a way that differs from how he has always previously entered. In his instructions to two disciples, how does he once again reveal his supernatural power (vv. 30–34)?

The event of Jesus's entry intro Jerusalem, often referred to as "The Triumphal Entry" and celebrated on Palm Sunday, fulfills prophecy found in Zechariah 9:9:

> Rejoice greatly, daughter of Zion!
> Shout, daughter of Jerusalem!
> Look! Your king is coming to you:
> He is legitimate and victorious,
> humble and riding on a donkey—
> on a young donkey, the foal of a female donkey.

Zechariah personified the daughter of Jerusalem as a female herald, rejoicing that their king has come. And Jesus is reenacting a key event in Israel's monarchy, the coronation of Solomon, son of David. We find the record of that event in 1 Kings 1, where the text says the aged King David gave these instructions: "Put my son Solomon on my mule, and lead him down to Gihon. There Zadok the priest and Nathan the prophet will anoint him king over Israel; then blow the trumpet and declare, 'Long live King Solomon!' Then follow him up as he comes and sits on my throne. He will be king in my place; I have decreed that he will be ruler over Israel and Judah" (1 Kings 1:33–35). Everyone did as told, and the people sounded a trumpet and shouted, "Long live King Solomon." Following him, they played flutes and rejoiced so much that the ground shook with the sound (vv. 39–40).

Fast forward to Jesus's actions on his arrival outside the city. He has never outright declared himself the king. But what do his actions say? The people certainly interpret his actions as regal. So they cry out with words from Psalms: "Blessed is the king who comes in the name of the Lord! Peace in heaven and glory in the highest!" (Luke 19:38).

Jesus has crafted a highly symbolic act. By riding into the City of David on the pure, never-before-ridden colt of a donkey, Jesus is declaring his right to the throne. Compare the psalm itself (Psalm 118:26) with what the people cry out (Luke 19:38). What similarities do you see?

> Please, Lord, deliver!
> Please, Lord, grant us success!
> May the one who comes in the name of the Lord be blessed.
> We will pronounce blessings on you in the Lord's temple
> (Ps. 118:25–26)

> "Blessed is the king who comes in the name of the Lord! Peace in heaven and glory in the highest!" (Luke 19:38)

12. What response does this exclamation by Jesus's followers evoke in some Pharisees (v. 39)?

____

____

13. One way or another the prophecy will be fulfilled here, regardless of whether the people in the cheering crowd fulfill it or stones do. Why does Jesus refuse to comply with the demand to silence those referring to him as the king who comes in the name of the Lord (v. 40)?

____

____

14. *Jerusalem* means City of Peace, as "Salem" is a derivative of the Hebrew word "shalom." One might think Jesus would be euphoric to approach this city at such a moment in such a way to such a reception, especially after a long journey. But instead, when he draws near, what is his response (vv. 41–42)?

____

____

15. The disciples' and the Pharisees' responses to Jesus perfectly reflect the nation's divided response. Jesus has harsh words for those who

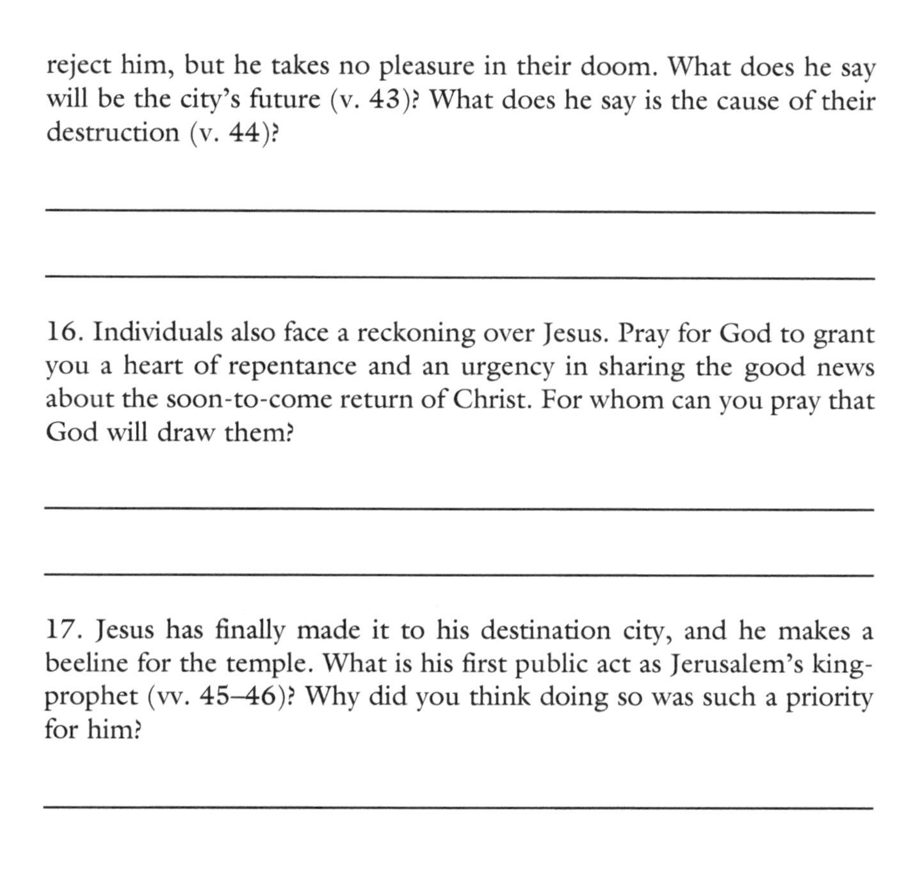

reject him, but he takes no pleasure in their doom. What does he say will be the city's future (v. 43)? What does he say is the cause of their destruction (v. 44)?

16. Individuals also face a reckoning over Jesus. Pray for God to grant you a heart of repentance and an urgency in sharing the good news about the soon-to-come return of Christ. For whom can you pray that God will draw them?

17. Jesus has finally made it to his destination city, and he makes a beeline for the temple. What is his first public act as Jerusalem's king-prophet (vv. 45–46)? Why did you think doing so was such a priority for him?

"It is written, 'My house will be a house of prayer,' but you have turned it into a den of robbers!" (v. 46). God, through the prophets, had spoken against temple profits. Here Jesus cites a combination of two such statements in which God has expressed his vision for the temple:

> Isa 56:7 – I will bring them to my holy mountain;
> I will make them happy in the temple where people pray to me.
> Their burnt offerings and sacrifices will be accepted on my altar,
> for my temple will be known as a temple where all nations may pray."
>
> Jer 7:11 Do you think this temple I have claimed as my own is to be a hideout for robbers?

Upon his arrival, Jesus finds in the temple the very things that God has long since prohibited. People are "selling things there" (v.

45)—creating "*scandalons*" that trip up others seeking God. Instead of being a place where all nations are welcome to pray, the temple has become—thanks to greedy people—a profit center. But Jesus will have none of it. Note his double meaning of the word "my" in "my house." He is quoting the words of God as spoken through the prophets, but Jesus is also taking ownership of his house.

18. For a few days during Jesus's earthly life, the temple is cleansed, and the Lord himself instructs people there. Imagine it! What are the contrasting responses to Jesus's daily teaching in the temple's courts (vv. 47–48)?

____

____

Friday: The Evil Treatment

1. Pray for the Holy Spirit's help in understanding before reading Luke 20.

20:1 Now one day, as Jesus was teaching the people in the temple courts and proclaiming the gospel, the chief priests and the experts in the law with the elders came up 2 and said to him, "Tell us: By what authority are you doing these things? Or who is it who gave you this authority?" 3 He answered them, "I will also ask you a question, and you tell me: 4 John's baptism—was it from heaven or from people?" 5 So they discussed it with one another, saying, "If we say, 'From heaven,' he will say, 'Why did you not believe him?' 6 But if we say, 'From people,' all the people will stone us because they are convinced that John was a prophet." 7 So they replied that they did not know where it came from. 8 Then Jesus said to them, "Neither will I tell you by whose authority I do these things."

9 Then he began to tell the people this parable: "A man planted a vineyard, leased it to tenant farmers, and went on a journey for a long time. 10 When harvest time came, he sent a slave to the tenants so that they would give him his portion of the crop. However, the tenants beat his slave and sent him away empty-handed. 11 So he sent another slave. They beat this one too, treated him outrageously, and sent him away empty-handed. 12 So he sent still a third. They even wounded this one and threw

him out. 13 Then the owner of the vineyard said, 'What should I do? I will send my one dear son; perhaps they will respect him.' 14 But when the tenants saw him, they said to one another, 'This is the heir; let's kill him so the inheritance will be ours!' 15 So they threw him out of the vineyard and killed him. What then will the owner of the vineyard do to them? 16 He will come and destroy those tenants and give the vineyard to others." When the people heard this, they said, "May this never happen!" 17 But Jesus looked straight at them and said, "Then what is the meaning of that which is written: 'The stone the builders rejected has become the cornerstone'? 18 Everyone who falls on this stone will be broken to pieces, and the one on whom it falls will be crushed." 19 Then the experts in the law and the chief priests wanted to arrest him that very hour because they realized he had told this parable against them. But they were afraid of the people.

20 Then they watched him carefully and sent spies who pretended to be sincere. They wanted to take advantage of what he might say so that they could deliver him up to the authority and jurisdiction of the governor. 21 Thus they asked him, "Teacher, we know that you speak and teach correctly, and show no partiality, but teach the way of God in accordance with the truth. 22 Is it right for us to pay the tribute tax to Caesar or not?" 23 But Jesus perceived their deceit and said to them, 24 "Show me a denarius. Whose image and inscription are on it?" They said, "Caesar's." 25 So he said to them, "Then give to Caesar the things that are Caesar's, and to God the things that are God's." 26 Thus they were unable in the presence of the people to trap him with his own words. And stunned by his answer, they fell silent.

27 Now some Sadducees (who contend that there is no resurrection) came to him. 28 They asked him, "Teacher, Moses wrote for us that if a man's brother dies leaving a wife but no children, that man must marry the widow and father children for his brother. 29 Now there were seven brothers. The first one married a woman and died without children. 30 The second 31 and then the third married her, and in this same way all seven died, leaving no children. 32 Finally the woman died too. 33 In the resurrection, therefore, whose wife will the woman be? For all seven had married her."

34 So Jesus said to them, "The people of this age marry and are given in marriage. 35 But those who are regarded as worthy to share in that age and in the resurrection from the dead neither marry nor are given in marriage. 36 In fact, they can no longer die because they are equal to angels and are sons of God, since they are sons of the resurrection. 37 But even Moses revealed that the dead

are raised in the passage about the bush, where he calls the Lord the God of Abraham and the God of Isaac and the God of Jacob. 38 Now he is not God of the dead, but of the living, for all live before him." 39 Then some of the experts in the law answered, "Teacher, you have spoken well!" 40 For they did not dare any longer to ask him anything.

41 But he said to them, "How is it that they say that the Christ is David's son? 42 For David himself says in the book of Psalms,

'The Lord said to my lord,
"Sit at my right hand,
43 until I make your enemies a footstool for your feet."'
44 If David then calls him 'Lord,' how can he be his son?"

45 As all the people were listening, Jesus said to his disciples, 46 "Beware of the experts in the law. They like walking around in long robes, and they love elaborate greetings in the marketplaces and the best seats in the synagogues and the places of honor at banquets. 47 They devour widows' property, and as a show make long prayers. They will receive a more severe punishment."

2. During the week Jesus is in Jerusalem for Passover, what is he doing (20:1)?

____

____

3. Who questions Jesus's authority (vv. 1–2)?

____

4. Notice how Jesus answers a question with a question. By whose [implied] authority is Jesus teaching and sharing the good news (v. 4)?

____

____

5. In Thursday's reading, we read a story Jesus told of a nobleman who went away for a long time before returning (20:9). Jesus includes that same dynamic of time in his story about the vineyard owner

(21:9). Why do you think this “long wait” detail is important?

____

____

6. Fill in the chart according to Luke 20:9–16.

Person sent	How tenants treat the person
Slave 1	
Slave 2	
Slave 3	
Beloved son of the owner	

7. What two things will the owner do in response to such rejection (v. 16)?

____

____

8. What is the response to this story by those represented as the “tenants” (v. 19)? Why don’t these opponents do anything?

____

____

____

____

9. Think about Luke and his insider/outsider themes. In this story who is the owner, who were the slaves, and who is the owner’s dear

son? What is Jesus communicating through this story without stating it outright?

____

____

"The stone the builders rejected has become the cornerstone" (v. 17). Psalm 118 is cited for the third time in the Gospel of Luke. In each instance the quotation comes in connection with the city of Jerusalem. Luke has been presenting Jesus as the king who will be rejected, suffer, and be exalted. In his final usage of the psalm, he captures this in one image: Jesus is the stone rejected by builders that will become the building's exalted cornerstone—the foundation upon which the entire structure is built.

10. What is Jesus's body language as he speaks of the rejected stone being exalted (v. 17)?

____

____

11. People either fall on the stone, or the stone will fall on them (v. 18). If Jesus is the stone, what do you think are the responses he has in mind? What is your response to him?

____

____

____

12. What actions reveal that the hypocritical and two-faced leaders are continuing to fall on this "stone" (vv. 19–20)?

____

____

13. **"The authority and jurisdiction of the governor"** (v. 20) – The next challenge to Jesus is more political than religious. Will he pass the test of appropriate nationalism? Or will he side with Rome?

____

____

14. Luke has revealed the religious insiders' motives (v. 20). Why do you think they would say, "Teacher, we know that you speak and teach correctly, and show no partiality, but teach the way of God in accordance with the truth" (v. 21)?

____

____

"Is it right for us to pay the tribute tax to Caesar or not?" (v. 22). Jewish people at this time are under Roman subjugation, and their question is about the ethics of paying a poll tax to their colonizers. Jesus is not a Zealot; that is, he is not a member of a first-century political movement that seeks to incite the people of the Province of Judea to expel Rome by force. In this advent, Jesus has not come as a partisan political leader. He had a more important task in view.

"Show me a denarius" (v. 24). A *denarius*, a dime-sized coin, is the wage for about one typical day's labor. It bears a picture of Caesar (see image) and has a Latin inscription:

"TI CAESAR DIV AUG F AUGUSTUS"
meaning "Tiberius Caesar Augustus, son of divine Augustus."

"Whose image and inscription are on it?" (v. 24). Jesus's opponents have tried to trap him, but he outwits them—and with a sobering truth. Every religious person in his context would know the phrase "image and likeness" comes right out of Genesis, where the Scriptures say God made male and female in His image and likeness (Gen. 1:27). Caesar's image attributes to Caesar's imperial divine honors. Jesus's point is that the coin bears Caesar's image, so it goes to Caesar. But humans bear the image of God, so they (and we) belong to God.

15. How do they respond to Jesus's answer (v. 26)? Do you think they repented? Why or why not?

Next, the Sadducees, (who didn't believe in resurrection) have a question about life in the world after death. Their question relates to Levirate (Latin: *levir* means "brother-in-law") law. This law instructs that in the event of death, a biological brother must marry his deceased sibling's childless widow to father children in the name of the lost brother (Deut. 25:5–10). Remember from Luke 16 how Jesus didn't name the rich man, but he named Lazarus? Having a "name that lasts" was a big deal.

16. What did the Sadducees want Jesus to tell them (v. 33)?

Not only does Jesus answer their question, but he also provides details about life in "that age"—an age in which the Sadducees do not even believe. Fill in the description of each thing Jesus reveals:

State of marriage (v. 35)	
State of death (v. 36)	

Position of the righteous in the presence of angels (v. 36)	
Family status in that day (v. 36)	
Reason for such status (v. 36)	

17. Jesus suggests that when death ends, there is no longer a reason for reproduction. That is why many rightly teach that celibacy chosen for the sake of Christ in the present age stands as a sign of a future when death will die. Is celibacy an honored or discouraged state in your own sphere of influence? Explain your answer.

___

___

___

"Moses revealed that the dead are raised in the passage about the bush" (v. 37). Jesus goes on to give the Sadducees more than they asked for—a correction of their wrong views on life after death. He does so by citing a story found in Exodus 3. Moses is shepherding a flock in the desert, and the Angel of the LORD appears to him in a flame of fire from within a bush. Although the bush is aflame, it remains intact instead of burning up. And God calls to Moses from within that bush. After telling Moses to take off his shoes, the Lord announces himself as "the God of Abraham, the God of Isaac and the God of Jacob." In this story, Jesus tells the Sadducees, "Even Moses revealed that the dead are raised...where he calls the Lord the God of Abraham and the God of Isaac and the God of Jacob." Jesus concludes, "Now he is not God of the dead, but of the living, for all live before him."

18. Notice it is not a Sadducee who responds to Jesus after this story. While the Law experts are no fans of Jesus, they probably enjoyed it

when he outwitted their theological opponents. What is the expert's assessment of Jesus's answer, and what is the result of Jesus's theology lesson (vv. 39–40)?

____

____

19. Having silenced his opponents, Jesus has a question for them based on an observation from a psalm written by David (Psalm 110). What is Jesus's point, and what does it reveal about his identity (vv. 41–44)?

____

____

20. Jesus has one final warning. What six things reveal the hypocrisy of those in Jesus's circle who were typically most familiar with God's word?

____

____

21. Why do you think the experts in the law will receive an extra severe punishment (v. 47)?

____

____

Saturday: Remember Lot's Wife

Scripture: "Remember Lot's wife! Whoever tries to keep his life will lose it, but whoever loses his life will preserve it" (Luke 17:32–33).

Jesus's "Exhibit A" to illustrate "Whoever tries to keep one's life will lose it, but whoever loses one's life will preserve it" (Luke 17:30–32) is Lot's wife. In Genesis 19 we find the tragic end of this woman married to Abraham's nephew.

As the story goes, two angels arrive at evening in Sodom, where Lot is sitting at the city gate—the typical location for those who hold judicial office. In Proverbs 31, we see a similar reference, as the "husband is respected at the city gate, where he takes his seat among the elders of the land" (Prov. 31:23). This detail about Lot suggests he is deeply embedded in Sodom and fully aware of what goes on there.

When Lot sees the figures approaching, he gets up to greet them, bows his face to the ground, and urges them to lodge with him. Hospitality was and is a core value in the Middle East.

The visitors decline, saying they'll stay in the town square.

But Lot insists, so they enter his house, and Lot makes a feast for them. But before they have a chance to rest, the unthinkable happens. Both old and young men from Sodom surround Lot's house demanding access to these visitors. "Where are the men who came to you tonight?" they ask. "Bring them out to us so we can 'know' them!" The word "know" here suggests a Semitic euphemism for sex. These men in Sodom want to have forced sex with Lot's visitors.

Imagine Lot's horror! Not only is this a huge violation of hospitality—the very suggestion of gang rape is evil. But Lot shows he's no Boy Scout. In response, he steps outside his house and beyond the angels' earshot, calls the men of Sodom "brothers." He then offers an alternative: "I have two daughters who have never 'known' a man. Let me bring them out to you, and you can do to them whatever you please" (v. 8). Great dad, huh?

But Lot's proposal fails. The men of Sodom don't want women. They want men. They turn on Lot, insulting him by calling him a "foreigner" and threatening to hurt him even more than they planned to hurt his guests (v. 9). The men press in on Lot so much that they almost break down the door.

The visitors inside quickly rescue Lot by pulling him in, shutting the door, and striking their attackers with blindness. They urge Lot to flee with his family and get them to safety because God has sent these men to destroy this city. The angels say "The outcry against this place is so great before the Lord" that they have come to destroy it (v. 13).

But Lot sees a complication. His daughters are betrothed, so he delays long enough to go urge his future sons-in-law to escape with the family. But they think Lot is mocking them.

At dawn, the angels tell Lot to hurry up and get his family out, or they'll be destroyed along with all the cities in the area. But Lot hesitates, so his visitors grab the hands of Lot and his family, "because the Lord had compassion on them" (v. 16). The angels then lead the group out of the city.

Once outside the gates, the angels urge, "Run for your lives! Don't look behind you or stop anywhere in the valley! Escape to the mountains or you will be destroyed!"

Instead, Lot digs in his heels and negotiates to go to a nearby town rather than all the way to the mountains, so God agrees to spare this one town for Lot.

Finally, when the sun has risen, the Lord rains down sulfur and fire from the sky on Sodom and Gomorrah (v. 24). God overthrows the entire region except the town where Lot and his family have taken refuge.

God has shown mercy upon mercy to this family. They had only one job—run without looking back!

But what does Lot's wife do? She flagrantly disobeys by looking back. What's more, she does so with longing.

That's why she is destroyed along with ßthat which she loves. She dies with her old life rather than experiencing the rescue and new life God mercifully offers.

Jesus said that "in the days of Lot, people were eating, drinking, buying, selling, planting, building" but suddenly one day when they least expected it, they were destroyed (v. 29). The Lord adds "It will be the same on the day the Son of Man is revealed. On that day, anyone who is on the roof, with his goods in the house, must not come down to take them away, and likewise the person in the field must not turn back" (vv. 30–32). He will appear suddenly: "There will be two people in one bed; one will be taken and the other left." And "There will be two women grinding grain together; one will be taken and the other left."

The point? We must always be ready.

God spared Noah's family as he pulled them from a wicked generation. God plucked Lot's family from destruction. But Lot's wife chose, with longing, destruction over life. She preferred a community that accepted gang rape over a chance to start over with her family. Jesus told his followers to remember her—to let her serve as a warning. She tried to keep her life, but she lost it. She longed for what destroyed, and ultimately it destroyed her.

We face a similar choice. What are your longings? Do they contribute to your ultimate flourishing or to your ruin? Falling on the mercy of God, what will you choose?

For memorization: "Whoever tries to keep their life will lose it, and whoever lose their life will preserve it." (Luke 17:33, NIV).

Prayer: *Heavenly Father, Thank you for your loving mercy! I offer to you my life and longings. You created me. I belong to you. I was made for you. I repent of the evil in my heart. Cleanse me of all hypocrisy and self-righteous and self-justification. Wash me and I will be clean. Help me choose life. And rescue me through your Son, that I might walk in newness of life. I ask this in His name and through the power of the Spirit, Amen.*

Week 7 of 7

Jesus: The Risen Savior (Luke 21–24)

Sunday: Mary Tower

Scripture: "Now it was Mary Magdalene, Joanna, Mary the mother of James, and the other women with them who told these things to the apostles." (Luke 24:10)

Who was Mary Magdalene? Because early New Testament manuscripts were more difficult to search than today's books, Mary M. has at times been confused or combined with other Marys.

Some have conflated Mary Magdalene with the sinful woman whom we read about in Luke 7. Thus, this Mary has been described in prose and depicted in art as a reformed prostitute.

Others have suggested she had a romantic relationship with Jesus—or even married him!

But the Scriptures suggest none of these things about her past. The actual details in Luke's Gospel are that Jesus cast out seven demons from Mary Magdalene, and she was among the healed women who traveled with Jesus and supported him from their own means (Luke 8:2–3). She went on to be an eyewitness to the sufferings of Jesus, the first witness to see the risen Christ, and the first evangelist—announcing the Lord's resurrection to the apostles with "I have seen the Lord!" (John 20:18). The latter is why Thomas Aquinas, the great thirteenth-century philosopher and theologian, described Mary

Magdalene as "the apostle to the apostles." The word *apostle* means "sent one," and she was sent to relay the best news ever to the "sent ones"—the Twelve.

Some say this Mary was from a Galilean fishing village called Migdal, meaning "tower," thus "Mary from Midgal." But about six different Galilean towns had the word "tower" in them; and that little connector "of" or "from" Migal was missing. And one possible alternative is that she was nicknamed "Mary Tower."

In the New Testament, we often find people with two names: sometimes they had a Hebrew and a Latin name; sometimes a Latin and Greek one. There's John who is "also called Mark" (Acts 12:12), Dorcas who is also Tabitha (9:36), Nathanael is probably Bartholomew, Silas is also Silvanus, and perhaps Junia is Joanna.

Then there were the nicknames. Jesus named James and John the "Sons of Thunder" (Mark 3:17). Our Lord also emphasized the "Peter" in Simon "Peter" (Matt. 16:18), calling him "this rock"—since that's what "Peter" means. Thomas was "also called Didymus," or "twin" (John 11:16). The "Iscariot" in "Judas Iscariot" probably means "man of Kerioth" (a place in Palestine), distinguishing him from other men by the same name. And the "Barsabbas" in "Judas Barsabbas" means "Son of the Sabbath" (Acts 15:22). The custom of having more than one name combined with our Lord's habit of nicknaming people in his inner circle have led some to suppose that "Mary Tower" is a description not of geography but of her personality.

We don't know for sure. But here's what we do know: through the life of Mary Magdalene, we see that Christ has the power to release someone—man or woman—from spiritual bondage. Interestingly, we also learn something about the validity of the New Testament. Anyone trying to fabricate a convincing history surely would have made men the key witnesses at a time when a woman's testimony counted as little to nothing in a court of law. Yet other than the husband of the Virgin Mary or John the Apostle, women were the primary witnesses of Jesus's birth, death, and resurrection. God chose women as witnesses when their word in the legal culture carried as much weight as a dust bunny.

Yet, the best part about Mary is what we learn of Jesus through her. The great British author, Dorothy L. Sayers, summed it up beautifully in a timeless observation piece she penned more than eighty years ago:

> Perhaps it is no wonder that the women were first at the Cradle and last at the Cross. They had never known a man like this Man—there has never been such another. A prophet and teacher who never nagged at them, flattered or coaxed or patronised; who never made arch jokes about them, never treated them either as 'The women, God help us!' or 'The ladies, God bless them!'; who rebuked without querulousness and praised without condescension; who took their questions and arguments seriously; who never mapped out their sphere for them, never urged them to be feminine or jeered at them for being female; who had no axe to grind and no uneasy male dignity to defend; who took them as he found them and was completely unself-conscious. There is no act, no sermon, no parable in the whole Gospel that borrows its pungency from female perversity; nobody could possibly guess from the words and deeds of Jesus that there was anything 'funny' about woman's nature.

Mary Magdalene speaks across the years, testifying that Jesus the Christ changes lives, setting prisoners free from all kinds of bondage. And after he has taken us from bondage to flourishing, he urges us to go and tell.

For memorization: "Some time afterward he [Jesus] went on through towns and villages, preaching and proclaiming the good news of the kingdom of God. The twelve were with him, and also some women who had been healed of evil spirits and disabilities: Mary (called Magdalene), from whom seven demons had gone out, and Joanna the wife of Cuza (Herod's household manager), Susanna, and many others who provided for them out of their own resources." (Luke 8:1–2)

Prayer: *Thank you, Father, for creating women in your own image. Thank you, Lord Christ, for being born of a woman, dwelling in a world half full of women, and granting the joy of announcing your resurrection to such a disciple as Mary Magdalene. Thank you, Spirit, for filling and empowering women on mission fields around the globe to spread the good news. O, three-personed God, grant the women of our time the strength to persevere, the courage to obey, and the faith to believe in you. Use them to show your face on earth, that it might be seen in all its beauty. Thank you for the hope of your coming kingdom, when men and women* *will be whole, and the earth filled with your glory. We ask these things of the Father, in the name of the Son, through the power of the Holy Spirit. Amen.*

Monday: From Jerusalem to Bethany

1. Pray for the Spirit to guide you and read Luke 21–24. Underline each time Jesus tells his disciples to do something. What are his instructions?

21:1 Jesus looked up and saw the rich putting their gifts into the offering box. 2 He also saw a poor widow put in two small copper coins. 3 He said, "I tell you the truth, this poor widow has put in more than all of them. 4 For they all offered their gifts out of their wealth. But she, out of her poverty, put in everything she had to live on."

5 Now while some were speaking about the temple, how it was adorned with beautiful stones and offerings, Jesus said, 6 "As for these things that you are gazing at, the days will come when not one stone will be left on another. All will be torn down!" 7 So they asked him, "Teacher, when will these things happen? And what will be the sign that these things are about to take place?" 8 He said, "Watch out that you are not misled. For many will come in my name, saying, 'I am he,' and, 'The time is near.' Do not follow them! 9 And when you hear of wars and rebellions, do not be afraid. For these things must happen first, but the end will not come at once."

10 Then he said to them, "Nation will rise up in arms against nation, and kingdom against kingdom. 11 There will be great earthquakes, and famines and plagues in various places, and there will be terrifying sights and great signs from heaven. 12 But before all this, they will seize you and persecute you, handing you over to the synagogues and prisons. You will be brought before kings and governors because of my name. 13 This will be a time for you to serve as witnesses. 14 Therefore be resolved not to rehearse ahead of time how to make your defense. 15 For I will give you the words along with the wisdom that none of your adversaries will be able to withstand or contradict. 16 You will be betrayed even by parents, brothers, relatives, and friends, and they will have some of you put to death. 17 You will be hated by everyone because of my name. 18 Yet not a hair of your head will perish. 19 By your endurance you will gain your lives.

20 "But when you see Jerusalem surrounded by armies, then know that its desolation has come near. 21 Then those who are in

Judea must flee to the mountains. Those who are inside the city must depart. Those who are out in the country must not enter it, 22 because these are days of vengeance, to fulfill all that is written. 23 Woe to those who are pregnant and to those who are nursing their babies in those days! For there will be great distress on the earth and wrath against this people. 24 They will fall by the edge of the sword and be led away as captives among all nations. Jerusalem will be trampled down by the Gentiles until the times of the Gentiles are fulfilled.

25 "And there will be signs in the sun and moon and stars, and on the earth nations will be in distress, anxious over the roaring of the sea and the surging waves. 26 People will be fainting from fear and from the expectation of what is coming on the world, for the powers of the heavens will be shaken. 27 Then they will see the Son of Man arriving in a cloud with power and great glory. 28 But when these things begin to happen, stand up and raise your heads because your redemption is drawing near."

29 Then he told them a parable: "Look at the fig tree and all the other trees. 30 When they sprout leaves, you see for yourselves and know that summer is now near. 31 So also you, when you see these things happening, know that the kingdom of God is near. 32 I tell you the truth, this generation will not pass away until all these things take place. 33 Heaven and earth will pass away, but my words will never pass away.

34 "But be on your guard so that your hearts are not weighed down with dissipation and drunkenness and the worries of this life, and that day close down upon you suddenly like a trap. 35 For it will overtake all who live on the face of the whole earth. 36 But stay alert at all times, praying that you may have strength to escape all these things that must happen, and to stand before the Son of Man."

37 So every day Jesus was teaching in the temple courts, but at night he went and stayed on the Mount of Olives. 38 And all the people came to him early in the morning to listen to him in the temple courts.

22:1 Now the Feast of Unleavened Bread, which is called the Passover, was approaching. 2 The chief priests and the experts in the law were trying to find some way to execute Jesus, for they were afraid of the people.

3 Then Satan entered Judas, the one called Iscariot, who was one of the twelve. 4 He went away and discussed with the chief priests and officers of the temple guard how he might betray Jesus, handing him over to them. 5 They were delighted and arranged to

give him money. 6 So Judas agreed and began looking for an opportunity to betray Jesus when no crowd was present.

7 Then the day for the feast of Unleavened Bread came, on which the Passover lamb had to be sacrificed. 8 Jesus sent Peter and John, saying, "Go and prepare the Passover for us to eat." 9 They said to him, "Where do you want us to prepare it?" 10 He said to them, "Listen, when you have entered the city, a man carrying a jar of water will meet you. Follow him into the house that he enters, 11 and tell the owner of the house, 'The Teacher says to you, "Where is the guest room where I may eat the Passover with my disciples?"' 12 Then he will show you a large furnished room upstairs. Make preparations there." 13 So they went and found things just as he had told them, and they prepared the Passover.

14 Now when the hour came, Jesus took his place at the table and the apostles joined him. 15 And he said to them, "I have earnestly desired to eat this Passover with you before I suffer. 16 For I tell you, I will not eat it again until it is fulfilled in the kingdom of God." 17 Then he took a cup, and after giving thanks he said, "Take this and divide it among yourselves. 18 For I tell you that from now on I will not drink of the fruit of the vine until the kingdom of God comes." 19 Then he took bread, and after giving thanks he broke it and gave it to them, saying, "This is my body which is given for you. Do this in remembrance of me." 20 And in the same way he took the cup after they had eaten, saying, "This cup that is poured out for you is the new covenant in my blood.

21 "But look, the hand of the one who betrays me is with me on the table. 22 For the Son of Man is to go just as it has been determined, but woe to that man by whom he is betrayed!" 23 So they began to question one another as to which of them it could possibly be who would do this.

24 A dispute also started among them over which of them was to be regarded as the greatest. 25 So Jesus said to them, "The kings of the Gentiles lord it over them, and those in authority over them are called 'benefactors.' 26 Not so with you; instead the one who is greatest among you must become like the youngest, and the leader like the one who serves. 27 For who is greater, the one who is seated at the table, or the one who serves? Is it not the one who is seated at the table? But I am among you as one who serves.

28 "You are the ones who have remained with me in my trials. 29 Thus I grant to you a kingdom, just as my Father granted to me, 30 that you may eat and drink at my table in my kingdom, and you will sit on thrones judging the twelve tribes of Israel.

31 "Simon, Simon, pay attention! Satan has demanded to have you all, to sift you like wheat, 32 but I have prayed for you, Simon, that your faith may not fail. When you have turned back, strengthen your brothers." 33 But Peter said to him, "Lord, I am ready to go with you both to prison and to death!" 34 Jesus replied, "I tell you, Peter, the rooster will not crow today until you have denied three times that you know me."

35 Then Jesus said to them, "When I sent you out with no money bag, or traveler's bag, or sandals, you didn't lack anything, did you?" They replied, "Nothing." 36 He said to them, "But now, the one who has a money bag must take it, and likewise a traveler's bag too. And the one who has no sword must sell his cloak and buy one. 37 For I tell you that this scripture must be fulfilled in me, 'And he was counted with the transgressors.' For what is written about me is being fulfilled." 38 So they said, "Look, Lord, here are two swords." Then he told them, "It is enough."

39 Then Jesus went out and made his way, as he customarily did, to the Mount of Olives, and the disciples followed him. 40 When he came to the place, he said to them, "Pray that you will not fall into temptation." 41 He went away from them about a stone's throw, knelt down, and prayed, 42 "Father, if you are willing, take this cup away from me. Yet not my will but yours be done." [43 Then an angel from heaven appeared to him and strengthened him. 44 And in his anguish he prayed more earnestly, and his sweat was like drops of blood falling to the ground.] 45 When he got up from prayer, he came to the disciples and found them sleeping, exhausted from grief. 46 So he said to them, "Why are you sleeping? Get up and pray that you will not fall into temptation!"

47 While he was still speaking, suddenly a crowd appeared, and the man named Judas, one of the twelve, was leading them. He walked up to Jesus to kiss him. 48 But Jesus said to him, "Judas, would you betray the Son of Man with a kiss?" 49 When those who were around him saw what was about to happen, they said, "Lord, should we use our swords?" 50 Then one of them struck the high priest's slave, cutting off his right ear. 51 But Jesus said, "Enough of this!" And he touched the man's ear and healed him. 52 Then Jesus said to the chief priests, the officers of the temple guard, and the elders who had come out to get him, "Have you come out with swords and clubs like you would against an outlaw? 53 Day after day when I was with you in the temple courts, you did not arrest me. But this is your hour, and that of the power of darkness!"

54 Then they arrested Jesus, led him away, and brought him into the high priest's house. But Peter was following at a distance.

55 When they had made a fire in the middle of the courtyard and sat down together, Peter sat down among them. 56 Then a slave girl, seeing him as he sat in the firelight, stared at him and said, "This man was with him too!" 57 But Peter denied it: "Woman, I don't know him!" 58 Then a little later someone else saw him and said, "You are one of them too." But Peter said, "Man, I am not!" 59 And after about an hour still another insisted, "Certainly this man was with him because he too is a Galilean." 60 But Peter said, "Man, I don't know what you're talking about!" At that moment, while he was still speaking, a rooster crowed. 61 Then the Lord turned and looked straight at Peter, and Peter remembered the word of the Lord, how he had said to him, "Before a rooster crows today, you will deny me three times." 62 And he went outside and wept bitterly.

63 Now the men who were holding Jesus under guard began to mock him and beat him. 64 They blindfolded him and asked him repeatedly, "Prophesy! Who hit you?" 65 They also said many other things against him, reviling him.

66 When day came, the council of the elders of the people gathered together, both the chief priests and the experts in the law. Then they led Jesus away to their council 67 and said, "If you are the Christ, tell us." But he said to them, "If I tell you, you will not believe, 68 and if I ask you, you will not answer. 69 But from now on the Son of Man will be seated at the right hand of the power of God." 70 So they all said, "Are you the Son of God, then?" He answered them, "You say that I am." 71 Then they said, "Why do we need further testimony? We have heard it ourselves from his own lips!"

23:1 Then the whole group of them rose up and brought Jesus before Pilate. 2 They began to accuse him, saying, "We found this man subverting our nation, forbidding us to pay the tribute tax to Caesar and claiming that he himself is Christ, a king." 3 So Pilate asked Jesus, "Are you the king of the Jews?" He replied, "You say so." 4 Then Pilate said to the chief priests and the crowds, "I find no basis for an accusation against this man." 5 But they persisted in saying, "He incites the people by teaching throughout all Judea. It started in Galilee and ended up here!"

6 Now when Pilate heard this, he asked whether the man was a Galilean. 7 When he learned that he was from Herod's jurisdiction, he sent him over to Herod, who also happened to be in Jerusalem at that time. 8 When Herod saw Jesus, he was very glad, for he had long desired to see him because he had heard about him and was hoping to see him perform some miraculous sign. 9 So Herod

questioned him at considerable length; Jesus gave him no answer. 10 The chief priests and the experts in the law were there, vehemently accusing him. 11 Even Herod with his soldiers treated him with contempt and mocked him. Then, dressing him in elegant clothes, Herod sent him back to Pilate. 12 That very day Herod and Pilate became friends with each other, for prior to this they had been enemies.

13 Then Pilate called together the chief priests, the leaders, and the people, 14 and said to them, "You brought me this man as one who was misleading the people. When I examined him before you, I did not find this man guilty of anything you accused him of doing. 15 Neither did Herod, for he sent him back to us. Look, he has done nothing deserving death. 16 I will therefore have him flogged and release him.

18 But they all shouted out together, "Take this man away! Release Barabbas for us!" 19 (This was a man who had been thrown into prison for an insurrection started in the city, and for murder.) 20 Pilate addressed them once again because he wanted to release Jesus. 21 But they kept on shouting, "Crucify, crucify him!" 22 A third time he said to them, "Why? What wrong has he done? I have found him guilty of no crime deserving death. I will therefore flog him and release him." 23 But they were insistent, demanding with loud shouts that he be crucified. And their shouts prevailed. 24 So Pilate decided that their demand should be granted. 25 He released the man they asked for, who had been thrown in prison for insurrection and murder. But he handed Jesus over to their will.

26 As they led him away, they seized Simon of Cyrene, who was coming in from the country. They placed the cross on his back and made him carry it behind Jesus. 27 A great number of the people followed him, among them women who were mourning and wailing for him. 28 But Jesus turned to them and said, "Daughters of Jerusalem, do not weep for me, but weep for yourselves and for your children. 29 For this is certain: The days are coming when they will say, 'Blessed are the barren, the wombs that never bore children, and the breasts that never nursed!' 30 Then they will begin to say to the mountains, 'Fall on us!' and to the hills, 'Cover us!' 31 For if such things are done when the wood is green, what will happen when it is dry?"

32 Two other criminals were also led away to be executed with him. 33 So when they came to the place that is called "The Skull," they crucified him there, along with the criminals, one on his right and one on his left. 34 [But Jesus said, "Father, forgive them, for they don't know what they are doing."] Then they threw dice to

divide his clothes. 35 The people also stood there watching, but the leaders ridiculed him, saying, "He saved others. Let him save himself if he is the Christ of God, his chosen one!" 36 The soldiers also mocked him, coming up and offering him sour wine, 37 and saying, "If you are the king of the Jews, save yourself!" 38 There was also an inscription over him, "This is the king of the Jews."

39 One of the criminals who was hanging there railed at him, saying, "Aren't you the Christ? Save yourself and us!" 40 But the other rebuked him, saying, "Don't you fear God, since you are under the same sentence of condemnation? 41 And we rightly so, for we are getting what we deserve for what we did, but this man has done nothing wrong." 42 Then he said, "Jesus, remember me when you come in your kingdom." 43 And Jesus said to him, "I tell you the truth, today you will be with me in paradise."

44 It was now about noon, and darkness came over the whole land until three in the afternoon, 45 because the sun's light failed. The temple curtain was torn in two. 46 Then Jesus, calling out with a loud voice, said, "Father, into your hands I commit my spirit!" And after he said this he breathed his last.

47 Now when the centurion saw what had happened, he praised God and said, "Certainly this man was innocent!" 48 And all the crowds that had assembled for this spectacle, when they saw what had taken place, returned home beating their breasts. 49 And all those who knew Jesus stood at a distance, and the women who had followed him from Galilee saw these things.

50 Now there was a man named Joseph who was a member of the council, a good and righteous man. 51 (He had not consented to their plan and action.) He was from the Judean town of Arimathea, and was looking forward to the kingdom of God. 52 He went to Pilate and asked for the body of Jesus. 53 Then he took it down, wrapped it in a linen cloth, and placed it in a tomb cut out of the rock, where no one had yet been buried. 54 It was the day of preparation, and the Sabbath was beginning. 55 The women who had accompanied Jesus from Galilee followed, and they saw the tomb and how his body was laid in it. 56 Then they returned and prepared aromatic spices and perfumes.

On the Sabbath they rested according to the commandment.

24:1 Now on the first day of the week, at early dawn, the women went to the tomb, taking the aromatic spices they had prepared. 2 They found that the stone had been rolled away from the tomb, 3 but when they went in, they did not find the body of the Lord Jesus. 4 While they were perplexed about this, suddenly two men stood beside them in dazzling attire. 5 The women were terribly frightened and bowed their faces to the ground, but the men said to them, "Why do you look for the living among the dead? 6 He is not here, but has been raised! Remember how he told you, while he was still in Galilee, 7 that the Son of Man must be delivered into the hands of sinful men, and be crucified, and on the third day rise again." 8 Then the women remembered his words, 9 and when they returned from the tomb, they told all these things to the eleven and to all the rest. 10 Now it was Mary Magdalene, Joanna, Mary the mother of James, and the other women with them who told these things to the apostles. 11 But these words seemed like pure nonsense to them, and they did not believe them. 12 But Peter got up and ran to the tomb. He bent down and saw only the strips of linen cloth; then he went home, wondering what had happened.

13 Now that very day two of them were on their way to a village called Emmaus, about seven miles from Jerusalem. 14 They were talking to each other about all the things that had happened. 15 While they were talking and debating these things, Jesus himself approached and began to accompany them 16 (but their eyes were kept from recognizing him). 17 Then he said to them, "What are these matters you are discussing so intently as you walk along?" And they stood still, looking sad. 18 Then one of them, named Cleopas, answered him, "Are you the only visitor to Jerusalem who doesn't know the things that have happened there in these days?" 19 He said to them, "What things?" "The things concerning Jesus the Nazarene," they replied, "a man who, with his powerful deeds and words, proved to be a prophet before God and all the people; 20 and how our chief priests and leaders handed him over to be condemned to death, and crucified him. 21 But we had hoped that he was the one who was going to redeem Israel. Not only this, but it is now the third day since these things happened. 22 Furthermore, some women of our group amazed us. They were at the tomb early this morning, 23 and when they did not find his body, they came back and said they had seen a vision of angels, who said he was alive. 24 Then some of those who were with us went to the tomb and found it just as the women had said, but they did not see him." 25 So he said to them, "You foolish people—how slow of heart to believe all that the prophets have spoken! 26 Wasn't it necessary for the Christ to suffer these things and enter into his glory?" 27 Then beginning with Moses and all the prophets, he interpreted to them the things written about himself in all the scriptures.

28 So they approached the village where they were going. He acted as though he wanted to go farther, 29 but they urged him, "Stay with us because it is getting toward evening and the day is almost done." So he went in to stay with them.

30 When he had taken his place at the table with them, he took the bread, blessed and broke it, and gave it to them. 31 At this point their eyes were opened and they recognized him. Then he vanished out of their sight. 32 They said to each other, "Didn't our hearts burn within us while he was speaking with us on the road, while he was explaining the scriptures to us?" 33 So they got up that very hour and returned to Jerusalem. They found the eleven and those with them gathered together 34 and saying, "The Lord has really risen and has appeared to Simon!" 35 Then they told what had happened on the road, and how they recognized him when he broke the bread.

36 While they were saying these things, Jesus himself stood among them and said to them, "Peace be with you." 37 But they were startled and terrified, thinking they saw a ghost. 38 Then he said to them, "Why are you frightened, and why do doubts arise in your hearts? 39 Look at my hands and my feet; it's me! Touch me and see; a ghost does not have flesh and jbones like you see I have." 40 When he had said this, he showed them his hands and his feet. 41 And while they still could not believe it (because of their joy) and were amazed, he said to them, "Do you have anything here to eat?" 42 So they gave him a piece of broiled fish, 43 and he took it and ate it in front of them.

44 Then he said to them, "These are my words that I spoke to you while I was still with you, that everything written about me in the law of Moses and the prophets and the psalms must be fulfilled." 45 Then he opened their minds so they could understand the scriptures, 46 and said to them, "Thus it stands written that the Christ would suffer and would rise from the dead on the third day, 47 and repentance for the forgiveness of sins would be proclaimed in his name to all nations, beginning from Jerusalem. 48 You are witnesses of these things. 49 And look, I am sending you what my Father promised. But stay in the city until you have been clothed with power from on high."

50 Then Jesus led them out as far as Bethany, and lifting up his hands, he blessed them. 51 Now during the blessing he departed and was taken up into heaven. 52 So they worshiped him and returned to Jerusalem with great joy, 53 and were continually in the temple courts blessing God.

2. What things does Jesus want his disciples to do?

____

____

3. Which of these things still apply to all of his followers?

____

____

Tuesday: Things to Come

1. Pray for the Holy Spirit to grant insight into God's word and read Luke 21—22:23. Circle all references to the "end" and "near" in chapter 21, and references to "Passover" in the verses in chapter 22. Underline signs that the end is near.

> 21:1 Jesus looked up and saw the rich putting their gifts into the offering box. 2 He also saw a poor widow put in two small copper coins. 3 He said, "I tell you the truth, this poor widow has put in more than all of them. 4 For they all offered their gifts out of their wealth. But she, out of her poverty, put in everything she had to live on."
>
> 5 Now while some were speaking about the temple, how it was adorned with beautiful stones and offerings, Jesus said, 6 "As for these things that you are gazing at, the days will come when not one stone will be left on another. All will be torn down!" 7 So they asked him, "Teacher, when will these things happen? And what will be the sign that these things are about to take place?" 8 He said, "Watch out that you are not misled. For many will come in my name, saying, 'I am he,' and, 'The time is near.' Do not follow them! 9 And when you hear of wars and rebellions, do not be afraid. For these things must happen first, but the end will not come at once."
>
> 10 Then he said to them, "Nation will rise up in arms against nation, and kingdom against kingdom. 11 There will be great earthquakes, and famines and plagues in various places, and there will be terrifying sights and great signs from heaven. 12 But before all this, they will seize you and persecute you, handing you over to the synagogues and prisons. You will be brought before kings and governors because of my name. 13 This will be a time for you to serve as witnesses. 14 Therefore be resolved not to rehearse ahead of time how to make your defense. 15 For I will give you the words along with the wisdom that none of your adversaries will be able to withstand or contradict. 16 You will be betrayed even by parents, brothers, relatives, and friends, and they will have some of you put

to death. 17 You will be hated by everyone because of my name. 18 Yet not a hair of your head will perish. 19 By your endurance you will gain your lives.

20 "But when you see Jerusalem surrounded by armies, then know that its desolation has come near. 21 Then those who are in Judea must flee to the mountains. Those who are inside the city must depart. Those who are out in the country must not enter it, 22 because these are days of vengeance, to fulfill all that is written. 23 Woe to those who are pregnant and to those who are nursing their babies in those days! For there will be great distress on the earth and wrath against this people. 24 They will fall by the edge of the sword and be led away as captives among all nations. Jerusalem will be trampled down by the Gentiles until the times of the Gentiles are fulfilled.

25 "And there will be signs in the sun and moon and stars, and on the earth nations will be in distress, anxious over the roaring of the sea and the surging waves. 26 People will be fainting from fear and from the expectation of what is coming on the world, for the powers of the heavens will be shaken. 27 Then they will see the Son of Man arriving in a cloud with power and great glory. 28 But when these things begin to happen, stand up and raise your heads because your redemption is drawing near."

29 Then he told them a parable: "Look at the fig tree and all the other trees. 30 When they sprout leaves, you see for yourselves and know that summer is now near. 31 So also you, when you see these things happening, know that the kingdom of God is near. 32 I tell you the truth, this generation will not pass away until all these things take place. 33 Heaven and earth will pass away, but my words will never pass away.

34 "But be on your guard so that your hearts are not weighed down with dissipation and drunkenness and the worries of this life, and that day close down upon you suddenly like a trap. 35 For it will overtake all who live on the face of the whole earth. 36 But stay alert at all times, praying that you may have strength to escape all these things that must happen, and to stand before the Son of Man."

37 So every day Jesus was teaching in the temple courts, but at night he went and stayed on the Mount of Olives. 38 And all the people came to him early in the morning to listen to him in the temple courts.

1 Now the Feast of Unleavened Bread, which is called the Passover, was approaching. 2 The chief priests and the experts in the law were trying to find some way to execute Jesus, for they were afraid of the people.

3 Then Satan entered Judas, the one called Iscariot, who was one of the twelve. 4 He went away and discussed with the chief priests and officers of the temple guard how he might betray Jesus, handing him over to them. 5 They were delighted and arranged to give him money. 6 So Judas agreed and began looking for an opportunity to betray Jesus when no crowd was present.

7 Then the day for the feast of Unleavened Bread came, on which the Passover lamb had to be sacrificed. 8 Jesus sent Peter and John, saying, "Go and prepare the Passover for us to eat." 9 They said to him, "Where do you want us to prepare it?" 10 He said to them, "Listen, when you have entered the city, a man carrying a jar of water will meet you. Follow him into the house that he enters, 11 and tell the owner of the house, 'The Teacher says to you, "Where is the guest room where I may eat the Passover with my disciples?"' 12 Then he will show you a large furnished room upstairs. Make preparations there." 13 So they went and found things just as he had told them, and they prepared the Passover.

14 Now when the hour came, Jesus took his place at the table and the apostles joined him. 15 And he said to them, "I have earnestly desired to eat this Passover with you before I suffer. 16 For I tell you, I will not eat it again until it is fulfilled in the kingdom of God." 17 Then he took a cup, and after giving thanks he said, "Take this and divide it among yourselves. 18 For I tell you that from now on I will not drink of the fruit of the vine until the kingdom of God comes." 19 Then he took bread, and after giving thanks he broke it and gave it to them, saying, "This is my body which is given for you. Do this in remembrance of me." 20 And in the same way he took the cup after they had eaten, saying, "This cup that is poured out for you is the new covenant in my blood.

According to a report in *The London Economic*, the wealthiest Americans donate 1.3 percent of their income, while the poorest donate 3.2 percent. Why do you think poor people tend to be more generous?

"Into the offering box" (v. 1) – The Jerusalem temple had multiple offering boxes that were wide at the bottom and narrow at the top like trumpets. People would bring their free-will offerings and place their cash in one of these boxes.

"A poor widow" (v. 2) – Imagine a world without social security or welfare. A woman's dowry, her children, and the mercy of God's people were her main sources of food. Widows were truly vulnerable and among "the least of the least." Notice how the last chapter—Luke 20—ends. Jesus describes religious people who devour widows' property. Having said this, he looks up and sees a widow whose life stands in contrast with such duplicity.

"Two small copper coins" (v. 2) – The word translated "coins" here is the plural form of lepton. A lepton was the smallest and least valuable coin in circulation in Jesus's world. It represented five to six minutes' labor at minimum wage and was small enough to fit on a thumbnail.

2. For how long do you think you could eat on ten minutes' wages?

____

____

3. What does her action reveal about the woman Jesus is observing?

____

____

4. How can you be more like her?

____

____

"Everything she had to live on" (v. 4) – Or "her entire livelihood."

5. Luke transitions from talking about this woman's huge-to-her contribution to talking about offerings and stones that adorn the temple. What does Jesus say will happen to all the adornment (vv. 5–6)?

____

____

6. The disciples want to know when Jesus's prediction will happen (v. 7). The Lord does not give a date, but he gives his disciples signs to notice as well as warnings and encouragements that accompany the signs. Fill in the middle section of the chart that shows Jesus's teaching about the future.

Signs	Exhortation, instruction and/ or reason
Many come in my name (v. 8)	Watch out that you are not misled. Don't follow them.
Wars, rebellions (v. 9)	Don't be afraid.
Nations/kingdoms rising in arms (v. 10) Earthquakes, famines, plagues (v. 11) Terrifying signs from heaven (v. 11) Christ-followers seized (v. 12)	This will be a time to serve as witnesses. Be resolved not to rehearse your defense for I will give you words to say.
Betrayal by relatives, some of you put to death, hated by everyone because of my name (vv. 16, 17)	(v. 18, 19)
Jerusalem surrounded by armies (v. 20)	(vv. 20–21)
Woe to pregnant, nursing women (v. 23) Great distress on earth and wrath against this people (v. 23). They will fall by the edge of the sword and be led away captives. Jerusalem will be under the yoke of conquering nations till the times of the Gentiles are fulfilled (v. 24). Signs in sun, moon, and stars; earth's nations in distress, anxious over the sea and surging waves. People faint from fear (vv. 25–26). The powers of heaven shaken (v. 26).	(vv. 21–26)
They will see the Son of Man arriving in a cloud with power and great glory (v. 27)	Stand and raise your heads, for your redemption is drawing near (v. 28)

7. What does a fig tree have to do with the events Jesus has described (vv. 29–31)?

"I tell you the truth, this generation will not pass away until all these things take place" (v. 32). Jesus prefaces his promise with an emphatic assurance—I tell you the truth. What exactly is he stressing as true? Actually, the most difficult saying of all! Everything Jesus has predicted is supposed to take place before "this generation" passes away. But what does he mean by "this generation"? Since Luke has used the word "generation" to refer to people alive in his day, one would expect all of Jesus's predictions to have been fulfilled within several decades of these statements. Yet, we're still waiting for his return. Others think "generation" means "race." If so, Jesus was saying the Jewish race or nation would not pass away till all these things happened. Yet such a meaning for "generation" would be an odd use of the word. A third option is that Jesus meant when the birth pangs of fulfillment start, the generation that sees the beginning of signs will also see the end of them—the signs and their fulfillment will not be drawn out for hundreds of years or over millennia. If so, "this generation" means the generation that sees the birth pangs of the end will also see their fulfillment (vv. 25–26). A fourth possibility, and one I'm inclined toward, is that Jesus's use of "generation" here refers to "this kind of generation"—that is, wicked humanity. If so, humanity will not pass away until all is fulfilled, even if we blow each other up with nuclear wars. Jesus seems to use the word this way elsewhere in referring to "an evil and adulterous generation" which "asks for a sign" (Matt. 12:39). Wicked humanity is still expecting signs from God, even though we have the "sign" of Jesus's resurrection.

"Heaven and earth will pass away, but my words will never pass away" (v. 33). Lest anyone doubt, Jesus says his own words are more sure than heaven and earth. Every last thing he predicted will happen. How many humans can say this?

8. In light of the coming events, why does Jesus say to be on guard (vv. 34–35)?

---

9. What two things does he say to pray for while staying alert and praying at all times (v. 36)?

____

____

10. Jesus has come to Jerusalem to lay down his life. How is he spending his final days and nights (vv. 37–38)?

____

____

11. Are you ready for Jesus's return at any time? How can you prepare?

____

____

12. Think of how you spend your days and nights. Do you have Jesus's priorities? Why or why not?

____

____

13. Jesus has an earnest desire to do something before he suffers. What is that desire (v. 15)?

____

____

"The Feast of Unleavened Bread, which is called the Passover, was approaching" (v. 1). The Feast of Unleavened Bread and Passover were actually separate events, but they were often combined as "Passover." The feast, described in Exodus 11, commemorates the event of "the Exodus." After the descendants of Jacob/Israel were slaves in Egypt for more than four centuries, God raised up Moses to free them. After nine plagues, the tenth and final blow to the

Egyptians was that God killed every firstborn person and creature. Yet God spared every family that painted lamb's blood on their doorpost; for them, the angel of death "passed over." Knowing this, God's people "under the blood' were spared, while every Egyptian household "not covered by the blood" suffered. All the deaths were the final straw for Pharaoh, who finally allowed Moses's people the freedom to go to their Promised Land. The nation of Israel commemorated this deliverance by observing an annual feast. Jesus and his disciples—all being observant Jews—were in Jerusalem for the events. The temple would have been especially crowded during this time.

14. While Jesus is having this very public ministry, what do the chief priests and law experts want, and what prevents them (v. 2)?

____

____

15. List Judas's acts of betrayal (vv. 4–6).

____

____

16. What supernatural powers does Jesus demonstrate in his Passover plans (vv. 7–13)?

____

____

17. After this Passover, when does Jesus say will be the next time he observes the Passover supper (v. 16)?

____

18. For whom does Jesus say his body is given and his blood is poured out (v. 19)?

____

____

Wednesday: Betrayed!

1. Pray for wisdom and read Luke 22:21–71. Circle all references to "Passover." Underline the sections where Jesus is betrayed in some way.

> 22:21 "But look, the hand of the one who betrays me is with me on the table. 22 For the Son of Man is to go just as it has been determined, but woe to that man by whom he is betrayed!" 23 So they began to question one another as to which of them it could possibly be who would do this.
>
> 24 A dispute also started among them over which of them was to be regarded as the greatest. 25 So Jesus said to them, "The kings of the Gentiles lord it over them, and those in authority over them are called 'benefactors.' 26 Not so with you; instead the one who is greatest among you must become like the youngest, and the leader like the one who serves. 27 For who is greater, the one who is seated at the table, or the one who serves? Is it not the one who is seated at the table? But I am among you as one who serves.
>
> 28 "You are the ones who have remained with me in my trials. 29 Thus I grant to you a kingdom, just as my Father granted to me, 30 that you may eat and drink at my table in my kingdom, and you will sit on thrones judging the twelve tribes of Israel.
>
> 31 "Simon, Simon, pay attention! Satan has demanded to have you all, to sift you like wheat, 32 but I have prayed for you, Simon, that your faith may not fail. When you have turned back, strengthen your brothers." 33 But Peter said to him, "Lord, I am ready to go with you both to prison and to death!" 34 Jesus replied, "I tell you, Peter, the rooster will not crow today until you have denied three times that you know me."
>
> 35 Then Jesus said to them, "When I sent you out with no money bag, or traveler's bag, or sandals, you didn't lack anything, did you?" They replied, "Nothing." 36 He said to them, "But now, the one who has a money bag must take it, and likewise a traveler's bag too. And the one who has no sword must sell his cloak and buy one. 37 For I tell you that this scripture must be fulfilled in me, 'And he was counted with the transgressors.' For what is written about me is being fulfilled." 38 So they said, "Look, Lord, here are two swords." Then he told them, "It is enough."
>
> 39 Then Jesus went out and made his way, as he customarily did, to the Mount of Olives, and the disciples followed him. 40 When he came to the place, he said to them, "Pray that you will not fall into temptation." 41 He went away from them about a stone's throw, knelt down, and prayed, 42 "Father, if you are willing,

take this cup away from me. Yet not my will but yours be done." [43 Then an angel from heaven appeared to him and strengthened him. 44 And in his anguish he prayed more earnestly, and his sweat was like drops of blood falling to the ground.] 45 When he got up from prayer, he came to the disciples and found them sleeping, exhausted from grief. 46 So he said to them, "Why are you sleeping? Get up and pray that you will not fall into temptation!"

47 While he was still speaking, suddenly a crowd appeared, and the man named Judas, one of the twelve, was leading them. He walked up to Jesus to kiss him. 48 But Jesus said to him, "Judas, would you betray the Son of Man with a kiss?" 49 When those who were around him saw what was about to happen, they said, "Lord, should we use our swords?" 50 Then one of them struck the high priest's slave, cutting off his right ear. 51 But Jesus said, "Enough of this!" And he touched the man's ear and healed him. 52 Then Jesus said to the chief priests, the officers of the temple guard, and the elders who had come out to get him, "Have you come out with swords and clubs like you would against an outlaw? 53 Day after day when I was with you in the temple courts, you did not arrest me. But this is your hour, and that of the power of darkness!"

54 Then they arrested Jesus, led him away, and brought him into the high priest's house. But Peter was following at a distance. 55 When they had made a fire in the middle of the courtyard and sat down together, Peter sat down among them. 56 Then a slave girl, seeing him as he sat in the firelight, stared at him and said, "This man was with him too!" 57 But Peter denied it: "Woman, I don't know him!" 58 Then a little later someone else saw him and said, "You are one of them too." But Peter said, "Man, I am not!" 59 And after about an hour still another insisted, "Certainly this man was with him because he too is a Galilean." 60 But Peter said, "Man, I don't know what you're talking about!" At that moment, while he was still speaking, a rooster crowed. 61 Then the Lord turned and looked straight at Peter, and Peter remembered the word of the Lord, how he had said to him, "Before a rooster crows today, you will deny me three times." 62 And he went outside and wept bitterly.

63 Now the men who were holding Jesus under guard began to mock him and beat him. 64 They blindfolded him and asked him repeatedly, "Prophesy! Who hit you?" 65 They also said many other things against him, reviling him.

66 When day came, the council of the elders of the people gathered together, both the chief priests and the experts in the law. Then they led Jesus away to their council 67 and said, "If you are

the Christ, tell us." But he said to them, "If I tell you, you will not believe, 68 and if I ask you, you will not answer. 69 But from now on the Son of Man will be seated at the right hand of the power of God." 70 So they all said, "Are you the Son of God, then?" He answered them, "You say that I am." 71 Then they said, "Why do we need further testimony? We have heard it ourselves from his own lips!"

2. Jesus knows all about his betrayer's actions (v. 21). Why do you think Jesus does not stop him?

____

____

3. What does Jesus suggest is Judas's future (v. 22)?

____

____

4. The disciples seem to have no idea which one of them is capable of betraying Jesus. What does that suggest about Judas?

____

____

5. How do you think Jesus feels, knowing one of his friends, someone with whom he has shared a thousand meals—including this one—is cooperating to have him murdered? How do you think Jesus feels when, in response to the news someone will betray him, his disciples argue over who will be greatest (v. 24)?

____

____

____

6. Compare and contrast how the nations rule and lead with how Jesus views greatness (vv. 24–27)?

____

____

7. What does Jesus promise his faithful followers (vv. 28–30)?

____

____

8. How has Jesus specially prepared Peter for the trauma he is about to face (vv. 31–32)?

____

____

9. Peter has a high view of his own faithfulness (v. 33). In what way does Jesus say Peter is about to fail (v. 34)? Consider ways in which we are at risk of being like Peter.

____

____

10. Things are changing now. Opposition will come. So, in contrast with previous guidelines (v. 35), Jesus has new instructions (v. 36). How do the two sets of instructions differ?

____

____

"This scripture must be fulfilled in me, 'And he was counted with the transgressors.' For what is written about me is being fulfilled" (v. 37). Notice Jesus uses the word "fulfilled" twice. None of the events about to happen are hitting him by surprise, nor are they out of his control. Jesus quotes from Isaiah's "Suffering Servant" passage, in which this prophet predicted Messiah's sufferings eight centuries earlier:

"So I will assign him a portion with the multitudes,
he will divide the spoils of victory with the powerful,
because he willingly submitted to death
and was numbered with the rebels,
when he lifted up the sin of many
and intervened on behalf of the rebels." (Isaiah 53:12, italics added)

In this chapter and the next, Luke emphasizes how the innocent willingly lays down his life for the unrighteous.

11. Jesus is focused on fulfilling prophecy. On what are the disciples focused (v. 38)? It would be easy to criticize, but Jesus's followers today are not all that different, are we?

____

____

12. We read earlier that Jesus has been spending his nights at the Mount of Olives (v. 39), which overlooks Jerusalem from across a valley. On this evening, what does he instruct his disciples to do (v. 40)?

____

____

13. What does Jesus pray (v. 42)? How do you think he felt at this point?

____

____

As if Judas's betrayal were not enough (added to knowing Peter will deny him), how do you think Jesus felt when he found his disciples asleep (vv. 45–46)?

____

____

14. In Jesus's very moment of aloneness, Judas shows up leading a crowd. He approaches Jesus and kisses him. Jesus seems to find Judas's means of betrayal particularly bitter (v. 48). What title does Jesus use of himself here—which suggests Judas has done far more than betray a friend?

Not all manuscripts include vv. 43–44. A good case can be made both for omission and inclusion. The events doubtless happened, even if Luke was not the one who first recorded them.

---

15. Realizing what's about to happen, the disciples jump into action. What are their first impulses (vv. 49–50) and how does Jesus's response differ (v. 51)?

---

16. Jesus addresses the religious leaders who have come to seize him. He has just healed one of his attackers. Why do you think Jesus finds their swords and clubs so repulsive (vv. 52–53)?

---

17. Jesus predicted Peter would betray him, and outside the high priest's house, this prediction is sadly fulfilled (vv. 54–62). What is Peter's response? What do you think was the worst part for Peter?

---

18. Jesus is an innocent man. He understands how it feels to suffer injustice of the worst kind. List the injustices done to him as recorded in v. 63–65.

____

____

19. Notice how the leaders equate Jesus's self-identification as the "Son of Man" with the title "Son of God" (vv. 69–70). How do you think Jesus sees himself (v. 71)?

____

____

20. Who do they think Jesus is? Who do you think Jesus is?

____

____

Thursday: The Innocent For The Guilty

1. Pray for the Spirit to grant wisdom and read Luke 23. Circle references to guilt and innocence.

> 23:1 Then the whole group of them rose up and brought Jesus before Pilate. 2 They began to accuse him, saying, "We found this man subverting our nation, forbidding us to pay the tribute tax to Caesar and claiming that he himself is Christ, a king." 3 So Pilate asked Jesus, "Are you the king of the Jews?" He replied, "You say so." 4 Then Pilate said to the chief priests and the crowds, "I find no basis for an accusation against this man." 5 But they persisted in saying, "He incites the people by teaching throughout all Judea. It started in Galilee and ended up here!"
>
> 6 Now when Pilate heard this, he asked whether the man was a Galilean. 7 When he learned that he was from Herod's jurisdiction, he sent him over to Herod, who also happened to be in Jerusalem at that time. 8 When Herod saw Jesus, he was very glad, for he

had long desired to see him because he had heard about him and was hoping to see him perform some miraculous sign. 9 So Herod questioned him at considerable length; Jesus gave him no answer. 10 The chief priests and the experts in the law were there, vehemently accusing him. 11 Even Herod with his soldiers treated him with contempt and mocked him. Then, dressing him in elegant clothes, Herod sent him back to Pilate. 12 That very day Herod and Pilate became friends with each other, for prior to this they had been enemies.

13 Then Pilate called together the chief priests, the leaders, and the people, 14 and said to them, "You brought me this man as one who was misleading the people. When I examined him before you, I did not find this man guilty of anything you accused him of doing. 15 Neither did Herod, for he sent him back to us. Look, he has done nothing deserving death. 16 I will therefore have him flogged and release him."

18 But they all shouted out together, "Take this man away! Release Barabbas for us!" 19 (This was a man who had been thrown into prison for an insurrection started in the city, and for murder.) 20 Pilate addressed them once again because he wanted to release Jesus. 21 But they kept on shouting, "Crucify, crucify him!" 22 A third time he said to them, "Why? What wrong has he done? I have found him guilty of no crime deserving death. I will therefore flog him and release him." 23 But they were insistent, demanding with loud shouts that he be crucified. And their shouts prevailed. 24 So Pilate decided that their demand should be granted. 25 He released the man they asked for, who had been thrown in prison for insurrection and murder. But he handed Jesus over to their will.

26 As they led him away, they seized Simon of Cyrene, who was coming in from the country. They placed the cross on his back and made him carry it behind Jesus. 27 A great number of the people followed him, among them women who were mourning and wailing for him. 28 But Jesus turned to them and said, "Daughters of Jerusalem, do not weep for me, but weep for yourselves and for your children. 29 For this is certain: The days are coming when they will say, 'Blessed are the barren, the wombs that never bore children, and the breasts that never nursed!' 30 Then they will begin to say to the mountains, 'Fall on us!' and to the hills, 'Cover us!' 31 For if such things are done when the wood is green, what will happen when it is dry?"

32 Two other criminals were also led away to be executed with him. 33 So when they came to the place that is called "The Skull," they crucified him there, along with the criminals, one on his right and one on his left. 34 [But Jesus said, "Father, forgive them, for

they don't know what they are doing."] Then they threw dice to divide his clothes. 35 The people also stood there watching, but the leaders ridiculed him, saying, "He saved others. Let him save himself if he is the Christ of God, his chosen one!" 36 The soldiers also mocked him, coming up and offering him sour wine, 37 and saying, "If you are the king of the Jews, save yourself!" 38 There was also an inscription over him, "This is the king of the Jews."

39 One of the criminals who was hanging there railed at him, saying, "Aren't you the Christ? Save yourself and us!" 40 But the other rebuked him, saying, "Don't you fear God, since you are under the same sentence of condemnation? 41 And we rightly so, for we are getting what we deserve for what we did, but this man has done nothing wrong." 42 Then he said, "Jesus, remember me when you come in your kingdom." 43 And Jesus said to him, "I tell you the truth, today you will be with me in paradise."

44 It was now about noon, and darkness came over the whole land until three in the afternoon, 45 because the sun's light failed. The temple curtain was torn in two. 46 Then Jesus, calling out with a loud voice, said, "Father, into your hands I commit my spirit!" And after he said this he breathed his last.

47 Now when the centurion saw what had happened, he praised God and said, "Certainly this man was innocent!" 48 And all the crowds that had assembled for this spectacle, when they saw what had taken place, returned home beating their breasts. 49 And all those who knew Jesus stood at a distance, and the women who had followed him from Galilee saw these things.

50 Now there was a man named Joseph who was a member of the council, a good and righteous man. 51 (He had not consented to their plan and action.) He was from the Judean town of Arimathea, and was looking forward to the kingdom of God. 52 He went to Pilate and asked for the body of Jesus. 53 Then he took it down, wrapped it in a linen cloth, and placed it in a tomb cut out of the rock, where no one had yet been buried. 54 It was the day of preparation, and the Sabbath was beginning. 55 The women who had accompanied Jesus from Galilee followed, and they saw the tomb and how his body was laid in it. 56 Then they returned and prepared aromatic spices and perfumes.

On the Sabbath they rested according to the commandment.

"Brought Jesus before Pilate" (v. 1) – Marcus Pontius Pilate, according to tradition, was a Roman citizen from the clan of the Pontii, hence his name "Pontius." He was the Roman prefect, or governor, of Judea (hence "Pilate") at the time when Tiberius was emperor. Pilate presided at the trial of Jesus and gave the order to have him crucified.

Rome allowed conquered peoples to have a degree of self-government. In Judea, the Jews' highest court was the Sanhedrin, comprised of chief priests, elders, and scribes. They could rule on religious matters, but Roman law superseded when civil and religious laws came into conflict. The religious leaders were prohibited from carrying out capital punishment, which they wanted to do in the case of Jesus, because in their eyes he had committed blasphemy. Although a claim to be God's anointed one was not punishable under Roman law, claiming to be king was a capital offense. Part of why the phrase "suffered under Pontius Pilate" is included in the Apostles' Creed is because the events of Christianity are rooted in historical and not simply "spiritual" events.

2. What non-religious accusations do Jesus's accusers bring against him (v. 2)?

____

____

3. Does Pilate initially find Jesus guilty or innocent (v. 4)? Such being the case, what would have been the just response?

____

____

4. What additional secular charge do Jesus's accusers bring (v. 5)?

____

____

5. How does Pilate get out of having to displease the crowd if he does the right thing (vv. 6–7)?

____

____

"He was from Herod's jurisdiction" (v. 7). Herod Antipas is the same ruler who ordered Jesus's relative, John the Baptist, beheaded and whom Jesus called a "fox."

6. What is Herod's response to the news that Jesus is coming his way, and what does he hope will happen (v. 8)?

---

7. Imagine facing the person who had your relative beheaded. What is Jesus's response to Herod's considerable questioning (v. 9)?

---

8. What are the responses of the Jewish leaders, Herod, and Herod's soldiers (vv. 10–12)?

---

9. Why do you think they dressed Jesus in elegant clothes (v. 11)?

---

10. Pilate repeats his own finding—and he adds Herod's. Does Pilate say Herod considers Jesus innocent or guilty of a capital offense (vv. 14–15)?

"I will therefore have him flogged and release him" (v. 16) – Jewish law had a forty-lash maximum, but the Romans had no such limit. In a typical whipping, soldiers stripped prisoners naked, tied them to posts, and whipped them across the back, buttocks, and legs.

Sometimes soldiers would inflict further pain by cutting off the tongue or gouging out the eyes.

11. What is the crowd's response to Pilate's decision to flog a man he has declared innocent (vv. 18–19, 21)?

____

____

12. How many times has Pilate stated Jesus's innocence (v. 22)? Consider the irony that Peter denied his Lord three times.

____

____

13. The innocent (Jesus) will die so the guilty (Barabbas) can go free (v. 25). What do all humans have in common with Barabbas?

____

____

14. Why do you think Jesus did not carry his own cross (v. 26)?

____

____

"Daughters of Jerusalem...weep for yourselves" (v. 28). Remember how Jesus's Triumphal Entry fulfilled this prophecy of Zechariah?

Rejoice greatly, daughter of Zion!
Shout, daughter of Jerusalem!
Look! Your king is coming to you:
He is legitimate and victorious,
humble and riding on a donkey—
on a young donkey, the foal of a female donkey. (Zech. 9:9)

Zechariah mentions a daughter of Zion/Jerusalem who heralds the king's arrival in the city. But now in a great reversal, Jesus tells "the daughters of Jerusalem" to weep not for him but for themselves.

15. What is Jesus's word to Jerusalem (vv. 28–31)?

____

____

"For if such things are done when the wood is green, what will happen when it is dry?" (v. 31). Jesus likens his own suffering to a fire made with green wood. In comparison, Jerusalem's inhabitants are like dry lumber. The judgment for sin laid on God's own Son is like a mere struggling campfire compared with the conflagration coming for those who have rejected their king.

16. Jesus was flanked by two people as he was crucified. How does Luke describe them (vv. 32–33)? How does their presence add to the public shaming of Jesus?

____

____

17. What further shame is added to Jesus's suffering (vv. 34–39)?

____

____

"There was also an inscription over him, "This is the king of the Jews" (v. 38). The state intends the inscription as ironic. But in an ironic twist, they declare the actual truth.

18. Luke emphasizes in numerous ways the innocence of Jesus. Here one more person declares Jesus innocent (vv. 40–41). What does Jesus promise the one who believes (v. 43)?

____

____

19. What two supernatural events happen as Jesus is dying (vv.

44–45)? What do you think is significant about creation's response to the passion (suffering and death) of the Christ?

____

____

Consider renting the film *The Passion of the Christ* and viewing a retelling of the last week of Jesus's earthly life. Although the film is rated "R" for violence, New Testament scholars say the events that happened to Jesus were probably much more violent than depicted.

"The temple curtain was torn in two" (v. 45). The word "curtain" is broad enough to allow for two possibilities: (1) the curtain that separated the outer court from the temple itself and (2) the curtain that guarded the way into the Holy of Holies, behind which only the high priest passed once a year. Although we cannot be certain, it would seem that the tearing of the curtain when Jesus dies suggests that Jesus himself is the one who has torn it, concluding the ultimate atonement sufficient for sin, and granting access to the Holy of Holies to male and female, Jew and Gentile for all time. The tearing also suggests the inauguration of a transition from God inhabiting one physical temple to an era in which the Spirit—once sent—will indwell every human body where Christ is worshiped as Lord.

20. Yet another person declares Jesus innocent. Who is this person, and what does he say (v. 47)?

____

____

21. Luke makes no mention of the twelve apostles during these events, but some of his female followers witness his death. Where are the women from Galilee as Jesus is dying on the cross (v. 49)?

____

"A member of the council" (v. 50) – At the beginning of this chapter, Luke mentions the Jews' highest court, the Sanhedrin, comprised of chief priests, elders, and scribes. At this point, Luke mentions one member of this group who comes forward and provides a glimmer of hope that a remnant of Jewish leaders believe.

22. What do we learn about this member of the council (vv. 50–53)?

____

____

"It was the day of preparation, and the Sabbath was beginning" (v. 54). Friday was preparation day for the Sabbath, which lasted twenty-four hours beginning at sundown. A person observing the Sabbath laws would spend part of Friday preparing special meals, setting out Sabbath artifacts, cleaning, and arranging for prayer and worship time. Preparing a body for burial was considered work, so those preparing Jesus's body had to wait until Sunday morning to complete their task.

"Aromatic spices and perfumes" (v. 56) – Jewish custom did not include cremation or embalming, so those treating a body for burial prepared fragrances to cover the stench of decomposition. The fact that Jesus's female followers from Galilee chose to honor his body in this way suggests they had no idea he would rise from the dead.

23. Imagine yourself in the scene. What is going through your mind as you prepare spices and perfumes for the body of the one you love, whom you thought would be king?

____

____

____

Friday: He Is Not Here!

1. Pray for the Spirit to grant insight and read Luke 24. Underline references to the women.

> 24:1 Now on the first day of the week, at early dawn, the women went to the tomb, taking the aromatic spices they had prepared. 2 They found that the stone had been rolled away from the tomb, 3 but when they went in, they did not find the body of the Lord Jesus. 4 While they were perplexed about this, suddenly two men stood beside them in dazzling attire. 5 The women were ter-

ribly frightened and bowed their faces to the ground, but the men said to them, "Why do you look for the living among the dead? 6 He is not here, but has been raised! Remember how he told you, while he was still in Galilee, 7 that the Son of Man must be delivered into the hands of sinful men, and be crucified, and on the third day rise again." 8 Then the women remembered his words, 9 and when they returned from the tomb, they told all these things to the eleven and to all the rest. 10 Now it was Mary Magdalene, Joanna, Mary the mother of James, and the other women with them who told these things to the apostles. 11 But these words seemed like pure nonsense to them, and they did not believe them. 12 But Peter got up and ran to the tomb. He bent down and saw only the strips of linen cloth; then he went home, wondering what had happened.

13 Now that very day two of them were on their way to a village called Emmaus, about seven miles from Jerusalem. 14 They were talking to each other about all the things that had happened. 15 While they were talking and debating these things, Jesus himself approached and began to accompany them 16 (but their eyes were kept from recognizing him). 17 Then he said to them, "What are these matters you are discussing so intently as you walk along?" And they stood still, looking sad. 18 Then one of them, named Cleopas, answered him, "Are you the only visitor to Jerusalem who doesn't know the things that have happened there in these days?" 19 He said to them, "What things?" "The things concerning Jesus the Nazarene," they replied, "a man who, with his powerful deeds and words, proved to be a prophet before God and all the people; 20 and how our chief priests and leaders handed him over to be condemned to death, and crucified him. 21 But we had hoped that he was the one who was going to redeem Israel. Not only this, but it is now the third day since these things happened. 22 Furthermore, some women of our group amazed us. They were at the tomb early this morning, 23 and when they did not find his body, they came back and said they had seen a vision of angels, who said he was alive. 24 Then some of those who were with us went to the tomb and found it just as the women had said, but they did not see him." 25 So he said to them, "You foolish people—how slow of heart to believe all that the prophets have spoken! 26 Wasn't it necessary for the Christ to suffer these things and enter into his glory?" 27 Then beginning with Moses and all the prophets, he interpreted to them the things written about himself in all the scriptures.

28 So they approached the village where they were going. He acted as though he wanted to go farther, 29 but they urged him, "Stay with us because it is getting toward evening and the day is almost done." So he went in to stay with them.

30 When he had taken his place at the table with them, he took the bread, blessed and broke it, and gave it to them. 31 At this point their eyes were opened and they recognized him. Then he vanished out of their sight. 32 They said to each other, "Didn't our hearts burn within us while he was speaking with us on the road, while he was explaining the scriptures to us?" 33 So they got up that very hour and returned to Jerusalem. They found the eleven and those with them gathered together 34 and saying, "The Lord has really risen and has appeared to Simon!" 35 Then they told what had happened on the road, and how they recognized him when he broke the bread.

36 While they were saying these things, Jesus himself stood among them and said to them, "Peace be with you." 37 But they were startled and terrified, thinking they saw a ghost. 38 Then he said to them, "Why are you frightened, and why do doubts arise in your hearts? 39 Look at my hands and my feet; it's me! Touch me and see; a ghost does not have flesh and bones like you see I have." 40 When he had said this, he showed them his hands and his feet. 41 And while they still could not believe it (because of their joy) and were amazed, he said to them, "Do you have anything here to eat?" 42 So they gave him a piece of broiled fish, 43 and he took it and ate it in front of them.

44 Then he said to them, "These are my words that I spoke to you while I was still with you, that everything written about me in the law of Moses and the prophets and the psalms must be fulfilled." 45 Then he opened their minds so they could understand the scriptures, 46 and said to them, "Thus it stands written that the Christ would suffer and would rise from the dead on the third day, 47 and repentance for the forgiveness of sins would be proclaimed in his name to all nations, beginning from Jerusalem. 48 You are witnesses of these things. 49 And look, I am sending you what my Father promised. But stay in the city until you have been clothed with power from on high."

50 Then Jesus led them out as far as Bethany, and lifting up his hands, he blessed them. 51 Now during the blessing he departed and was taken up into heaven. 52 So they worshiped him and returned to Jerusalem with great joy, 53 and were continually in the temple courts blessing God.

2. What part do the women have in the resurrection story?

____

____

"Now on the first day of the week, at early dawn" (v. 1) – The Sabbath is over, so at the first possible moment, the women who have mixed spices go to Jesus's tomb to prepare his body for burial.

3. What do the women discover (vv. 2–3)?

____

____

4. What is the women's emotion (v. 4)? Imagine you are one of them. What are you thinking? What are the possible options you consider for what has happened?

____

____

"Suddenly two men stood beside them in dazzling attire" (v. 4). Later in the chapter (v. 23) Luke confirms that these "men" are actually angels. It's possible they have come as a pair because the Law said "At the mouth of two witnesses, or at the mouth of three witnesses, shall the matter be established" (Deut. 19:15). The first witnesses of the empty tomb are angels. The next witnesses are the women from Galilee who have traveled with Jesus.

5. How do these women respond (v. 5)? What do you think would be your response if you saw two men standing in the empty tomb in dazzling or brilliantly shining clothing?

____

____

____

"Why do you look for the living among the dead?" (v. 5). At first the angels are subtle. They ask why the women are looking for a living body where corpses are kept. This suggests Jesus is not a corpse but he is alive, so the women won't find him here. Then the angels get more direct: "He is not here, but has been raised!"

6. What do the angels remind the women that Jesus taught them (vv. 6–7)?

____

____

"The Son of Man" (v. 7) – Notice the title here. Angels are calling Jesus the Son of Man.

"Must be delivered" (v. 7) – Or "it is necessary that..." Jesus' death had to happen. We find God's sovereignty in this statement. What happened to Jesus was necessary and not an accident of history. That reality does not make the evil actions okay—those who committed them will be held responsible. But the events were never out of God's control. God had a plan in it all.

"On the third day rise again" (v. 7) – We must be careful not to confuse "three days" with "seventy-two hours." Perhaps a helpful parallel is thinking of a weekend photo essay with entries starting Friday afternoon and ending early Sunday morning. The file has entries for three days—Friday, Saturday, and Sunday.

7. What do the women do with the information they've been given (vv. 8–9)?

____

____

8. Luke names them. Make a list of the women who witnessed the resurrection (v. 10).

____

____

____

9. Remember, Luke did not record that the apostles were even present at the crucifixion nor as witnesses of the resurrection. What is the initial response of the Twelve to the women's testimony (vv. 11–12)?

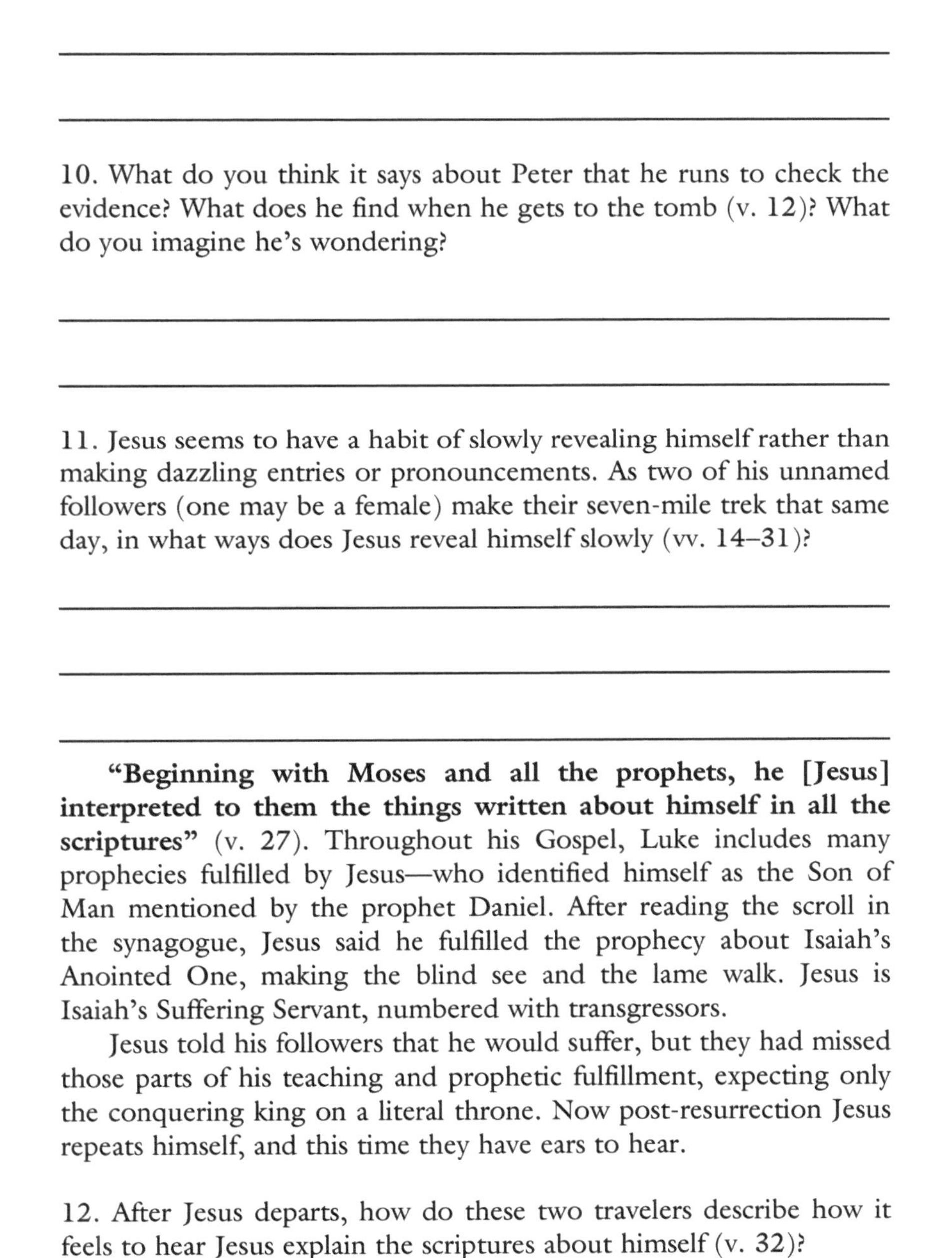

10. What do you think it says about Peter that he runs to check the evidence? What does he find when he gets to the tomb (v. 12)? What do you imagine he's wondering?

11. Jesus seems to have a habit of slowly revealing himself rather than making dazzling entries or pronouncements. As two of his unnamed followers (one may be a female) make their seven-mile trek that same day, in what ways does Jesus reveal himself slowly (vv. 14–31)?

"Beginning with Moses and all the prophets, he [Jesus] interpreted to them the things written about himself in all the scriptures" (v. 27). Throughout his Gospel, Luke includes many prophecies fulfilled by Jesus—who identified himself as the Son of Man mentioned by the prophet Daniel. After reading the scroll in the synagogue, Jesus said he fulfilled the prophecy about Isaiah's Anointed One, making the blind see and the lame walk. Jesus is Isaiah's Suffering Servant, numbered with transgressors.

Jesus told his followers that he would suffer, but they had missed those parts of his teaching and prophetic fulfillment, expecting only the conquering king on a literal throne. Now post-resurrection Jesus repeats himself, and this time they have ears to hear.

12. After Jesus departs, how do these two travelers describe how it feels to hear Jesus explain the scriptures about himself (v. 32)?

13. Even though the sky is close to dark, if not dark already, in a world without streetlights or flashlights, what do they do in response to their new-found knowledge (v. 33)?

14. What are the disciples saying upon their return (v. 34)?

15. The Emmaus disciples tell everyone that they recognized Jesus when he broke bread (v. 35). How have they seen Jesus break bread in the past? What about the specific action of bread-breaking, do you think, might have clued them in?

16. Jesus appears out of nowhere to a gathering of his disciples in the City of Peace. This is his first appearance to the full group. What are his first words (v. 36)?

17. Not only are Jesus's followers startled and terrified, but they think they are seeing a ghost (v. 37). What non-ghost actions does Jesus do (vv. 39–43)?

18. What is the new reaction of Jesus's followers based on this data (v. 41)?

____

____

19. Name times you can recall from the Gospel of Luke that Jesus has used fish as an object lesson.

____

____

20. Each day as you have read the Gospel of Luke, you have been instructed to ask for the Spirit to help you understand. Why were the disciples finally able to understand the Scriptures (v. 45)?

____

____

21. According to Jesus, what did the Scriptures predict about the Christ (vv. 46–47)?

____

____

22. Who are to be the recipients of the proclamation about Jesus (v. 47)? What is the role of the listeners in this proclamation (v. 48)?

____

____

"I am sending you what my Father promised" (v. 49). Eight or nine centuries before Christ, God communicated a prophetic word through the prophet Joel: 'I will pour out my Spirit on all people. Your sons and daughters will prophesy, your old men will dream dreams, your young men will see visions. Even on my servants, both men and women, I will pour out my Spirit in those days" (Joel 2:28–29). Jesus knows this promise, and he tells his followers that there is yet more prophecy to be fulfilled. They are to be his witnesses, but first his disciples need to wait in Jerusalem until they receive supernatural power to testify. The Spirit will descend in Jerusalem, but not immediately.

Jesus promised to send the Holy Spirit (fulfilled on the day of Pentecost, or fifty days after Passover and recorded in the Book of Acts), and he led his disciples out of Jerusalem to Bethany, which you located on the map in the section on Luke 19.

23. Once in Bethany what three things does Jesus do to their instructions (vv. 50–51).

____

____

24. What is Jesus's disciples' response (vv. 52–53)? How can you be like them?

____

____

SATURDAY: FOLLOWING IN THE STEPS OF JOANNA

Scripture: "Now it was Mary Magdalene, Joanna, Mary the mother of James, and the other women with them who told these things to the apostles" (Luke 24:10).

In his book, *Gospel Women: Studies of the Named Women in the Gospels*, biblical scholar Richard Bauckham argues that Junia—whom the apostle Paul refers to as being "among the apostles" (Rom. 16:7)—is the Latinized version of the Hebrew name *Yehohannah* or *Yohannah*. That name rendered in English is Joanna. Do you see the connection? Bauckham equates the apostle Junia (Rom. 16:7) with Joanna, the follower of Jesus whom Luke mentions twice in his Gospel (8:3, 24:10). Didn't she travel alongside Jesus and witness the teachings, miracles, crucifixion, and resurrection? Indeed, she did!

Remember how I listed people in Jesus's circle who had more than one name—Simon Peter, John Mark, and Judas Barsabbas? Well, Jewish people in Jesus's world commonly adopted Greek or Latin names that sounded similar to their given Hebrew names, like Simon for Simeon or Rufus for Reuben. Their doing so helped their Greek and Roman neighbors who had difficulty pronouncing their Hebrew names. Sometimes my students from outside the English-speaking world adopt a similar practice to help their professors and classmates—even though we know it's important to learn people's actual names.

Dr. Bauckham thinks that after the resurrection, Joanna adopted a Latinized version of her name, making it "Junia," when she traveled to spread the good news, or perhaps even before she left Galilee to follow Christ. You'll recall she was the wife of Cuza, steward of Herod (Luke 8:3), so that made her a member of the Herodian elite. Remember Luke's words?

> "The twelve were with him, and also some women who had been healed of evil spirits and disabilities: Mary (called Magdalene), from whom seven demons had gone out, and Joanna the wife of Cuza (Herod's household manager), Susanna, and many others who provided for them out of their own resources." (Luke 8:1–3)

Dr. Bauckham notes,

> Consider how appropriate it would have been for Joanna, the wife of Herod's steward, member of the Romanized Herodian elite of Tiberias, to become a Christian missionary specifically in Rome. She would have known some Latin, doubtless a rare accomplishment among the first Jewish Christians of Jerusalem. She had the means to support herself and a degree of acculturation to Roman ways.

Paul mentions "Andronicus and Junia" (Rom. 16:7) as first-century Jewish Christians who were his fellow prisoners-of-war. In fact, he says, these two believed in Christ even before he did—perhaps while he was persecuting them. If so, that would place their conversion within a year or two of the events in the Gospel of Luke. And if such were the case, by the time Paul wrote the Book of Romans, Junia would have already been a gospel-proclaimer for more than two decades. Such timing further supports Dr. Bauckham's claim that Junia and Joanna might have been the same person because that would make Junia one of the earliest Christians—which Joanna was.

Jesus told his disciples to wait for the promise of the Father to be fulfilled. Within fifty days, he sent the Holy Spirit. Once empowered from on high, Jesus's followers spread out from Jerusalem, Judea, Samaria, and to all the earth.

Regardless of whether Joanna and Junia are one woman or two, she or they had an appropriate response to Jesus's birth, life, death, burial, resurrection, ascension, and promised kingdom: Obedience. Sacrifice. Worship. And testifying.

Joanna witnessed it all. Her next assignment: Go and tell!

Our task is the same. We have great news! Who needs to hear it?

For memorization: Then they worshiped him and returned to Jerusalem with great joy. And they stayed continually at the temple, praising God. (Luke 24:52–53)

Prayer: *Almighty God, who for our redemption gave your only-begotten Son to the death of the cross, granted access to the holy place, and by his glorious resurrection delivered us from the power of our enemy: Grant us the desire to die daily to sin, the joy in living new life in obedience to you, and the power to bring tidings of great joy to those in our own Jerusalem, Judea, Samaria, and all the earth. Through Jesus Christ your Son our Lord, who lives and reigns with you and the Holy Spirit, one God, now and forever. Amen.*

Leader's Guide

Do you sense God leading you to facilitate a group? To lead a Bible study, you do not need a seminary degree or skill as a public speaker. You don't even need to have the gift of teaching. You need only a desire to see people grow through God's Word and a genuine concern for their spiritual growth. Often the person best suited to the facilitator's role is someone who prefers drawing out others and listening to them rather than teaching. So, no matter your skill level, offer yourself to God as a willing conduit of his grace.

Get started. Determine if you will meet virtually, in person, or in a hybrid setup. Pray about what person or people you should invite to join you. Determine the best way to communicate to others about the chance to do a group study—Church bulletin? Web site? Blog? Podcast? Text? Email? Flier? Poster? Phone call? Social media? Ask potential participants and set a deadline for commitments.

If you envision a church-sponsored study, aim to give participants several months' notice so you can schedule a room and people can plan ahead. Work with the appropriate church staff member or volunteer to schedule the time and place.

If you plan to gather a group of friends online, in an office, living room, or coffee house, decide as a group the best time and place to meet. For optimum interaction, small groups should be limited to eight or ten members—or even fewer.

Handle the business stuff. Take book orders, collect payment, and distribute books in advance or have each individual obtain her own. The former is recommended, as bulk discounts are often available, and people are more likely to follow through in participating if they have a study in hand. Before your first meeting, determine whether to distribute studies in advance or to hand them out at an event. Also, do you want to incorporate a service project, such as collecting used glasses for donation? If so, make arrangements. Something else you'll need to determine—do you want to complete each chapter in one week, or do you want to spread out your seven-week study over a fourteen-week period? If the latter, determine where to divide the book's layout in half for each week.

Hold the kick-off. Before your first Bible discussion time, consider holding a kick-off brunch or dinner, getting your group together at church, a coffee shop, or in a home—or online. Pray for each person who plans to attend, asking that God's presence would be present and that each would have a desire to learn the word. When you do meet, open with prayer.

Include an icebreaker. Provide opportunities for members to get acquainted if they don't already know each other. Do so by providing introductions or offering some questions that include each participant giving her name and some background information. Ask something benign such as "What's your favorite household appliance" (Water heater? Blender? Coffee maker?). Such a non-threatening question will help people open up to each other. One artist-led group asked the household-appliance question and provided Play-Doh so each participant had to make an image of her appliance. The others had to guess what it was.

Obtain permission to distribute contact information among the members to encourage discussion and fellowship throughout the week.

Hold your first discussion meeting. Begin each session with prayer and do your best to start on time, depending on the formality of the group. Set a clear ending time, and respect participants' schedules.

When the group meets for the first discussion, be sure all participants have met each other. Distribute contact information for late joiners, and make sure everyone has a study handy.

You will spend most of your time in discussion. If your group members hardly know each other or seem reluctant to talk, use a prepared icebreaker question to get them started. Try to come up with something that relates to the topic without requiring a spiritual answer. You may have people in your group who feel uncomfortable talking about spiritual things, and the icebreaker can help them participate in a way that's less threatening. In fact, you might want to include an icebreaker at the beginning of each discussion to get lighthearted conversation going. See the list of suggestions below for each week's possible questions. Also, remember that the leader sets the level of vulnerability. If you share openly, you create an environment that feels safer for others to do so as well. When someone does share, don't leave that person to endure a long silence afterward. Provide affirmation that you heard and that you care.

After prayer, ask the icebreaker question, if you plan to use one. Then move to discussion. Plan to allow about forty-five minutes for this time. Select the questions you'll ask by going back through the lesson for the week and choosing about seven open-ended questions. You can simply circle in your guide the questions you want to ask. Be sure at least one of your choices covers what you feel is the most important point from the text for that week. And make sure you get some application in there—not just facts and observations, but how Jesus's life changes us.

If you're an extrovert, consciously avoid dominating as the leader. Remember, your job is less about instruction and more about drawing people out. If one member rarely says anything, periodically direct an easy question specifically to that person.

When you finish the final question, ask members if they have a question or issue they wanted to cover that you missed. Then ask them to share prayer requests, items for thanksgiving, and announcements. Make sure each prayer request is actually prayed for and encourage the group to refrain from answering prayer requests with advice or related stories (e.g., "I know someone else with that kind of cancer, and she used XYZ herbal supplement").

When you're finished, review info about what's due the following week, as well as the meeting time and place for your next study.

Between meetings, pray for participants. Also, it will mean a lot if you can follow up with a phone call, particularly when people have shared urgent requests. If you can make one visit to each person's home during the study, you will likely reap a huge dividend in time invested. "Just showing up" goes a long way toward building community and aiding spiritual growth. And meeting people in their own environments is also a great way to build relationships.

Icebreakers:
Week 1 – This week, before launching into the trees, we got an overview of the forest by reading the entire Book of Luke. Luke seems to

love the insider/outsider theme. Can you think of a television show, film, or popular book with a main character that people consider an outsider?

Week 2 – This week in our reading, the elderly Elizabeth is a key character, and Luke leaves the reader with the impression that Elizabeth mentored Mary. Who is an elderly person that you admire or that has helped you?

Week 3 – Jesus spoke of the kind of family in which "Spirit is thicker than blood." Share about a person outside of this group to whom you are not biologically related but who is like family to you.

Week 4 – One of my students once designed a mockup of a Playbill magazine issue for an imaginary production of the story of Philemon. So ask: If you were directing a production of the Gospel of Luke, who would you identify as the main characters, and who would you cast to play each person selected?

Week 5 – This week we read how Jesus healed a woman who was bent over for eighteen years. What were you doing eighteen years ago?

Week 6 – In our reading this week, Jesus told a story about a man who went away and left others in charge, but not everybody left behind acted responsibly. Share a time when a fiasco happened in your absence (no names please). OR Lot's wife was destroyed by her own longings. What are some longings you or a friend have successfully let go of for your own good?

Week 7 – The "Magdalene" in Mary Magdalene might be a nickname meaning "tower." What are some nicknames in your life, either what others call you or names you have given others? Explain.

Remember that these icebreaker questions are simply to get discussion started by opening with an easy question for which everyone should be able to give an answer without feeling intimidated. Feel free to craft questions that better fit your own group.

More than Bible Study

Perhaps you would like to combine your time in Bible study with service. By linking time in God's word with time serving others, you will help group members move from compartmentalizing to integrating their discipleship time and the stewardship of their resources. Choose from the following or come up with your own ideas:

Have each person bring something every week to donate. One week, they can bring their used cell phones to recycle. Then another week you can send used Bibles to an organization that distributes them to the needy or in countries where Bibles are difficult to obtain. And then one week you could bring books to donate to the public library or your church library. Other possibilities are combining your time with a "baby shower" to benefit a pregnancy resource center, collecting coats for the homeless, or making potholders for a soup kitchen. Involve the group in deciding what they want to do.

Combine your study with your church's missionary needs. One week have everyone bring supplies for someone's ministry trip, such as power bars, dried soup, and seeds. Often short-term teams need items to give to translators as gifts, or maybe they could use some VBS prizes. My congregation's sister-church in Mexico once asked for school supplies in September and for Spanish Bibles. You could ask your congregation's webmaster to set up an Amazon Associates' account with a link through your church's web page and direct all members to order through the link. Choose a mission to benefit from all proceeds. Another possibility is to bring office and bathroom supplies for your church. Or host a group garage sale and use the proceeds to grant scholarships for a church conference or retreat.

Target a people group to learn about and pray for as part of your time together.

"Adopt" a missionary or ministry of the week/month to correspond with, pray for, and learn about each time you meet.

Choose a group within your community to serve. If a nursing home, visit it together one week. Or volunteer to pick up trash in an area where your city has a need. Or take homemade cookies to your local fire fighters.

Work together as a group on a craft to donate, such as sewing blankets for a women's shelter. Local homeless shelters often have ongoing demand for pillowcases—which are easy to make. Or learn to knit and donate scarves.

Perhaps you have some artists in your group who need more right-brained interaction. Songs, jewelry, paintings, photos, collages, poetry, prayers, psalms—the options for creative interaction in response to the truths learned in the Gospel of Luke are endless. Brainstorm about how to incorporate the arts into your interaction with the text. You can find some art links in the Coffee Cup Bible Study section at the author's web site, www.aspire2.com

Finally, if your group meets at a coffee shop or restaurant, learn and use the name of the barista, the waiter, and/or the person cleaning your table. You may be the only people they meet all day who paid attention to that detail.

MEETING THE
DEEPEST NEEDS

WE BELIEVE THE GOSPEL IS TRANSFORMATIVE

And you can change the world one child at a time.

Thousands of children in the world are born into a cycle of poverty that has been around for generations, leaving them without hope for a safe and secure future. For a little more than $1 a day you can provide the tools a child needs to break the cycle in the name of Jesus.